THE ANTHOLOGY OF BLACK MOUNTAIN COLLEGE POETRY

THE ANTHOLOGY OF BLACK MOUNTAIN COLLEGE POETRY

EDITED BY

Blake Hobby

Alessandro Porco

Joseph Bathanti

The University of
North Carolina Press,
Chapel Hill,
in association with the
Black Mountain College
Museum + Arts Center

Published by the University of North Carolina Press in association with the Black Mountain College Museum + Arts Center.

Designed by April Leidig
Set in Garamond Premier Pro by Copperline Book Services, Inc.

Cover art: Dew covered web at Black Mountain College, 1948.
Photograph by Kenneth Snelson. Courtesy of the Western Regional Archives, State Archives of North Carolina, Asheville.

Frontispiece: S. Tsuchiya, unsplash.com

Library of Congress Cataloging-in-Publication Data
Names: Hobby, Blake, editor. | Porco, Alessandro, editor. | Bathanti, Joseph, editor.
Title: The anthology of Black Mountain College poetry / edited by Blake Hobby, Alessandro Porco, and Joseph Bathanti.
Description: Chapel Hill : The University of North Carolina Press/Black Mountain College Museum + Arts Center, 2025. | Includes bibliographical references.
Identifiers: LCCN 2024045622 | ISBN 9781469641133 (cloth) | ISBN 9781469683447 (paperback) | ISBN 9781469641157 (epub) | ISBN 9798890855770 (pdf)
Subjects: LCSH: American poetry—20th century. | American poetry—21st century. | Black Mountain College (Black Mountain, N.C.) | BISAC: POETRY / Anthologies (multiple authors) | HISTORY / United States / State & Local / South (AL, AR, FL, GA, KY, LA, MS, NC, SC, TN, VA, WV)
Classification: LCC PS584 .A58 2025 | DDC 811/.008—dc23/eng/20241007
LC record available at https://lccn.loc.gov/2024045622

publication supported by a grant from
The Community Foundation for Greater New Haven
as part of the *Urban Haven Project*

Jargon 115

CONTENTS

PART II | VISITING FACULTY

in order of appointment

PART III | STUDENTS

in order of enrollment

PART IV | AFFILIATES

who visited Black Mountain College or published in the *Black Mountain Review* by year

PREFACE | Blake Hobby

Sometimes, when lovers of wisdom meet, community forms and, through shared experience, new knowledge comes into being. The speech of Diotima in Plato's *Symposium* refers to this phenomenon as *poiesis*—not the creation of an isolated object or idea to be contemplated but a process flowing from the love of things that yields irreducible and ever-shifting sound happenings, which reverberate when read or performed. We call these dynamic works of art "poetry"—not fixed objects bound to two-dimensional space but active creations that celebrate the love of invention, the desire to explore, and the will to create.[1]

Between 1933 and 1957, a radical form of learning infused with the arts and animated by democratic ideals formed the Black Mountain College (BMC) experience. The school's curriculum included lectures, classes, study time, performances, and even daily work on a farm. As lovers of wisdom who believed in the power of *poiesis*, the school's founders, faculty, and associates envisioned a better, progressive, open, tolerant, and inclusive community and, by analogy, a better world. *The Anthology of Black Mountain College Poetry* celebrates that community and aims to follow the school's inclusive mission. By collecting a disparate band of poetic voices under one cover, this anthology aims first and foremost to arouse. To help understand how *The Anthology of Black Mountain College Poetry* showcases the fruit of the college's labors, I turn to the story of two friends who share a mutual love of this small institution in the Western North Carolina mountains.

In the summer of 2003, I accepted a position at the University of North Carolina Asheville. In August, before the school year began, a group of professors held a meet and greet to welcome new faculty. That is where I first came to know my dear colleague and friend Brian Butler, with whom I taught for eleven years. At that time, Brian was a philosophy professor and artist, and I was a newly hired English lecturer and musician. As Brian and I quickly learned about each other, we shared sensibilities. We resisted boundaries. We made connections. We sought to transcend the confines and jargon of our disciplines and forge relationships. And, significantly, we were *doers*. While juggling heavy teaching loads, serving on campus committees, traveling to conferences, doing academic advising, serving in leadership positions, and publishing widely in our fields, we practiced the arts.

As we got to know each other over a six-year period, Brian and I often talked about the community that existed at BMC among faculty, students, and those who were closely associated with the school. In the summer of 2009, after many conversations, Brian and I founded the *Journal of Black Mountain College Studies*. Our aim was to create an informational and authoritative open-access resource that would provide an outlet for scholars. We hoped researchers from a variety of disciplines would come together and make connections. With the resources of a nonprofit organization in Asheville—the Black Mountain College Museum + Arts Center (BMCM + AC)—and the dedication and support of Alice Sebrell, then program director, we established an editorial board, enlisted the help of scholars, and compiled our first journal issue, which appeared in 2010. As we went along, we noticed gaps in the scholarship and hoped to make other BMC resources available. The first thing we wanted to publish was a collection of BMC poetry. That was this book's genesis. Since then, a lot has happened. While Brian has supported me every step of the way, he moved out of the limelight and trusted me with the investigation process, the compiling of the manuscript, and the editing. But as you will see, I needed a lot of help and have had the good fortune to receive it.

First, I collected poems and artifacts and dug into the research. As I did, I began thinking that the way Donald Allen identified Black Mountain poets in his groundbreaking and widely acclaimed 1960 book, *The New American Poetry: 1945–1960*, needed to be revisited. To his credit, Allen recognized BMC as a locus of creativity and invention in the poetic arts. He demonstrated the influence those associated with the college had. He also showed how the writing and thinking departed from other collections of poetry. Allen knew these new voices had then "appeared only in a few little magazines" and in "broadsheets, pamphlets, and limited editions" but were catching on because of dynamic poetry readings held across the United States.[2] Allen's "Black Mountain" moniker stuck. His widely sold book is famous, and his geographic groupings still form a powerful corrective to the teaching of accepted academic literary history and prescribed poetic forms.

I began with respect and admiration for Donald Allen and first traced the many luminaries associated with the institution. Then, mindful of Allen's monumental achievement and thankful for the corrective vision of poetry Allen's book provided, I sought to enlarge the scope for poetics at BMC. Why? Because many more than ten poetic luminaries taught, visited, studied, and were associated with the school. While Allen carefully selected ten figures to represent BMC, I knew from researching and from reading poems by BMC faculty, visiting faculty, students, and affiliates during my visits to BMCM + AC in Asheville and to the BMC holdings in the North Carolina Western Regional Archives in Oteen, just outside of Asheville, that the diversity of the BMC experience transcended Allen's group. Following the inspiring example set by Mary Emma Harris in her highly influential book *The Arts at Black Mountain College*, which aimed to be faithful to the historical record and to be inclusive, I vowed to show how BMC's lived creed of "democracy as a way of life" was reflected in the poetry of the college's faculty, visiting faculty, students, and affiliates.[3]

This was no small task. It took years of research and correspondence and the generous assistance of many dedicated to the cause, most especially BMC scholar and pioneer Mary Emma Harris, an invaluable resource, champion of BMC, and faithful correspondent who also provided a detailed review of an early manuscript version of this anthology. It was also indispensable to have BMCM + AC just down the street from the university. BMCM + AC is a repository of archival materials, a living embodiment of the school's mission, and a carefully connected network of BMC lovers and scholars with close ties to many students who attended BMC.

My work progressed for years before I became acquainted with two dynamic teachers and scholars: Alessandro Porco and Joseph Bathanti. During the spring of 2013, I invited them to join me in bringing the anthology together. Researchers recognized for their scholarship and creativity, they were BMC obsessives who taught, performed, researched, and practiced the creative arts. I am thankful for Alessandro Porco's strong knowledge of BMC's poets and of contemporary poetics and am very appreciative for the support the University of North Carolina Wilmington provided for the archival visits he and I made. I am equally thankful for the vision, experience, knowledge, commitment, and unfailing support that Joseph Bathanti, the seventh named North Carolina poet laureate (2012–14), provided and wish to thank Appalachian State University for its support. Without these experts, without the support of their institutions, and without the support of Alice Sebrell, Jeff Arnal, and Erin Dickey (BMCM + AC), as well as Lucas Church, Andrew Winters, and Andrew Hachey (UNC Press), who dutifully obtained many permissions, this book would not exist. Their gift of time, their willingness to brainstorm ideas, their commitment, and the many hours they freely gave as we sat together, read poetry, and made selections moved me to keep going, even when the task seemed impossible.

In the late summer of 2013 and continuing through that fall, Brian Butler, Alice Sebrell, Alessandro Porco, Joseph Bathanti, and I gathered for lengthy sessions to discuss the book's contents. After careful consideration, we developed criteria for including writers and then sought representative poems for those who taught at

BMC, those who studied there, and those who had strong college affiliations. While we chose to include all ten Black Mountain poets Donald Allen anthologized in *The New American Poetry: 1945–1960*, we expanded Allen's vision and included faculty and visiting faculty who taught at the college, students who wrote poetry either during their BMC studies or later in life, and affiliates who were associated with the print culture and the social network of the college. While we certainly knew that other criteria could have been followed, we imposed limits to produce a manageable book that would represent the BMC experience and be affordable.

As a way of orienting readers and of providing context for the writers and selections included, Alessandro Porco and I fashioned informative header notes that appear at the beginning of each entry. These notes supply context, emphasizing each poet's relationship to the college. Rather than provide the last word, they are designed to move readers to find out more about BMC.

What emerges while reading the book is a fuller, more complete picture of the BMC experience. When weighing what to include, we did not confine ourselves to poems written only between 1933 and 1957, the period when the college held classes. Instead, we included representative selections from faculty, visiting faculty, students, and affiliates written at the college and after, attempting to show BMC connections and the school's lasting influence. While the college accomplished remarkable things in a very short period of time, it exerted a strong influence long after its doors closed. And it continues to do so today. The book is organized by sections—Faculty, Visiting Faculty, Students, and Affiliates. Within each section, writers appear in the order they were associated with BMC. Publication dates for poems are included, except in rare occasions where the precise years are unknown or the poems are unpublished. In cases of the former, estimates are provided based on contextual information; in cases of the latter, we simply indicate "unpublished" and supplement, when possible, with dates of composition. Designed to be practical, this arrangement invites readers to make connections and to forge relationships.

While I first learned of BMC's significance and influence in the early 1980s, I did not understand then the truly transnational nature of the college and the worldwide influence it had and continues to exert. For me, *The Anthology of Black Mountain College Poetry* affirms the school's international reputation, opens the Black Mountain poetry canon, and brings us to reconsider the BMC experience. Donald Allen's "Black Mountain" section contained poems by nine men and one woman and portrayed the school as a regional and a national phenomenon. *The Anthology of Black Mountain College Poetry* illustrates the transnational nature of the school. It also attempts to fill glaring gaps, especially when it comes to the inclusion of women writers, perhaps most significant, with two key faculty members,

M. C. Richards and Hilda Morley, both first-rate poets. All too often, Charles Olson and Robert Creeley have been raised to the height of gods dwelling on high in a BMC pantheon and lauded as the literary zenith of the school's creativity, with their poems and writings praised as the school's primary contribution to contemporary poetics. But the college was a place where everyone practiced the arts, and many wrote poetry. Thus, we included writers known primarily for other art forms—such as Josef Albers and Ray Johnson—who also wrote poems. We also selected poems from students who have continued the school's far-reaching legacy. We employ "students" as the standard convention among BMC scholars and distinguish, as necessary, between students who attended and who graduated.

As I reread *The Anthology of Black Mountain College Poetry*, I continue to make new associations. Importantly, as Brian Butler has said, when you dig into the life and works of these writers, you often fall into a "rabbit hole," discovering new things and continually becoming aware that there is much more than either this anthology's header notes or front material indicate or you might have imagined. Thus, we hope this anthology will encourage others to learn and seek and know and understand and, above all, to create. For what is labeled and codified often becomes calcified, dictatorial, and imprisoning, but what appears as irreducible expression often proves vital, open to interpretation, and delirious with possibilities. In following this ethos, we have tried to be true to the BMC experience: to not only study and theorize but also practice, to not only think and learn about but also do and make. In this sense both this anthology and the BMC community laud *poiesis*. For poetry is not a tool of the state or a fixed metrical form but a radical way of doing that often topples the very foundations to which we cling. In the end, this anthology is for everyone interested in poetry, for those seeking to learn more about BMC, for those who are interested in BMC's influence, for teachers seeking a great collection that instills a love of poetry as it informs, and for scholars who are busy at work enlarging our understanding of the college and continuing the conversation.

I wish to extend a heartfelt thanks to the leaders, faculty, students, and staff of UNC Asheville. With administrative approval, I taught three courses on BMC poetry. As I introduced undergraduates to BMC, I was renewed by their enthusiasm for the project and their love of the poetry. They fueled my passion and helped perform research and transcribe poems. I also am most thankful for Corina Heich, a talented UNC Asheville alumna, who spent the summer of 2014 with me working as a faithful editorial assistant and helped assemble the first manuscript draft with a grant from BMCM + AC.

It is one thing to experience meaning as one does research. It is another thing to know the sheer joy of seeing others learn and fall in love with BMC. Along the way,

I have corresponded with many who attended BMC. During these discussions and through illuminating correspondence, BMC students expressed excitement, gave their blessing, and shared their stories. In the end, I am humbled by their gift of time and by the profound influence BMC had and continues to have on their lives. I also want to extend grateful thanks to Heather South, archivist at the Western Regional Archives of North Carolina, for fielding many queries and for her dedication and support of this project.

My experience with BMC began in 1983 in an honors music theory and history course taught by Charles McKnight and Paul Langston in the School of Music at Stetson University, where I first encountered the music of John Cage. I returned again and again to BMC throughout my graduate studies. But my academic formation alone did not give me the tools to bring this collection together. I needed to be near the locus of BMC activity. Thus, I am thankful for the wonderful years in Asheville, where resources and experts were readily available. This collection fills me with life as I continue to marvel at the many BMC writers who experimented with poetry, believed in democratic ideals, saw education as a form of liberation, and fought to challenge the status quo. May it also inspire you to live and learn and create.

ABBREVIATIONS

The following abbreviations are used in the anthology's biographical header notes:

BMC Black Mountain College

BMR *Black Mountain Review*

NAP *The New American Poetry: 1945–1960*

THE ANTHOLOGY OF BLACK MOUNTAIN COLLEGE POETRY

INTRODUCTION | Alessandro Porco

In September 1933, nineteen students and ten faculty members gathered in Western North Carolina for the opening of Black Mountain College (BMC).[1] For twenty-four years, from 1933 to 1957, BMC exemplified the experimental spirit in American education, culture, and letters.

The school grew largely out of the vision, imagination, and efforts of John Andrew Rice. An Oxford graduate, Guggenheim fellow, classics scholar, and essayist promoting John Dewey's educational reforms, Rice believed in a student-centered, hands-on approach to learning that emphasized method over content and process over product.[2] Altering the course of higher education, he, Theodore Dreier, and other students and staff formerly of Rollins College helped establish BMC.[3] The chosen location was just outside the town of Black Mountain, North Carolina, approximately sixteen miles east of Asheville. Rice served as the school's official rector from 1934 to 1938.

Although Rice is now seen as the admired founder and leader of a radical, experimental institution, that wasn't so in 1933, when Central Florida socialites and the administration at Rollins College—a small liberal arts school in Winter Park, Florida—deposed him. Rice had objected to many educational policies and practices at Rollins, taking a stand, for example, against the newly regimented eight-hour school day, the presence of sororities and fraternities on campus, compulsory chapel services, lecture-based instruction in the classroom, and the practice of competitive debate.[4] Instead, he followed a more progressive philosophy, championing the intellectual freedom of faculty and students over and against standardized teaching methods and learning objectives. Aiming to facilitate independent thinking, Rice insisted that students pursue their own interests and, most important, that they connect knowledge to personal action.[5] "To know is not enough," insisted Rice.[6] Dismissed as a rogue by the school's president and board of trustees, Rice lost his tenured faculty position, learning firsthand the lack of understanding from which visionaries often suffer.[7] What might have been a curse at Rollins, however, became a blessing at BMC in the fall of 1933.

Rice established four key principles of education at the newly founded college. First, he sought to make creative practices integral to the BMC curriculum.[8] Rice believed that aesthetic experience prepared students not to be artists necessarily but, rather, citizens capable of imaginatively re-creating "a public world" that was otherwise far too "ready-made, stern, [and] demanding."[9] Second, he kept a low student-to-faculty ratio and, thus, ensured an intense, intimate learning environment both inside and outside the classroom.[10] Professors offered partisan views on art, literature, and music while supporting and developing the particular interests of individual students. Third, he divided up labor, with both students (male and female) and faculty required to work together, sharing responsibility for the campus's upkeep.[11] Success at the college meant acquiring the know-how to discuss Arnold Schoenberg's twelve-tone technique *and* to mend a sewage pipe. Fourth, he distributed power equally among the faculty, avoiding an authoritative, external administrative force.[12] Even students had representational rights as officers on various committees, including the board of fellows.[13]

From 1933 to 1941, faculty, staff, and students congregated daily at Robert E. Lee Hall, a plantation-style building with three-story Doric columns and a sprawling portico. Part of the Blue Ridge Assembly (a group of buildings used by the local YMCA), Lee Hall served as the college's epicenter, the site of classes, performances, dorms, and parties; it even housed the school's library in the basement.[14] By decade's end, the college demonstrated significant growth, with as many as seventy-four students enrolled in the fall of 1939.[15]

In 1941, BMC moved to Lake Eden, a 674-acre summer resort and camp that the school had purchased a few years earlier, in 1937. The site featured buildings originally designed by E. W. Grove (e.g., the dining hall, stone cottage, and north and south lodges), and A. Lawrence Kocher, head of the Department of Architecture at the University of Virginia, was hired to design additions to the campus, including the Jalowetz House and iconic Studies Building, the latter of which looked more like a surreal glass-box flotilla than an antiseptic educational facility. Faculty and students worked together to build the Lake Eden campus—an example of the "living" and "learning" ethos that defined the college.[16]

From the moment of their arrival, Josef and Anni Albers assumed key leadership roles on campus, helping the college blossom in those early years despite the hardships and interruptions caused by the Great Depression and the Second World War. The Bauhaus-trained émigrés—Josef was a painter, Anni was a textile designer—first came to BMC from Germany, escaping political persecution and censorship under the Third Reich. In late November of 1933, the couple took refuge in North Carolina's Swannanoa Valley.[17] They had accepted an offer to develop the BMC art program and, in the years that followed, transformed the small rural campus into a cosmopolitan hub of creativity, with connections as far as Mexico, Canada, Cuba, France, Germany, Spain, Japan, and India.[18]

Like Rice, Josef Albers was a forward-thinking educator, and BMC experienced a golden age due, in part, to his support of the college's special summer sessions in the mid-1940s. The original idea for the summer sessions—or "institutes," as they were officially called—came from faculty member Heinrich Jalowetz, who organized the 1944 Summer Music Institute around the occasion of Arnold Schoenberg's seventieth birthday.[19] An inspired Albers organized the complementary Art Institute.[20] Thereafter, each summer provided an influx of visiting students and faculty who reenergized the campus with new ideas about art, music, literature, dance, and science.[21] The institutes reached their interdisciplinary apotheosis in 1948: seventy-four students enrolled, and the now-legendary faculty included John Cage, Merce Cunningham, Buckminster Fuller, Willem de Kooning, and Isaac Rosenfeld. That summer, Fuller developed his prototype for the geodesic dome (he would successfully build it in the summer of 1949), and Cage curated a music festival in celebration of Erik Satie.[22]

Visual art, music, and drama dominated the arts curriculum at BMC almost exclusively until after the Second World War. However, creative writing courses *were* offered in the early days of the college.[23] In the 1930s, poets Jane Mayhall and Ruth Herschberger enrolled in writing classes led by John Andrew Rice; Frederick Mangold and Robert Wunsch also taught creative writing.[24] In 1939, playwright William McLeery joined the faculty as a writer in residence for the spring semester, composing the libretto for *Let Me Have Air*, a comedy with music by John Evarts.[25] Charles Norman and May Sarton also dropped by the campus, reciting poems, giving lectures, and reading student writing.[26] In 1944, BMC hired a young poet named George Zabriskie, who had recently graduated from Duke University. He taught modern poetry, verse writing (with an emphasis on prosody), and a popular course called the Psychodynamics of Creativity, introducing students to modernists such as Hart Crane, T. S. Eliot, Wallace Stevens, and William Carlos Williams.[27] By the fall of 1946, M. C. Richards was hosting an unofficial creative writing workshop for students on Friday nights in her living quarters, with participants including Mervin Louis Lane and Jesse Green, both of whom appear in the present anthology.[28]

Charles Olson began teaching at BMC as a visiting lecturer in 1948, accepted a permanent position in 1951, and eventually took over as the school's last rector in 1953.[29] His tenure signaled a major shift in emphasis at the college, with creative writing—especially poetry—taking priority over other artistic and intellectual disciplines. At Olson's invitation, poets Robert Creeley and Robert Duncan joined the faculty in 1954 and 1956, respectively.[30] But just as Olson and company attempted to transform the theory and practice of American poetry into a form of resistance in response to the conditions of postmodernity after the Second World War, the college fell, unfortunately, into disarray.[31]

Personal reminiscences of this late period in the school's history stress the psychological, emotional, and economic strains of everyday life. The campus was not impervious to the general existential malaise of the postwar period. "In anxiety and depression we felt trapped . . . *and we let each other suffer, in secret keeping watch*" (italics in the original), explains Fielding Dawson in his memoir.[32] Poet Hilda Morley recalls how "it was good, at Black Mountain, to wake up to the quiet, the space, the sound of birds, though at times these might be interrupted by the noise of beer bottles rolling on the floor above us, or the scream of a new mother in the throes of a nervous breakdown."[33] Increasingly, as Michael Rumaker writes, students came to the college as "damaged refugees from families, homes, and later, mental hospitals and the growing drug world out there."[34] One student attempted suicide, while others threatened it.[35] As the campus's physical conditions deteriorated (e.g., a fire destroyed the paintings of Joseph Fiore), so did the emotional conditions of students, faculty, and their families.[36] Enrollment steadily declined throughout the 1950s. In fall 1954, only nine students registered for classes. This significantly diminished student body contributed to the school's growing financial woes.

As rector, Olson faced the impossible task of fiscally salvaging the college. Throughout 1953 and 1954, he embarked on several fundraising campaigns that, despite his best efforts, ultimately failed.[37] For example, he created a mostly symbolic board of advisers that included Albert Einstein, Franz Kline, Carl O. Sauer, Norbert Wiener, and William Carlos Williams.[38] Olson hoped the board's big names would generate donor interest and capital, thus keeping the school's doors open and, at the same time, helping pay off the debt owed to its former faculty members. When nothing happened, Olson had no choice but to start selling and renting campus property. He even sold a herd of cows for $1,725.[39] BMC was forced to close its doors for good in 1957.[40] As Paul Metcalf describes, in those final months, Olson "stayed on alone, to preside over the distribution of the physical remains, landlord of the detritus of his educational ideals."[41]

The *Black Mountain Review* (*BMR*) was part of Olson's rescue plan. He envisioned *BMR* as a promotional tool—"an active advertisement for the nature and form of the college's program," explains Tim Woods.[42] To edit the magazine, Olson sought the help of Robert Creeley, who, in 1954, had set sail from Cadiz, Spain, to assume his new teaching position at BMC. Olson committed $2,000 per year to the magazine, and that was enough for Creeley to publish between 400 and 750 copies per issue. In 1954, Creeley edited the magazine's first volume's four issues; each issue was sixty-four pages. From 1955 to 1957, he edited one issue per year, with each issue coming in at well over 200 pages in length. Mossén Alcover Press in Mallorca, Spain, printed the first six issues. Creeley had worked with Mossén Alcover while living in Mallorca in 1953. The low-cost press also printed Creeley's Divers Press books, many of which are early publications by key BMC figures: Paul Blackburn's *The Dissolving Fabric*, Robert Duncan's *Caesar's Gate*, and Larry Eigner's *From the Sustaining Air*. Jonathan Williams's Jargon Society, in Highlands, North Carolina, printed the final issue.[43]

A well-edited and provocative magazine had the potential to attract students to the college, increasing enrollment and, by extension, tuition revenue. But Olson and Creeley also envisioned *BMR* as a critical and creative intervention into the institutional formation of midcentury American literature. In a letter from 14 December 1953 to Cid Corman, Olson explains how he wants *BMR* to "compete with Kenyon, Partison [*sic*], NMQ (what else is there, are Hudson, & Sewanee, still in existence?) Anyway, that sort of thing."[44] Creeley specifically looked to Corman's magazine *Origin* as an inspiring alternative model of publishing.[45] However, unlike *Origin*, *BMR* emphasized critical commentary, including essays, reviews, and manifestos, a difference that allowed it to provide a "context"—a key word for Creeley—for the reception of the new American poetry.[46]

Politically, the magazine's editors and contributors believed in self-reliance and community. Creeley describes *BMR* as "a place wherein we might make evident what we, as writers, had found to be significant, both for ourselves and for that world—no doubt often vague to us indeed—we hoped our writing might enter."[47] Writers affiliated with *BMR* were galvanized by Olson's projective poetics, embodying its formal and philosophical ideals in poetry, fiction, and criticism. They dared to disturb the universe and didn't think twice about it: for example, Martin Seymour-Smith's negative reviews of the extraordinarily popular Dylan Thomas and Theodore Roethke caused Kenneth Rexroth to resign from his position on the editorial board in 1954.[48] The magazine also adopted the college's interdisciplinary spirit, featuring cover art by Katue Kitasono as well as John Altoon, Dan Rice, and Ed Corbet; photography by Peter Mitchum, Aaron Siskind, and Diana Woelffer; reproductions of René Laubiès and Franz Kline paintings; and collage art by Jess.

BMR helped establish and connect a network of like-minded poets in San Francisco, New York, Chicago, Boston, Portland, and Taos, as well as Montréal, Toronto, and Vancouver in Canada and extending as far as Tokyo, Japan, and Stuttgart and Karlsruhe, Germany. It compelled young writers to publish similarly independent-minded literary magazines of their own in the late 1950s and early 1960s: LeRoi Jones/Amiri Baraka's *Yūgen* (coedited with Hettie Cohen for issues 6–8) and *Floating Bear* (coedited with Diane di Prima); Irving Rosenthal's *Chicago Review*; Paul Carroll's *Big Table*; John Wieners's *Measure*; Gilbert Sorrentino's *Neon*; Ron Padgett's *White Dove Review*; Daisy Aldan's *Folder*; Harry Matthews's *Locus Solus*; Raymond Souster's *Contact*; Louis Dudek's *CIV/n*; *TISH* (started by a collective of Vancouver poets, including George Bowering and Frank Davey); Katue Kitasono's *Vou*; Rainer Gerhardt's *Fragmente*; Gael Turnbull and Michael Shayer's *Migrant*; and Ian Hamilton Finlay's *Poor. Old. Tired. Horse.*

The Anthology of Black Mountain College Poetry includes poems that first appeared in the school's magazine: Creeley's "Old Song," Duncan's "For a Muse Meant," Denise Levertov's "Everything that Acts is Actual," and Olson's "On first Looking out through Juan de la Cosa's Eyes"—poems from the "big four"—but also William Bronk's "For an Early Italian Musician," Paul Carroll's "Plotinus Refuses to Sit for a Portrait," Larry Eigner's "F e s t e," Irving Layton's "Westmount Doll," Hilda Morley's "'Seldom Is A Gothic Head More Beautiful Than When Broken,'" Joel Oppenheimer's "Today an Ophelia," and Gael Turnbull's "Bjarni Spike-Helgi's Son."[49] The inclusion of Layton (from Canada) and Turnbull (from Scotland, although he lived and studied in the United States and Canada in the 1950s) in *BMR* exemplifies the international reach of a modest magazine produced by and for the small liberal arts college.

In *Leap Before You Look*, Helen Molesworth suggests that this internationalism was essential to BMC from the very start: "Cross-cultural exchange happened repeatedly at Black Mountain College; indeed, it could be argued that it typified the Black Mountain experience."[50] Faculty members in the 1930s hailed from Germany, Switzerland, Austria, England, and Cuba. With the war looming, European artists, musicians, and intellectuals escaped to the United States, living in exile. Many would visit the BMC campus to lecture, teach, or perform, including Herbert Bayer, Marcel Breuer, Albert Einstein, Serge Chermayeff, Ernst Krenek, José Luis Sert, and Edward Steuermann. Mary Emma Harris fittingly refers to the school during this period as "an American Salzburg."[51] Later, Natarash Vashi and Pra-Veena introduced Hindu dance to the campus, and Shōji Hamada and Sōetsu Yanagi taught ceramics.[52] A school brochure from the late 1940s announces, quite correctly, that "Black Mountain College is a small cosmopolitan community of students and teachers living together."[53]

The biographies of poets in the present anthology reveal the constant flow of intellectual and creative labor across borders at midcentury. Ruth Herschberger wins a grant from the Bollingen Foundation to translate Vladimir Mayakovsky, and

Paul Blackburn wins a Fulbright Fellowship to translate troubadour poetry; Hilda Morley is educated in Palestine, London, and New York, then takes a job with the Office of War Information, while Denise Levertov is born and raised in England, serving as a nurse during the Second World War before settling down in New York City in 1948; Charles Olson, in his capacity as an amateur archeologist, travels to Mexico in search of Mayan hieroglyphs and a more "human universe"; Gael Turnbull practices medicine in Northern Ontario, Canada; in the early 1950s, Jerrold Levy lives and works on a kibbutz in Israel, teaching printmaking to children; and Jonathan Williams is stationed in Germany in the early 1950s and splits his literary life *after* BMC between Appalachia and Cumbria.[54]

It's important to remember, however, that, in many instances, cross-cultural exchange often came at great personal cost to faculty, students, and affiliates—especially so for members of the Jewish Diaspora. They were often displaced from their homes, losing family, friends, and lovers.[55]

BMC did not enter the idiom of American poetry until 1960, the year Barney Rosset's New York City–based Grove Press—dedicated to avant-garde, countercultural, pornographic, and overall misfit literature—published Donald Allen's epoch-making *The New American Poetry: 1945–1960* (*NAP*).[56] It included forty-four upstarts, braggarts, mystics, hipsters, homosexuals, and iconoclasts, many of whom—John Ashbery, Barbara Guest, LeRoi Jones/Amiri Baraka, Kenneth Koch, Gary Snyder, and Jack Spicer—are now taken for granted as commonplace figures in twentieth-century American literature.[57]

NAP signaled a paradigm shift in American poetry in the years after the Second World War comparable to, and contiguous with, bebop in African American jazz and abstract expressionism in the visual arts. By the early 1950s, Creeley was as likely to expound upon the rhythmic properties of Miles Davis, Charlie Parker, and Bud Powell solos as he was William Carlos Williams's poetry. In fact, he did just that in his multivolume correspondence with Olson.[58] And as Steve Evans notes, there are clear aesthetic and existential similarities between Olson's notion of the poem as a "field of action" and Harold Rosenberg's description of Willem de Kooning's and Franz Kline's canvases in his essay "The American Action Painters."[59] It's no coincidence that the Museum of Modern Art's traveling exhibit of abstract expressionist paintings in 1958–59 was titled *The New American Painting*.

In his preface to *NAP*, Donald Allen argues that the new American poets are influenced by Ezra Pound (*The Cantos*), William Carlos Williams (*Paterson*), and H.D. (*Helen in Egypt*) rather than, say, T. S. Eliot or Robert Frost.[60] In addition, he states that the material conditions of poetry's production, circulation, and reception after 1945 have changed, with significant aesthetic and social consequences for these "new younger poets": "[They] have written a large body of work, but most of what has been published so far has appeared only in a few little magazines, as broadsheets, pamphlets, and limited editions, or circulated in manuscript."[61] The performance of poetry at public and private readings became increasingly popular, too, compelling these new American poets to think about voice, lineation, and diction in relation to live, attentive audiences. By 1970, Jeanetta L. Jones had established the New American Poetry Circuit, a Berkeley-based co-op involved in organizing readings and lectures across the country for poets associated with *NAP*.[62]

First published in 1950 in *Poetry New York*, Olson's "Projective Verse" is the defining poetics statement of *NAP*. In it, Olson theorizes "OPEN" verse or "COMPOSITION BY FIELD."[63] That is, a poem's form is not "inherited" (e.g., repeated stanza structure or accentual-syllabic lineation) but intuited and discovered in medias res.[64] Prosody, imagery, and diction are localized to, and guided by, the poet's breath, physis, and *energia*: "Get on with it, keep moving, keep in, speed, the nerves, their speed, the perceptions, theirs, the acts, the split second acts, the whole business, keep it moving as fast you can, citizen."[65] The spatialization of form (the "field" and its energy) is coordinated with a new temporality in which nothing "outside the unit of time local to the idea" enters the poem; and the typewriter, as writing implement, is suited to notating with precision "the personal and instantaneous."[66] This general desire for openness is echoed by Olson's fellow new American poets: Duncan's vowels serve as audible passages through which the occult and mystical enter and disturb the rational limits of the poem—what he calls "a disturbance of words within words" in "Often I Am Permitted to Return to a Meadow."[67] In "My Heart," Frank O'Hara explains,

> I want my face to be shaven, and my heart—
> you can't plan on the heart, but
> the better part of it, my poetry, is open.[68]

And Allen Ginsberg's "Howl" taps into and exposes the psychosocial trauma of an entire generation "destroyed by madness, starving hysterical naked, / dragging themselves through the negro streets at dawn looking for an angry fix."[69]

Allen organizes *NAP* into five grouped sections. Geography determines the first four groups: the Black Mountain poets; the San Francisco Renaissance; the Beats, who oscillated between San Francisco and New York; and the New York School. The fifth grouping possesses "no geographical definition": "It includes younger poets who have been associated with and in some cases influenced by the leading writers of the preceding groups."[70]

In order of appearance, Allen's Black Mountain poets are Charles Olson, Robert

Duncan, Denise Levertov, Paul Blackburn, Robert Creeley, Paul Carroll, Larry Eigner, Edward Dorn, Jonathan Williams, and Joel Oppenheimer. These ten figures meet at least one of Allen's three criteria: they teach at the college (Olson, Creeley, and Duncan); they study at the college under Olson, Creeley, and Duncan (Dorn, Oppenheimer, and Williams); or they publish in either *BMR* or *Origin* (Blackburn, Carroll, Eigner, and Levertov).

Allen acknowledges that his organizational "divisions are somewhat arbitrary and cannot be taken as rigid categories"[71]—though they have since circulated as dogma, causing Olson to dismiss, as early as 1968, "that whole 'Black Mountain poet' thing" as "a lot of bullshit" and "a topological error."[72] Case in point, Duncan works as an instructor at BMC briefly in 1956, and he contributes poetry and essays to *BMR* throughout the magazine's run. But, along with Helen Adam, Robin Blaser, Madeline Gleason, and Jack Spicer, Duncan is one of the major figures of the San Francisco Renaissance, his poetry and poetics socially, politically, and sexually grounded in that city's poetry community, institutions (e.g., San Francisco State University's Poetry Center), and the museum-like home he shared with the collage artist Jess. Similarly, Allen places John Wieners in the anthology's fifth group. However, as the Boston-born Wieners recalls, "I first met Charles Olson on the night of Hurricane Hazel, September 11, 1954, when I 'accidentally' heard him read his verse at the Charles St. Meeting House. They passed out complimentary copies of *BMR* #1, and I aint [*sic*] been able to forget."[73] An inspired Wieners enrolled at the college for one full semester and one summer session, and he is now regarded without much controversy as a Black Mountain poet while, at the same time, is also integral to the "occult school of Boston poetry," alongside poets such as Stephen Jonas and Gerritt Lansing.[74]

Alan Golding's scholarship on *NAP*'s editorial history points to the fluidity of Donald Allen's "Black Mountain" group.[75] Allen started the editorial process in earnest in April 1958, shaping a provisional table of contents through conversation and correspondence—often at cross-purposes and sometimes strained—with an advisory board that included, at various times, Olson, Creeley, and Duncan, as well as Blaser, O'Hara, Jones/Baraka, and James Schuyler.[76] In letters, for example, Olson urges Allen to categorize Edward Marshall as a Black Mountain poet.[77] *BMR* had published Marshall's "Leave the Word Alone," a poem that earned the admiration of Olson, Duncan, Creeley, Ginsberg, and Michael Rumaker. But Marshall suffered Wieners's fate: Allen placed him in the anthology's fifth section because of his age. William Bronk provides another interesting case study. He published his early poetry in *BMR* and *Origin*—thus satisfying one of Allen's three criteria. Allen's plan, in fact, had been to include Bronk in *NAP*. However, Bronk's Wallace

Stevens–esque poetry did not sufficiently impress Olson at the time (Olson, I should add, later came around to Bronk's work); Creeley originally recommended Bronk to Allen for inclusion, before, ultimately, withdrawing the suggestion and referring to him as "marginal, more Stevens than anything."[78] Unfortunately, Bronk was, as David W. Clippinger notes, the last poet cut from *NAP* in December 1959.[79] Fortunately, *The Anthology of Black Mountain College Poetry* includes Bronk's poetry for both its aesthetic and historical significance.

Several other poets satisfy one or more of Allen's criteria yet do not make *NAP*'s final table of contents. Edward Dahlberg (faculty), Paul Goodman (visiting faculty), and Michael Rumaker (student) each receive serious consideration from Allen and his various editorial confidants. In fact, Goodman is part of the final group of seven poets left out of the anthology. (The others are the aforementioned Bronk, as well as Judson Crews, Joanne Kyger, David Lyttle, Jack Micheline, and Stan Persky.)[80] Likewise, there is some support for Gael Turnbull and Irving Layton. In a letter to Olson on 9 September 1959, Allen writes, "Also think[ing] of throwing in a couple of poems by Layton & Gael Turnbull to round it out, taking American in the wider sense."[81] In the end, the more restrictive national purview of *NAP*—in contrast with the aforementioned international scope of the college and *BMR*—took precedence.

The Anthology of Black Mountain College Poetry recognizes and celebrates the historical importance of *BMR* and *NAP* but, at the same time, aims to transcend their respective limits, providing a far more inclusive sense of the BMC experience. It does include Goodman, Dahlberg, and Rumaker, as well as Turnbull and Layton. In addition, the anthology emphasizes the "people who were there," to borrow from Fielding Dawson.[82] For nearly twenty-five years, faculty, students, families, and visitors lived and learned together at Lee Hall or Lake Eden, though not necessarily in perfect harmony and not always under the easiest conditions. They hiked into the Smoky Mountains, seeking inspiration in nature's forms; they fertilized the soil, and they milked cows; they debated poems, plays, and novels; they enjoyed dancing on Saturday evenings, as well as the occasional romantic intrigue; they played football and softball (by all accounts, Fielding Dawson was an exceptional starting pitcher); they snuck out to Ma Peek's Tavern for drinks; and they played poker after dark, listening to the latest bebop records. Somewhere along the way, the faculty and students also found time to produce some of the most exhilarating poetry of the twentieth century.

Poets "who were there" often reflect on the meaningfulness of the BMC experience through their verse.[83] Marie Tavroges Stilkind's "To Fee Dawson," for example, recalls the tradition of Sunday afternoon softball games on campus:

Poetry that spring
was the crack of the ball
on wood.[84]

There's great irony in Stilkind's image of countercultural misfits at an experimental college indulging in the quintessential American pastime. In "The Black Mountain Blues," John Wieners imbues "old black mountain" with the promise of pastoral relief, personal freedom, and creative *communitas*:

I want to eat spaghetti every night
with the ladies who play gay guitars
and the boys who lie down.[85]

In his essay "Advance-Guard Writing, 1900–1950," Paul Goodman expresses a desire much like Wieners's but in more pointedly critical terms: "The essential present-day advance-guard is the physical reestablishment of community. This is to solve the crisis of alienation in the simple way: the persons are estranged from themselves, from one another, and from their artist; he takes the initiative precisely by putting his arms around them and drawing them together."[86] Published in 1951 in the *Kenyon Review*, Goodman's essay was, in fact, written as a reflection on, and celebration of, his transformative experience at BMC in 1950.

Martha Davis King's "Black Mountain Landscape" presents an account of everyday life on campus from a woman's perspective. Her poem begins with a description of the Western Carolina topography but ends with mention of a harrowing "dream" that throws Wieners's aforementioned queer pastoralism into sharp relief:

The valley rises and thins out
its up end curving like the handle of a spoon
Pancake clouds splotch across the valley floor
and rivers of light
spill past the sign for Stuckey's Pee cans
following the bent road
where farm boys park
gulp beer
and dream of beating city women[87]

King's poem suggests an intersection of town-and-gown conflict—the school's students and faculty spatially figured as interloping "city" people—and the omnipresent threat of violence against women who dared to get an education or, seemingly worse, to write and publish poetry.

Thankfully, of course, many women *did* dare to write poetry at BMC. While Denise Levertov is significant as the only woman included in Allen's "Black Mountain" section in *NAP*, she never, in fact, stepped foot on campus—her affiliation with the school is through *BMR* and a consequence of literary friendships with figures such as Olson, Creeley, Duncan, Richards, and Morley. In contrast, *The Anthology of Black Mountain College Poetry* includes poetry by women who served on faculty or comprised the student body across three decades: Sylvia Girsh Ashby, Peggy Bennett Cole, Ruth Herschberger, Cynthia Homire, Eva Schlein Jungermann, Martha Davis King, Jane Mayhall, Caroline Burton Michahelles, Hilda Morley, Barbara Stone Rice, M. C. Richards, Janet Heling Roberts, May Sarton, Marie Tavroges Stilkind, Martha Rittenhouse Treichler, Mary Parks Washington, and Susan Weil.

M. C. Richards started teaching at BMC in 1945, and she quickly became a favorite among the students. They enjoyed her classes—Richards taught Hardy, Conrad, Faulkner, Joyce, and Melville—but also her unusual professional temperament: "Youthful, enthusiastic, formal, aloof authority."[88] Richards shared her students' enthusiasm for and commitment to learning: while on faculty, she studied theater, dance, woodwork, printmaking, and, most important, pottery.[89] She devoted her post-BMC life to fully integrating poetry, pottery, and spirituality, resulting in the publication of *Centering in Pottery, Poetry, and the Person* in 1964. Richards's lyric poetry often emphasizes the Taoist concept of wu wei (the "getting out of one's own way") and Zen Buddhist concept of sunyata (emptiness) in order to present the world and its hidden, forgotten, or repressed connections more clearly:[90]

> Why is everything called
> by another name:
> water is smoky pearl this first bright morning of spring in the Mine-
>   sceonga at a depth of 14 inches over granite
> birds are flutes
> grass is having its hair streaked
> last week's sleds are beached in the field
> it's all a big double-take, a dédoublement as the French say, a
>   haunting:
> the world is full of phantoms walking around in bodies.
> The primal stuffing is leaking out all over the place.[91]

"Metaphor," argues Richards in *Centering*, is "the highest gift," the "intuition of union" between disparate objects, events, and experiences.[92] By contrast, earlier poems from her Black Mountain days, especially "Organization" and "For Political

Reasons," are more avant-garde in form and content, using prosaic, expository language to explore anarchist ideals and to critique institutional power politics. In a letter from June 1950, Charles Olson singled these two poems out as especially successful; they are composed, he says, "with the head" and without regard for "'the poetic.'"[93]

Inspired by Anaïs Nin, who visited BMC in 1947 and talked with students and faculty about self-publishing, Richards led the effort to revive an otherwise "dormant" print culture on campus in the years after the Second World War.[94] She did so with the help of students such as Jim Tite, Ann Mayer, and Harry Weitzer.[95] Tite, in particular, applied his technical know-how to salvage a Challenge Gordon press, and the college subsequently acquired a Kluge press through government surplus. "With our 'battery' of two presses we really went to town producing letterheads, bulletins, concert programs, student and faculty creative writing—you name it," recalls Tite.[96] One of the printshop's first publications was Richards's debut collection, *Poems* (1947), which circulated on campus in a limited edition of fifty copies. Other publications included Jerrold Levy and Richard Negro's *Poems by Gerard Legro* (1949), Jack Boyd and Fielding Dawson's *2 & 4* (1950), and Russell Edson's *Ceremonies in Bachelor Space* (1951), as well as the first and only issue of the *Black Mountain College Review* (1951)—not to be confused with the later *BMR*. Students eventually started up micropress imprints through the printshop: Joel Oppenheimer's Sad Devil Press, Carroll Williams's Black Cat Press, Tommy Jackson's Grapnel Press, Lou Harrison's Black Mountain College Music Press, and Nicholas Cernovich's Black Mountain Graphics Workshop.[97]

Hilda Morley—one of the great BMC poets (though still relatively unknown and underappreciated)—composes poems that are more painterly and emotive than those of M. C. Richards. In "The Poet and Painting," Morley writes,

> This darting swooping movement of the mind reflecting our world, a movement swift in its attack and at its most powerful, spherical or global in nature, is reflected in the spacing of words on a page of modern poetry, a movement full of stops, sudden coagulations and blockages, attempting to embody every turn of sensation or reflection in the way lines are broken to allow for ever-fresher emphases. A new kind of stillness can emerge from this use of space, for eye and ear at once, analogous, perhaps to the stillness of a crowded interior by Matisse.[98]

She imagines the page as a canvas. Each line is a brushstroke, tracing the mind's activity. It will not come as a surprise, then, to learn that Morley's poetry reflects a sustained interest in ekphrasis (i.e., the verbal representation of visual art), as demonstrated by her poems "Japanese Print" and "For Piet Mondrian." Whereas Olson emphasizes space and movement, Morley emphasizes space and stillness. Olson's poetry projects outward (to get inside), and Morley's projects inward (to get outside). This expansive interiority is most evident in the heartbreaking elegies she writes—including "The Shutter Clangs"—for her husband, avant-garde composer Stefan Wolpe, who taught music at BMC from 1952 to 1956. "The Shutter Clangs" is an exquisite poem, a forgotten classic in the Black Mountain canon. It equals, and perhaps even surpasses, the achievements of Carroll's "Father," Duncan's "Often I Am Permitted to Return to a Meadow," and Olson's "I, Maximus of Gloucester, to You."

Peggy Bennett Cole, Jane Mayhall, and Ruth Herschberger attended the college prior to 1945—before the arrivals of Richards and Olson. Cole writes light verse, using animals to communicate a clear moral lesson. For example, "Plain Talk for a Pachyderm" playfully dresses down the shabby chic of the hipster Bowery elite. By contrast, her "Parable" is far more serious in subject matter (i.e., an indictment of masculinity, misogyny, and violence) and modernist in its unadorned style. Mayhall is one of the few social satirists associated with BMC. Her poem "Re-Ejects" critiques the sexual and social politics of literary power and taste through the conceit of magazine rejection letters: a pretentiously named poetry editor, "John Esthetique Upsom" (a barely concealed John Crowe Ransom), refuses her poems "when [she] was twenty-one / . . . because / they were too hung up on social revolution."[99] Finally, Herschberger—who earned comparison to Elizabeth Bishop upon the publication of her first book of poems and the admiration of a young John Ashbery, who encountered her work in editor Oscar Williams's poetry anthologies of the 1940s[100]—writes formal verse representative of a well-wrought, midcentury style, with mannered metaphorical conceits that aspire to the heights of New Critical irony and ambiguity:

> We watched our love burn with the lumberyard,
> Bats in their wheeling showed our crazèd sense,
> We stood in fields where weeds with chiggers scrambled,
> And stood the heat flush in our face, immense.
>
> Softly the crowd acclaimed the devastation,
> And we, we smiled to see the embers twist,
> Tottering towers and poles with flashing wires.
> We shifted feet when shifting structures kissed.[101]

Herschberger's rhymed verse belies her otherwise radical spirit: in 1948, for example, she published *Adam's Rib*, a feminist tract that—in its advocacy of clitoral stimulation—was years ahead of its time; and in 1969, she wrote "The Battle Hymn of Women's Liberation" (a feminist parody of "The Battle Hymn of the Republic") in defense of Valerie Solanas.

The Anthology of Black Mountain College Poetry also presents a poem cowritten by Mary Parks Washington, one of the earliest African American students at BMC, following in the footsteps of Alma Stone Williams, who first enrolled in 1944, two years before Washington and a decade before *Brown v. Board of Education*. Debate over integration was intense and divisive at the college. Some faculty members felt morally and politically obligated to support the cause of integration in the Jim Crow South; others feared that accepting African American students would make the college the target of racists.[102] What's clear, though, is that BMC *students* actively championed civil rights at the college, demanding a more diverse student body, volunteering for the Southern Negro Youth Congress, and even providing refuge for early Freedom Riders associated with the Journey of Reconciliation.[103] Poet Jesse Green, for example, traveled to Charleston, South Carolina, for the congress, where he met W. E. B. Du Bois.[104] With the help of a Julius Rosenwald Fund Fellowship, Mary Parks Washington attended the 1946 Summer Institute, studying art with Josef Albers and Jean Varda and dance with Gwendolyn Knight Lawrence, wife of painter Jacob Lawrence. Her poem "A Downhome Recipe from a Black Soul Mother's Workshop" is a collaboration with Sarah Webster Fabio, the Black Arts Movement poet, performer, and critic.

This is not, however, the only connection between BMC and the Black Arts Movement. Olson played a significant role in the development of LeRoi Jones/Amiri Baraka's poetry and poetics, and Jones/Baraka was equally important to Olson, republishing Olson's "Projective Verse" as a Totem Press pamphlet in 1959 and, as Aldon Lynn Nielsen suggests, functioning as "a crucial representative for Olson of a further objective for projective verse."[105] Scholarship by Nathaniel Mackey, Joseph Pizza, Lorenzo Thomas, and Lewis Turco also explores this connection between Jones/Baraka and BMC at length.[106]

The purview of BMC poetry is further expanded in the present anthology by including work by figures traditionally thought of as visual artists, musicians, filmmakers, inventors, and theorists: Josef Albers, John Cage, Buckminster Fuller, Lou Harrison, Cynthia Homire, Ray Johnson, Basil King, Caroline Burton Michahelles, Gerd Stern, John Urbain, Stan VanDerBeek, and Susan Weil.

Josef Albers, for example, published a single volume of dual-language poetry

(German and English) in 1958, titled *Poems and Drawings.* "Poetry was," as Nicholas Fox Weber writes, "an essential part of Albers's life. He liked Schiller and Goethe; he also liked Haiku."[107] In his poetry, Albers proves especially adept at composing philosophical epigrams, such as

Calm down
whatever happens
happens mostly
without you.[108]

Buckminster Fuller is widely recognized for constructing and popularizing the geodesic dome, an example of which was the centerpiece of the American Pavilion at Expo 67; however, he also composed a discursive poetry—what George Quasha calls "a new lecture-poetry"—that earned the admiration of John Cage, Hugh Kenner, and Jonathan Williams and has been cited by critic Barry Alpert as a forerunner to David Antin's "talk" poetry.[109] Antin, in conversation with Alpert, once "singled out" for appreciation "Bucky's vernacular American anti-formalism."[110] John Urbain's "1930" tackles the effects of the Great Depression through an intimate William Carlos Williams–esque portrait of a married couple living in Detroit and struggling to make ends meet.[111] And an award-winning composer and BMC music professor, Lou Harrison, experimented with non-Western instrumentation and tunings; he was especially interested in the Indonesian gamelan, an ensemble-based musical style with its origins in eighth-century Yogyakarta. Yet Harrison also wrote moving verse in honor of fellow musicians, mentors, friends, and lovers, including Bill Colvig, his life partner, whom he met in 1967: "'He is the best decision you have made / in twenty-three years.'"[112] Poems such as "Of Bill" are significant because they represent the queer (literary) legacy of BMC, which is also represented in these pages.

The Anthology of Black Mountain College Poetry demonstrates that Olson's projective verse is only one compositional method among many at the college. Projective verse is correctly observed as a revolution in twentieth-century American poetry, and it informs much of the work included here, but the breadth of *other* poetic ideas, attitudes, forms, and genres studied and practiced at BMC, and beyond, is equally remarkable. Readers will encounter the blues (Wieners, "The Black Mountain Blues"), collage (Metcalf, "Willie's Throw"), and haiku (Blackburn, "16 Sloppy Haiku"); elegy (Carroll, "Father"), ode (Harrison, "Nines to John Cage on his 65th Birthday, 1977"), and sonnet (Rosenfeld, "The Dedication of a House in Spring"); ekphrasis (Basil King, "Pablo Picasso"), inventory (Janet Heling Roberts, "these things I love, 1944"), and mesostic (Cage, "Writing through the Cantos"); love lyric (Herschberger, "The Huron"), prayer (Levertov, "Prayer for Revolutionary Love"), and philosophical investigation (Bronk, "The Real World"); and parable (Cole, "Parable"), epistle (Sarton, "A Letter to the Students of Black Mountain College, written in homage and in faith"), and satire (Mayhall, "For the Well-Dressed Women Throwing Their Dirty Paper Towels on the Rest Room Floor at the Metropolitan Museum").

Paul Goodman's sonnet "Kent State, May 4, 1970" laments the murder of four Kent State University students by Ohio National Guardsmen who opened fire on a campus protest in response to the continued US presence in Vietnam and Cambodia. Nine students were also wounded in the shooting. "See, the children that we massacre / are our own children. Call the soldiers back," writes Goodman.[113] In that closing couplet, he establishes a correspondence between the violence of US military operations abroad and the violence simultaneously suffered at home. Poems such as Goodman's "Kent State, May 4, 1970," Charles Greenleaf Bell's "Bikini," Mervin Louis Lane's "The Army," Duncan's "Up Rising," Levertov's "Life at War," and Urbain's "BLACK VIGIL/Vietnam '67" are important because they demonstrate a protest line of poetics within the canon of BMC poetry. Furthermore, Goodman's poem indicates that the sonnet—symbolic bugaboo of *NAP*—has a place (albeit an uncomfortable one) in the history of BMC poetry, as the examples of Isaac Rosenfeld, Joel Oppenheimer, Irving Layton, and Ebbe Borregaard also confirm.

Poets such as John Cage, Susan Weil, and Jonathan Williams formally experiment with found materials. Cage's mesostics are variations on the acrostic and exemplify his chance-based composition methods. He identifies a key, typically a proper name, then "writes through" a predetermined source text using said key. In "Writing through the Cantos," for example, his key is "Ezra Pound": "and thEn with bronZe lance heads beaRing yet Arm's / sheeP slain Of plUto stroNg praiseD."[114] Weil's collage poems—she calls them "poemumbles"—flout the boundary between poetry and visual art.[115] Using an archive of linguistic and visual texts, Weil cuts and pastes found words, phrases, or sentences, as well as images, creating hybrid visual-verbal works. She continues today to compose poemumbles every morning, an ethical exercise of the imagination to start the day. Williams presents a documentary poetry of sorts in his book *Blues and Roots, Rue and Bluets*. The native North Carolinian hikes the southeastern Appalachian Trail with his ear to the ground and his notebook in hand, transcribing folk wisdom—often marked by the darkest of humor—in the vernacular of the area's longtime residents.

Finally, ekphrasis poems reflect the interdisciplinary ethos at BMC. Basil King's

"Paul Gauguin," for example, responds to the French symbolist's *The Yellow Christ* (1889). The poem gives collective voice to the peasant women of Brittany who pray for forgiveness at the feet of a crucified Jesus:

> Powerful men thought him bad trouble
> and framed it so he would be crucified.
> We're sorry. You know, we've
> begun to realize what he tried to do
> and we loved him.[116]

King is, in this particular instance, more interested in reinterpreting the painting's religious narrative than addressing its cloisonnist style. By contrast, his poem "Pablo Picasso" attempts to formally approximate cubist perspective on the page, doing so through slight variations on the poem's key words and phrases as well as its line breaks and typographic layout. Poets Jerrold Levy and Richard Negro compose a diptych, titled "Father Albers's Notebook," in which they similarly attempt to translate Josef Albers's *matière* into language (*matière* refers to the haptic rather than optical elements of a work of art):

> Snow with bird prints
> Saw marks on wood
> Tire marks in mud
> Wasp nests
> Bird nests
> Fluting
>
> Engraving
> Etching
> Woodcuts
> Hammered metal
>   (embossed)[117]

Surface textures of the compositional materials convey meaning—just as color, figuration, perspective, and space do.

Numerous instances of interdisciplinary exchange are, of course, present in the anthology. BMC poets such as Ray Johnson, Joel Oppenheimer, M. C. Richards, and Stan VanDerBeek look not only to visual art but music, dance, pottery, film, and new media for inspiration. In defense of this social, collaborative, and nonhierarchical spirit of making, Olson, in 1951, writes to W. H. Ferry, stating, "[I] do not think one can overstate . . . the importance of workers in different fields of the arts and of knowledge working so closely together some of the time of the year that they find out, from each other, the ideas, forms, energies, and the whole series of kinetics and emotions now opening up, out of the quantitative world."[118] It is BMC, observes Olson, that uniquely "offers this sort of chance, this sort of experimental locus."[119]

Some mornings, it is easy to imagine BMC poetry is as sharply defined, clear, and warm as the violet light Hilda Morley once described as Cézanne-like, falling across the Swannanoa Valley at dawn. Some nights, however, BMC poetry is as dark and smoky as the study rooms cum poker dens where students made art and socialized into the early hours. *The Anthology of Black Mountain College Poetry* preserves these seemingly irreconcilable impressions for the historical record, opening our eyes to the school's plenitude across three decades: visionary teachers, risk-taking students, and artistic friendships (and rivalries, too); vibrant material and print cultures that connected the campus to national and international audiences; and, most important, inimitable poems that reward reading and rereading.

The Anthology of Black Mountain College Poetry serves as an essential guide to be studied, tested, and debated by new generations of students, researchers, and general readers. The poets associated with BMC share in the responsibility to make a better world. They place civil disobedience and aesthetic experimentation in the service of progressive ideals, including political and formal autonomy. They see change—by way of movement or stillness, sound or silence—as a virtue to protect. They often wed personal ethics with community-building initiatives, including the editing and publishing of magazines and books. They insist that the self and language are grounded in local context but resonate globally. Finally, the poets in this anthology are suspicious of, and react against, consecrated forms of knowledge and power, using poetry as a means of inquiry and discovery, seeking out the unknown, explaining what is misunderstood or marginalized, and inventing new forms of being that exist beyond the readymade. The BMC poets anthologized here, to quote M. C. Richards, bring

> relevance to the human spirit
> in its quest for creative freedom
> and depth in learning.[120]

PART I | FACULTY

in order of appointment

JOSEF ALBERS | 1888–1976

Born in Bottrop, Germany, artist and designer Josef Albers entered the Weimar Bauhaus as a student in 1920. The Bauhaus curriculum combined fine and applied arts, including architecture, sculpture, graphic design, typography, textiles, and painting. When the school relocated to Dessau in 1925, Albers became a member of its faculty, which also boasted artists such as Paul Klee and Wassily Kandinsky. The Bauhaus focused on practical art-making and design problems and, at the same time, experimented with modern aesthetic, theoretical, and scientific ideas; its departure from tradition posed a threat to the ideology of Adolf Hitler and the ascendant Nazi Party. As a result, the school closed down under political pressure in 1933. That same year, Albers and his wife, Anni, fled Germany and, with the assistance of Philip Johnson, an architect and curator at the Museum of Modern Art in New York, obtained teaching positions at BMC. Significantly, Albers was influenced by the progressive educational philosophy of John Dewey, who visited the BMC campus in 1934 and again in 1935. While serving as art department head at the college (1933–49), Albers taught design and drawing as well as his *matière* studies; he also created a revolutionary course on color theory, which he later formalized in a book-length study, *Interaction of Color* (1963). Albers is best known for his prints and paintings, including *Homage to the Square*, a series of nested squares he began producing in 1950. Albers's *Poems and Drawings* (1958) features twenty-two drawings—known as "Structural Constellations"—and original poems appearing in both English and German.[1] "Poetry was an essential part of Albers's life," writes Nicholas Fox Weber, "and he was immensely proud of his own forays into the field—especially of [*Poems and Drawings*]."[2]

The aim of life
is living creatures

The aim of art
is living creations

Das Ziel des Lebens:
lebende Wesen

Das Ziel der Kunst:
lebende Werke

1958

Calm down
what happens
happens mostly
without you

Beruhige dich
das meiste was geschieht
geschieht ohne dich

1958

My earth
serves also others

my world
is mine alone

Meine Erde
dient auch andern

meine Welt
gehört nur mir

1958

To distribute material possessions
is to divide them
to distribute spiritual possessions
is to multiply them

Verteilen sachlicher Güter
    ist aufteilen – dividieren
Verteilen geistiger Güter
    ist verbreiten – multiplizieren

Ergreifen erwirkt Besitz
Begreifen bewirkt Einsicht

1958

When rhododendrons bloom
and fireflies light up

when there is sun and air and swimming
then there are holidays

then we believe in having time
to rest, to think, to gather our thoughts

before blank paper
and an empty canvas

Wenn Rhododendron blumen
und Feuerfliegen leuchten

Wenn Sonne, Luft, und Schwimmen
dann sind die Ferien

Dann glauben wir an freie Zeit
für ruhen, sinnen, sammeln

vor leerem Schreibpapier
und weisser Leinewand

1958

MARY CAROLINE "M. C." RICHARDS | 1916–1999

Born in Weiser, Idaho, Mary Caroline "M. C." Richards grew up in Portland, Oregon, where she attended St. Helen's Hall Junior College and earned her BA in literature and languages at nearby Reed College. Richards completed her MA and PhD at the University of California, Berkeley. After teaching English at Berkeley, the Central Washington College of Education, and the University of Chicago, Richards came to BMC in 1945, and she quickly became a popular instructor. Together with students, Richards helped establish the Black Mountain College Print Shop, which handset, printed, and bound her first book, *Poems*, in 1947. The next year, Richards translated Erik Satie's 1913 play *Le piège de Méduse* (*The Ruse of Medusa*). It was performed on 8 August 1948 as part of John Cage's Erik Satie festival. Richards later translated writings by Jean Cocteau and Antonin Artaud, including the latter's *The Theater and Its Double* (1958). In the spring of 1951, Richards's creative writing class at BMC published the first and only issue of the *Black Mountain College Review*, featuring work by faculty members and students (e.g., Fielding Dawson, Russell Edson, and Joel Oppenheimer). After helping to arrange Charles Olson's faculty appointment, Richards resigned from her BMC position and relocated to New York. Though Donald Allen did not select her as a member of his "Black Mountain" group in *NAP*, Richards's poetry was admired by students and faculty, including Olson, and she was anthologized alongside other BMC poets in Daisy Aldan's *A New Folder* (1959). In 1964, Richards published *Centering in Poetry, Pottery, and the Person*, a hybrid work of poetry, essays, and personal reflections on pedagogy, creativity, and the self. By espousing progressive ideas in her classes, demonstrating how the school's philosophy could be lived and practiced through her own studies in ceramics, and playing a vital leadership role on campus, Richards is, in Fielding Dawson's estimation, the "narrative center" of the BMC experience.[3]

For Political Reasons

The way a man eats is political.
For political reasons is for human reasons, confidence vote is
  not entirely politic.
We fired a man from our faculty one year
and students of course asked why. For political reasons?
If for political reasons unfair.
If for political reasons, then unjust, was it for political reasons.
Yes if politics are in the house, if they live across the cove then
  no.
No if politics is party, if the way a man governs himself
  yes only then.
I find it hard to answer honestly with care those who ask
is it for political reasons because I think about it differently:
I don't think politics when a man intimidates, I think human;
what he conceives politically grows face and hands,
image of government is self-portraiture.
I don't see departments, I see whole and I see features
some of them maybe political, pressing it outward.
Fruit grows on a tree, unless my eyes deceive me.
If I don't trust a man, his politics are not the cause,
though they too stem from roots. So all I finally say is
yes and no. And I find more and more that I say more and more
  yes and no
when I am asked if I think something is true, because
I don't think of what is true as any phrase one safely keeps.
I don't think ever so well-chosen words are likely to do the trick
or knowledge is now our homing-pigeon home.
I think of continually circling about and edging in,
but I wouldn't care much for a truth that was
"for political reasons." It would be smaller than a man.

1947

Imagine Inventing Yellow

Imagine inventing yellow or moving
For the first time in a cherry curve.

1947

Organization

Organization is not interesting, why.

If I am the chairman and you are on my committee it is not very interesting.

Or if you are the leader and we are your group and stay so who isn't bored.

Organization is all right while it is new until you thoroughly understand
what is expected of you and then what is expected of you
is soon no longer interesting.
It gets to be like a minuet or a masque that isn't play any longer but
the whole show.

Some people like to know what is expected of them and what
the consequences will be but not me.

Some like to set themselves goals and be clear about aims so that they can
formulate standards and have an institution to which they can feel they
belong

But I don't want to belong to an institution.

Organization is not interesting but sometimes necessary to get things done
if there is something that simply must get done and better done wrong
than not done at all, are there such things maybe.

Governments are well organized but the people in the governments
do they see it all so clearly, who makes the policy and is he well organized
with the right leadership and support or is he a house divided.

Organizations and institutions and government are not interesting to me
and perhaps that's not important

But I see more and more people expecting from them whatever they are
benefits they would not expect from any of the men composing them,
I mean what rare bliss will organized humanity bestow that a man will
not give his brother.

When I was a child I liked to be a member of a gang and have a leader
and a code and meetings and by-laws and a constitution and a declared
purpose and a stern loyalty to our side. What was good was that this
public life instructed me privately in the possibilities of attitudes.
But as I grew and filled the rooms inside me I found the converse true:
public life became a mirror. And so to play with governments
is to toy with mirrors rather than with men.

Will my bold anarchic dream come true and we will govern ourselves
unprofessionally, mirroring as universe our heart's terrain.
The private world is where men meet. It is much more interesting to look
than to see what is not there.

1947

What but a gesture can convey
the heart invisible?
No phrase may.
Body, opening, asks more eloquently
than syllables.

Gesture can accept abjection
as no voice shall.
Throat can close more slyly
than crying will.

1947

The Light This Late Day Casts

I sought for Love in the woods
where I had seen Him last

where in my trembling vision
He had awaked and fled

and now, in discouragement and grief,
I returned to search the place

drawn by a sense of infusion in the air
of that measureless union

pressed by a heart that swelled towards the pools
and hillsides of His visit.

To all the features of that space
I saw His face bequeathed: measuring
the atmosphere with summer's rapture
from within.

. . . sweeps His smile through the woods,
dashes light, the trickle of jet to the bright bomb,
mineral kings crowned colors of trees,
jade, agate, topaz, carnelian,
suspended cities, boardwalks, bridges,
mosaics and steppingstones dripped and flung,
visionary pueblos, flowering temples and pits,
a Presence
curls and floats and expires;
breathes through His pipe
warm music for life's slumbering oracles. Quick,
to the quick points the electric touch.

Truly, the farther into the woods I went,
the farther up the stream I climbed,
the more deeply I returned into His aura,

the more cleansed and naked . . . —
the more His pulse and ardor built
until in the chaste and voluptuous brake
I fainted dead away, and fell,
a dead leaf in His invisible arms.

His Being humped in the stream:
He was a dragon frothing and dragging the stones,
and the stones ground their teeth in blessedness.

His brown transparent watery body
flowed and humped and rattled the stones,
and the aroma of the stream smote me anew.

I sat on a granite island and assumed His shape;
sloped over the rock, and the back of my legs an arch
of His trouble, my toes tracing themselves in Him
and He leapt up and batted miraculous crystals.

I walked tenderly at the edge of the stream
and my tears fell with yearning into the body of Love
and they disappeared, and appeared again between the lashes of the spray.

I searched everywhere with my soul and my gaze,
and I lifted my eyes over the earth nearby.
On a rock at the base of a bank, a handful of gold—
limp and almost drained of its matter—and I suffered anew.

The summer is dying, the autumn is clear,
the autumn is dying, the winter is in flakes,
fast into the heart of the earth where the sun descends
runs the river, the loaves of its brown body rise
in the light this late day casts.

1964

Poem

Why is everything called
by another name:
water is smoky pearl this first bright morning of spring in the Mine-
sceonga at a depth of 14 inches over granite
birds are flutes
grass is having its hair streaked
last week's sleds are beached in the field
it's all a big double-take, a dédoublement as the French say, a
haunting:
the world is full of phantoms walking around in bodies.
The primal stuffing is leaking out all over the place,
it's bound to get mixed up either outside or inside man's speech.
What's the difference, the sages spend a lifetime trying to get to
that supreme point where
everything is everything else, and here it is happening down here
on my level.

1964

EDWARD DAHLBERG | 1900–1977

Born in Boston, Massachusetts, Edward Dahlberg, the son of Saul Gottdank (a barber) and Elizabeth Dahlberg (a hairdresser), had a troubled early life, which later became the subject of his 1929 novel, *Bottom Dogs*, and his 1964 memoir, *Because I Was Flesh*. He grew up primarily under the care of his mother, who moved often and ultimately settled in Kansas City, Missouri. From the ages of twelve to seventeen, Dahlberg was committed to the Jewish Orphan Asylum in Cleveland. At seventeen, he set off, traveling around the American West before ending up in Los Angeles, where he attended the University of California, Berkeley, from 1921 to 1923. In 1923, he transferred to Columbia University, where he earned a BS in 1925. While Dahlberg was a social activist who championed the cause of the downtrodden in his realist and naturalist novels of the early 1930s, he had begun experimenting with a more vatic literary style by the time he arrived at BMC in September 1948, when he temporarily replaced M. C. Richards, who was on leave. Although he appreciated the intimate and intensive student-teacher interactions, Dahlberg could not endure the campus's rural isolation. He stayed on for only two weeks, then recommended the school hire his friend Charles Olson as his replacement. Thus, Dahlberg inadvertently played a key role in the history of the college. His late works present radically new explorations of self and society, especially in the volume of poetry *Cipango's Hinder Door* (1965), which earned the praise of Allen Tate. A now-obsolete term that Marco Polo and medieval geographers gave to the group of islands that make up Japan, "Cipango" is one of the places Christopher Columbus believed he had discovered when he first landed in the New World. In this volume, Dahlberg literally and figuratively forges a new world and new understanding of his experience by juxtaposing his story against a mythologized version of American history.

Cipango's Hinder Door

For Rlene

I

I chant energy and chance to youth,
And to the old I bring
The mulled wine of ancient annals.
Strife is a demigod that parents our acts,
Eats the land,
And has created a race of dog-necked people
With bitter fangs of reason.

O people, take the purgative buckthorn
And the laurel for parturition.
Sons of little-born dust,
Your birth is in the bones of gods and fathers
Whose annals you know not;
Let history be your hymn of penance,
Farm your parents and the races in the ground,
Not for pelf but for remembrance,
And make ready for the festival of ruin.

II

The willow drank the pelting stream
Lipped by the goat at Lampsacus,
And on the Phaeacian bedrock
Nausicaä bruised the chaste cestus.
The woodlands were the fame of Diana.
In the Asopus and Maeander
The virgin sang water-songs
And the Naiad showed her breasts
Hurt with untaken milk and love.
Ulai was the pooled threshold
Where holy Gabriel stood by Daniel;
But no angel sighs or messengers intimations

To a spiky catfish or sea cow in the *da Prata*
Pouring its fresh furies for three leagues
Into the ocean.

Hercules and Father Liber cared for the vine, the fallow, the ladle, and the wine-lees that nurse savine; Hesiod went to the holm oak for honey, and Zeus plucked up dane wort and hemlock to heal the crop. The droppings of the thrush enlivened the furrow.

The Indies breeds no pining sorrow or domestic lament. *Nueva Firma* maddens the wit, drives the faculty to pasture with the pard, the mountain cat and black poplar. The man of the new world has a bison's brow, a jaguar's appetite and horse's bowels. His precepts are from the sumac, potherb, nettle branch, and the *Platte*, not ancient law.

Indian maidens chew a plant until the juice flows wine; balsam for pains is in the tree-bark scratched by wounded animals seeking a poultice; aboriginal beef is taken from the sea heifer that grazes upon the mangrove tree.

This is battle earth, forest is god,
And the loaves, wine and simple are from the tree;
But no Tree of Good and Evil has here been planted;
And the seamy rains and vapors of Peru
And the equinox
Are as the mists that went up before Creation.

The four rivers of Eden tamed the plum and the tuber-apple, and the winds pecked the fruits and seeds, carrying them to the Sierras and the Andean slopes.

The terebinth is Abraham's angelic branch;
The desert tamarisk is Saul's humble umbrella;
Samuel, God's olive,
Feeds the kids in Ramah;
The sibyl Deborah has a timbrel
No heavier than a peck of lupines,
Her skirts are an homer of apples,
And her petticoats an ephah of figs;
Aaron's tunic is table linen for Jacob and Rachel;
The springs in the Palmyra sands are Tamar's girdle;
Shun not Rahab, for through her gates
Are the shouting dates and palms of Jericho.

III

A hemisphere had slept like unknown John in the crypt at Ephesus, *Cipango*'s hinder door; the cartographer's honey, but hyssop to the bowels. Its plenteous fields were covered with the Indian yam, the vestal squill, a nuptial dessert in the pompion's mouth.

The Florida currents were seers, carrying the *ceiba* of the Antilles to Gomera, Norway, and the Orkneys. The tunnies that victual near the Pillars were intimations of a double fortune.

Western waters ran as April rivers;
The tern, frigate bird and weed
Tangled with cane, berries and ground-fruits
Wrung God from lips demon'd by woeful sea-salt.
But the race of men is bloat with boast,
And cunning in fast and vigil.

Touching the Antilles the voyagers gave sighing appellations to Indies' towns, bays, and coves in homage to the petrine saint and undefiled Mary. Aaron's rod nor Santiago James cast more prodigies than *Terra Firma.*

Rivers were salt at the mouth, a net brought up a sea pig, and rumor disclosed unicorns and monkeys with a human countenance. Cocoa-bodied Adams of flat faces swam with parrots to the boats; girls of lissomy nakedness, wives with but a clout, embalmed the island air, and so woo'd Cristobal Colon that he showed the savage cinnamon, pepper, pearl and gold, and breathing vice and dropping water for the rood, was sent left to leeward for ore in *Bohio.*

Plato's Atlantis had no gentler clime than *Española.* A calabash of its soft waters were enough to content the soul were it not that mountainous Pariacaca grieves the heart. On its summit an Indian beat his body against the earth for unreasoned sorrow.

Plants trammelled with dew
And ground in greenstone,
Plucked from a cock's maw,
Heal the desponding spaces
That send men's thoughts downwards to Tartarus.
Onion in honey is a simple for tumorous dreams
That wear away youth
And of a sudden bring sunset to the head.

A plaister of dragon's blood,
Juice of nettles and osier root
Ease the mind bereft of its destiny.

Canopus, the Fisher,
And the mastic at *Puerto Santo*
Fetch an Ave Maria.
A mullet leapt into the pinnace;
Ilex and myrtle were Cordoba's own,
But the river from *Sierras de Moa*
With the margaseta stones
Shone as Ophir.

When Colon's ship was aground a native arrived with a gourd of tears his king had shed.

Women, carrying hake, dory, gilt head, accompanied by men, trembling for no hurt but affection, approached the carracks in the river. The air, mild with aloes, arbutus, cedar, sweet reeds, and cane of *Española*, so affected Cristobal Colon that he named the harbor *Puerta de le Concepcion*. The morrow was the vigil of *Santo Tomas*, and he gave as tender another island to the Apostle.

Two girls, white as of Aragon, wore yellow grains in their noses, and a cacique brought gold leaf the size of a hand. The soil was guileless, but there are plants in the head, dodder and bind-weed, that ravish vetch; axe grass beheads the lentil; the sparrow, a freebooter, will avoid millet if the ground be the barrow of the toad.

Colon, with a turnip nose ruddling his face, was no robber Sisyphus; nor had Tantalus dowered him in the race's genius, insatiate of seizing seas and fruits, even in Erebus.

In *Española* the cacique had sent a mask with ears to porch rumor, and nostrils, gross with trade and old with proverbs, that was wrought of the ore which draws from the cheeks lumps of greed. The sailors filled their casks with water from the *Yaqui River*, but only small gold adhered to the hoops.

IV

Could he appear with begging leg before the Lady of the Earth with only a jakish claim to squash, maize, and the potato, heathen fellow in the furrow with Pythagoras's bean?

Devout Isabella was mortal, but goodness has a twin visage. My lady, of the space of a blush from Mary, has two breasts, only one tender of hearing. She would heed how a king brought three fat geese and cotton, or strain to her the sea cow in the *Rio del Oro* that carries in an arm the infant suckled, and would turn aside to wipe compassion from her bosom. But with no caravel of cloves or gold, and proffering only twelve Turk Indians in stoles embroidered with owls, she would press her hand to the other breast and feel a stone.

The earth rests upon the water
Which bears the title Ocean,
But Cristobal Colon has discovered a fillip of cockles.
He shook the dross of origin,
And imagined he was a cubit more of mortal dust.
Madeira had been gained, Ombrion too,
And this is St. Colon's day.

Am I, apprentice to Ptolemy, Isidorus, and King Juba, to commence a new evangel of geography, and walk the earth like forged knowledge? What Colchis have I found? The world tempted Origen who shore away the man in him as any sea dog would. What with a pippin face to vie with Anaximander and Hipparchus, with the genius to gull the cowslip, could I surmise a sea-vein to Ceylon where rice-winds are the summery prayers at St. Thomas's burial stone? I could have farmed a humble destiny beside two sons at Cordoba.

Zama is the borning-town of Augustine,
And Utica Cato's end.
Sargon was a gardener in Sumer
When Ishtar loved him,
But the Admiral of the Seas, vowing a candle
Six pounds of wax in weight
To the Virgin of Guadalupe,
Is a uterine Jew.

The sun is good,
The earth is dear,
How then was Golgotha?
O Atlantic grief, I die nonentity!
Maybe no; Salt Oceanus is my deity,
And the murex that empurples the saints

And Agrippina
Cannot live in fresh water.

There is a stygian dropsy sinks the blood;
The undyked spleen reduces all to gnome;
Had one a millennial pear in view
It would give the eye the gorgon's hue.

Let men cease their boast or lore be sere;
Caulk the boat and cast the Galilean weir.

Shrive my soul if I hid natural lineage;
Cape Verde green by name is horrid sterile;
At Scoria the amber grows.
I thought to stock Nativity, Indies entire,
With mares, sow, the jack,
As the Kassite brought the horse to Ur.
I carried my intellect in a salver
It made my eye so dote,
Yet I knew man is issue of Balaam's ass,
And the Lampsacus goat.

Blow Etesian gales
Dividing two harvests at the westerly Indus.
Go soft to fate;
The Inca treads a bridge of straw.
Suffer darkness;
In antarctic October, night is king three hours.
O grief without asylum,
That shame can be no more sunk
Than the camel on the Dead Sea.
Let it not purloin the mind,
Ransacked by remorse,
Gibbering its guilt in asphodel.
Quiet, and erect thy towers at Gerra
Of squares of salt.

1965

CHARLES OLSON | 1910–1970

Born in Worcester, Massachusetts, Charles Olson attended Wesleyan University, where he completed his BA in 1932 (with the distinction of Phi Beta Kappa) and his MA in 1933, writing a thesis on Herman Melville. By 1939, Olson had completed coursework for a PhD in American civilization at Harvard University, published the essay "Lear and Moby Dick," and received a Guggenheim Fellowship to continue research on Melville. During the Second World War, Olson worked for the Democratic Party and Office of War Information in Washington, DC. After the war, Olson became disenchanted with politics and instead dedicated his life to poetry and criticism. In 1947, he published *Call Me Ishmael*, a groundbreaking study of Melville's *Moby-Dick*; in 1948, upon the recommendation of Edward Dahlberg, Olson began teaching at BMC as a visiting lecturer. In the fall of 1951, he joined the faculty as a permanent instructor and, subsequently, became the school's rector in 1953, a position he held until its closing. He also published his first book of poems, *In Cold Hell, In Thicket*, in 1953, with Robert Creeley's Divers Press (in conjunction with Cid Corman's *Origin*); that book features Olson's "The Kingfishers," one of the defining poems of American postmodernism. BMC provided Olson with the social support, intellectual freedom, and material conditions to develop and disseminate his ideas, including some of the influential thinking found in his most famous essays—notably, "Projective Verse," "Human Universe," and "Against Wisdom as Such." Olson established *BMR* in 1954 to increase student enrollment and to provide an outlet for emergent postmodern writers, artists, and critics; he invited Creeley to edit this newly conceived magazine and to teach writing at the school. During his time at BMC, Olson also began working more intently on *The Maximus Poems* (1983), his epic poem set in Gloucester, Massachusetts, where he spent his childhood summers. He left an impressive body of work, voluminous correspondence, and a legacy of distinguished students, including Fielding Dawson, Ed Dorn, Joel Oppenheimer, and Michael Rumaker. An innovator, iconoclast, and renowned poet and intellectual, Olson has had a profound influence upon post–Second World War American literature and culture.

This

mexico)   could not
have guessed: wood, a
bowl of gray wood, of
an afternoon, already
shadowed (4
pm: very fast, high, sharp
rockets, a crazy trumpet
of a band, few
people, sloppy
cowboys picadors matadors bulls

but out there, on that dirt, in front, directly,
before your eyes, more, yr existence:

death, the
possibility of same, the certitude
right there in front of yr
eyes, god damn yr
eyes
this bull and this man (these men) can
kill
one another

What one knows
put out, & quietly out, put out right exactly I mean OUT
in front of all eyes, including
the bull's, who runs out so
lightly, with such
declarations of
his presence

the man, so
careful, such
preparations (the bull only about to find out), the man
so clothed, such tools, and
running back to

so ludicrously the
barricade, the bull, too, smelling
the wood, where an opening is, how
to get out of

Whoever
conceived this action, this
thing, this
instant declaration of that which you know is all
that constitutes both what you are and what is going on at all time
as of you or anyone since and as long as whatever
it is that it is, is

this
bullfight:

the bull so much not
animal (as the word
is) his
experience so very clear, there, his
bewilderment, tries, angers (no
fear, mere increasing sense from confrontation that
he is
involved

the men (the man) so much more
animal, so
aware, their
courage (fear) so
very clear, so very much the reason why
we too are
involved, why
we, here,

((the man, down in that dirt, so much
a scampering, so much (advancing) a
sort of picked bantam))

those horns

that voice repeating “to-ro” “to-ro” “to-ro”

those words, wooing

that head, the plain danger of

you

have been

asked

1952

Charles Olson, "This," broadside no. 1, Black Mountain College Graphics Workshop, 1952. Illustration by Nicholas Cernovich. Reprinted with the permission of the University of California Press.

Mailing envelope, "This," broadside no. 1, Black Mountain College Graphics Workshop, 1952. Poem by Charles Olson, design and printing by Nicholas Cernovich. Collection of Black Mountain College Museum + Arts Center. Gift of Brian Butler.

The Kingfishers

1

What does not change / is the will to change

He woke, fully clothed, in his bed. He
remembered only one thing, the birds, how
when he came in, he had gone around the rooms
and got them back in their cage, the green one first,
she with the bad leg, and then the blue,
the one they had hoped was a male

Otherwise? Yes, Fernand, who had talked lispingly of Albers & Angkor Vat.
He had left the party without a word. How he got up, got into his coat,
I do not know. When I saw him, he was at the door, but it did not matter,
he was already sliding along the wall of the night, losing himself
in some crack of the ruins. That it should have been he who said, "The kingfishers!
who cares
for their feathers
now?"

His last words had been, "The pool is slime." Suddenly everyone,
ceasing their talk, sat in a row around him, watched
they did not so much hear, or pay attention, they
wondered, looked at each other, smirked, but listened,
he repeated and repeated, could not go beyond his thought
"The pool   the kingfishers' feathers were wealth   why
did the export stop?"

It was then he left

2

I thought of the E on the stone, and of what Mao said
la lumiere"
                    but the kingfisher
de l'aurore"

but the kingfisher flew west
est devant nous!
he got the color of his breast
from the heat of the setting sun!

The features are, the feebleness of the feet (syndactylism of the 3rd & 4th digit)
the bill, serrated, sometimes a pronounced beak, the wings
where the color is, short and round, the tail
inconspicuous.

But not these things were the factors. Not the birds.
The legends are
legends. Dead, hung up indoors, the kingfisher
will not indicate a favoring wind,
or avert the thunderbolt. Nor, by its nesting,
still the waters, with the new year, for seven days.
It is true, it does nest with the opening year, but not on the waters.
It nests at the end of a tunnel bored by itself in a bank. There,
six or eight white and translucent eggs are laid, on fishbones
not on bare clay, on bones thrown up in pellets by the birds.

On these rejectamenta
(as they accumulate they form a cup-shaped structure) the young are born.
And, as they are fed and grow, this nest of excrement and decayed fish becomes
a dripping, fetid mass

Mao concluded:
nous devons
nous lever
et agir!

3

When the attentions change / the jungle
leaps in
even the stones are split
they rive

Or,
enter
that other conqueror we more naturally recognize
he so resembles ourselves

But the E
cut so rudely on that oldest stone
sounded otherwise,
was differently heard

as, in another time, were treasures used:

(and, later, much later, a fine ear thought
a scarlet coat)

> "of green feathers   feet, beaks and eyes
> of gold
>
> "animals likewise,
> resembling snails
>
> "a large wheel, gold, with figures of unknown four-foots,
> and worked with tufts of leaves, weight
> 3800 ounces
>
> "last, two birds, of thread and featherwork, the quills
> gold, the feet
> gold, the two birds perched on two reeds
> gold, the reeds arising from two embroidered mounds,
> one yellow, the other
> white.
>
> > "And from each reed hung
> > seven feathered tassels.

In this instance, the priests
(in dark cotton robes, and dirty,

their disheveled hair matted with blood, and flowing wildly
over their shoulders)
rush in among the people, calling on them
to protect their gods

And all now is war
where so lately there was peace,
and the sweet brotherhood, the use
of tilled fields.

4

Not one death but many,
not accumulation but change, the feed-back proves, the feed-back is
the law

> Into the same river no man steps twice
> When fire dies air dies
> No one remains, nor is, one

Around an appearance, one common model, we grow up
many. Else how is it,
if we remain the same,
we take pleasure now
in what we did not take pleasure before? love
contrary objects? admire and/or find fault? use
other words, feel other passions, have
nor figure, appearance, disposition, tissue
the same?
    To be in different states without a change
    is not a possibility

We can be precise. The factors are
in the animal and/or the machine the factors are
communication and/or control, both involve
the message. And what is the message? The message is
a discrete or continuous sequence of measurable events distributed in time

is the birth of the air, is
the birth of water, is
a state between
the origin and
the end, between
birth and the beginning of
another fetid nest

is change, presents
no more than itself

And the too strong grasping of it,
when it is pressed together and condensed,
loses it

This very thing you are

II

They buried their dead in a sitting posture
serpent   cane   razor   ray of the sun

And she sprinkled water on the head of my child, crying
"Cioa-coatl! Cioa-coatl!"
with her face to the west

Where the bones are found, in each personal heap
with what each enjoyed, there is always
the Mongolian louse

The light is in the east. Yes. And we must rise, act. Yet
in the west, despite the apparent darkness (the whiteness
which covers all), if you look, if you can bear, if you can, long enough

as long as it was necessary for him, my guide
to look into the yellow of that longest-lasting rose

so you must, and, in that whiteness, into that face, with what candor, look

and, considering the dryness of the place
the long absence of an adequate race

(of the two who first came, each a conquistador, one healed, the other
tore the eastern idols down, toppled
the temple walls, which, says the excuser
were black from human gore)

hear
hear, where the dry blood talks
where the old appetite walks

la piu saporita et migliore
che si possa truovar al mondo

where it hides, look
in the eye how it runs
in the flesh / chalk

but under these petals
in the emptiness
regard the light, contemplate
the flower

whence it arose

with what violence benevolence is bought
what cost in gesture justice brings
what wrongs domestic rights involve
what stalks
this silence

what pudor pejorocracy affronts
how awe, night-rest and neighborhood can rot
what breeds where dirtiness is law
what crawls
below

III

I am no Greek, hath not th'advantage.
And of course, no Roman:
he can take no risk that matters,
the risk of beauty least of all.

But I have my kin, if for no other reason than
(as he said, next of kin) I commit myself, and,
given my freedom, I'd be a cad
if I didn't. Which is most true.

It works out this way, despite the disadvantage.
I offer, in explanation, a quote:
si j'ai du goût, ce n'est guères
que pour la terre et les pierres.

Despite the discrepancy (an ocean   courage   age)
this is also true: if I have any taste
it is only because I have interested myself
in what was slain in the sun

    I pose you your question:

shall you uncover honey / where maggots are?

    I hunt among stones

1953

Merce of Egypt

1 I sing the tree is a heron
I praise long grass.
I wear the lion skin
over the long skirt
to the ankle. The ankle
is a heron

I look straightly backward. Or I bend to the side straightly
to raise the sheaf
up the stick of the leg
as the bittern's leg, raised
as slow as
his neck grows
as the wheat. The presentation,
the representation,
is flat

I am followed by women and a small boy in white carrying a duck,
all have flat feet and, foot before foot, the women with black wigs
And I intent
upon idlers,
and flowers

2 the sedge
as tall as I am, the rushes
as I am

as far as I am animal, antelope
with such's attendant carnivores

and rows of beaters
drive the game to the hunter, or into nets,
where it is thick-wooded or there are open spaces
with low shrubs

3 I speak downfall, the ball of my foot
on the neck of the earth, the hardsong
of the rise of all trees, the jay
who uses the air. I am the recovered sickle
with the grass-stains still on the flint of its teeth.
I am the six-rowed barley
they cut down.

I am tree. The boy of the back of my legs
is roots. I am water fowl
when motion is the season of my river, and the wild boar
casts me. But my time
is hawkweed,

4 I hold what the wind blows, and silt.
I hide in the swamps of the valley to escape civil war,
and marauding soldiers. In the new procession
I am first, and carry wine
made of dandelions. The new rites
are my bones

I built my first settlement
in groves

5 as they would flail crops
when the spring comes, and flood, the tassels
rise, as my head

1953

I, Maximus of Gloucester, to You

Off-shore, by islands hidden in the blood
jewels & miracles, I, Maximus
a metal hot from boiling water, tell you
what is a lance, who obeys the figures of
the present dance

1

the thing you're after
may lie around the bend
of the nest (second, time slain, the bird! the bird!

And there! (strong) thrust, the mast! flight
(of the bird
o kylix, o
Antony of Padua
sweep low, o bless

the roofs, the old ones, the gentle steep ones
on whose ridge-poles the gulls sit, from which they depart,

And the flake-racks

of my city!

2

love is form, and cannot be without
important substance (the weight
say, 58 carats each one of us, perforce
our goldsmith's scale

feather to feather added
(and what is mineral, what
is curling hair, the string
you carry in your nervous beak, these

make bulk, these, in the end, are
the sum

(o my lady of good voyage
in whose arm, whose left arm rests
no boy but a carefully carved wood, a painted face, a schooner!
a delicate mast, as bow-sprit for

forwarding

3

the underpart is, though stemmed, uncertain
is, as sex is, as moneys are, facts!
facts, to be dealt with, as the sea is, the demand
that they be played by, that they only can be, that they must
be played by, said he, coldly, the
ear!

By ear, he sd.
But that which matters, that which insists, that which will last,
that! o my people, where shall you find it, how, where, where shall you listen
when all is become billboards, when, all, even silence, is spray-gunned?

when even our bird, my roofs,
cannot be heard

when even you, when sound itself is neoned in?

when, on the hill, over the water
where she who used to sing,
when the water glowed,
black, gold, the tide
outward, at evening

when bells came like boats
over the oil-slicks, milkweed
hulls

And a man slumped,
attentionless,
against pink shingles

o sea city)

4

one loves only form,
and form only comes
into existence when
the thing is born

born of yourself, born
of hay and cotton struts,
of street-pickings, wharves, weeds
you carry in, my bird

of a bone of a fish
of a straw, or will
of a color, of a bell
of yourself, torn

5

love is not easy
but how shall you know,
New England, now
that pejorocracy is here, how
that street-cars, o Oregon, twitter
in the afternoon offend
a black-gold loin?

how shall you strike,
o swordsman, the blue-red black
when, last night, your aim
was mu-sick, mu-sick, mu-sick
And not the cribbage game?

(o Gloucester-man,
weave
your birds and fingers
new, your roof-tops,
clean shit upon racks
sunned on
American
braid
with others like you, such
extricable surface
as faun and oral,
satyr lesbos vase

o kill kill kill kill kill
those
who advertise you
out)

6

in! in! the bow-sprit, bird, the beak
in, the bend is, in, goes in, the form
that which you make, what holds, which is
the law of object, strut after strut, what you are, what you must be, what
the force can throw up, can, right now hereinafter erect,
the mast, the mast, the tender
mast!

The nest, I say, to you, I Maximus, say
under the hand, as I see it, over the waters
from this place where I am, where I hear,
can still hear

from where I carry you a feather
as though, sharp, I picked up,
in the afternoon delivered you
a jewel,
it flashing more than a wing,

than any old romantic thing,
than memory, than place,
than anything other than that which you carry

than that which is,
call it a nest, around the head of, call it
the next second

than that which you
can do!

1953

On first Looking out through Juan de la Cosa's Eyes

Behaim—and nothing
insula Azores to
Cipangu (Candyn
somewhere also there where spices

and yes, in the Atlantic,
one floating island: de
Sant
        brand
                an

1

St Malo, however.
Or Biscay. Or Bristol.
Fishermen, had,
for how long,
talked:
        Heavy sea,
snow, hail. At 8
AM a tide rip. Sounded.

Had 20 fath. decreased from that to
15, 10. Wore ship.

(They knew
Cap Raz

(As men, my town, my two towns
talk, talked of Gades, talk
of Cash's

drew, on a table, in spelt,
with a finger, in beer, a
portulans

But before La Cosa, nobody
could have
a mappemunde

2

(What he drew who drew Hercules
going by the Bear off from Calypso

Now, it would be breakers, Sable!
ahead, where, just off,
you could put buckets down

(You could go any coast
in such a raft as she taught,
as she taught him, favoring him

with cedar, & much niceties. It was only because the gods willed
that he could leave her, go away, determined though he had been the whole time
not to eat her food, not to wear gods' clothes,
to stick to what men eat

And wore

The Atlantic
just then,
was to take kings,
& fishermen

And Europe,
was being drained
of gold

II

but cod? The New Land was,
from the start, even by name was
Bacalhaos
there,
swimming, Norte, out of the mists

(out of Pytheus' sludge

out of mermaids & Monsters

(out of Judas-land

Tierra,
de bacalaos, out of

waters Massachusetts
my Newfoundlanders
My Portuguese: you

(Or Verrazano has it,
curiously, put down as
a Mud Bank

"Sounding
on George's
25 fath. sand. At the same time spoke
the Brig Albion, Packet,

John Dogget who told us
Cape Ann was 80 leag.
dis.

Terra nova sive Limo Lue
he wrote it who knew it
as only Corte Real (the first known lost
as Bertomez (as Cabot?

Who found you,

land,

of the hard gale?

1

Respecting the earth, he sd,
it is a pear, or,
like a round ball upon a part of which there is a prominence
like a woman's nipple, this protrusion
is the highest & nearest to
the sky

Ships
have always represented a large capital investment, and the manning,
the provisioning of same

It was the teredo-worm
was 1492: riddle a ship's hull
In one voyage ("pierced

with worm-holes
like a bee-hive
the report was

Ladies & Gentlemen,
he lost his pearl,
he lost the Indies
to a worm

2

North? Mud. 1480 John Lloyd, the most expert shipmaster of all England,
on behalf of John Jay and other merchants Bristol
set out to
the island of Brasylle, to
traverse the seas

Nine weeks. And storms
threw him back.

No worms. Storms,
Ladies &

to the bottom of the,

husbands, & wives,

little children lost their

(4,670 fishermen's lives are noticed. In an outgoing tide
of the Annisquam River, each summer, at the August full,
they throw flowers, which, from the current there, at the Cut,
reach the harbor channel, and go

these bouquets (there are few, Gloucester, who can afford florists' prices)
float out

you can watch them go out into,

the Atlantic

III

On ne doit aux morts nothing

else than

la vérité

1956

Variations Done for Gerald Van De Wiele

I. Le Bonheur

dogwood flakes
what is green

the petals
from the apple
blow on the road

mourning doves
mark the sway
of the afternoon, bees
dig the plum blossoms

the morning
stands up straight, the night
is blue from the full of the April moon

iris and lilac, birds
birds, yellow flowers
white flowers, the Diesel
does not let up dragging
the plow

                as the whippoorwill,
the night's tractor, grinds
his song

                and no other birds but us
are as busy (O saisons, O chateaux!

Délires!

                What soul
is without fault?

Nobody studies
happiness

Every time the cock crows
I salute him

I have no longer any excuse
for envy. My life

has been given its orders: the seasons
seize

the soul and the body, and make mock
of any dispersed effort. The hour of death

is the only trespass

II. The Charge

dogwood flakes
the green

the petals from the apple-trees
fall for the feet to walk on

the birds are so many they are
loud, in the afternoon

they distract, as so many bees do
suddenly all over the place

With spring one knows today to see
that in the morning each thing

is separate but by noon
they have melted into each other

and by night only crazy things
like the full moon and the whippoorwill

and us, are busy. We are busy
if we can get by that whiskered bird,

that nightjar, and get across, the moon
is our conversation, she will say

what soul
isn't in default?

can you afford not to make
the magical study

which happiness is? do you hear
the cock when he crows? do you know the charge,

that you shall have no envy, that your life
has its orders, that the seasons

seize you too, that no body and soul are one
if they are not wrought

in this retort? that otherwise efforts
are efforts? And that the hour of your flight

will be the hour of your death?

III. Spring

The dogwood
lights up the day.

The April moon
flakes the night.

Birds, suddenly,
are a multitude

The flowers are ravined
by bees, the fruit blossoms

are thrown to the ground, the wind
the rain forces everything. Noise—

even the night is drummed
by whippoorwills, and we get

as busy, we plow, we move,
we break out, we love. The secret

which got lost neither hides
nor reveals itself, it shows forth

tokens. And we rush
to catch up. The body

whips the soul. In its great desire
it demands the elixir

In the roar of spring,
transmutations. Envy

drags herself off. The fault of the body and the soul
—that they are not one—

the matutinal cock clangs
and singleness: we salute you

season of no bungling

1960

Maximus to Gloucester, Letter 27 [withheld]

I come back to the geography of it,
the land falling off to the left
where my father shot his scabby golf
and the rest of us played baseball
into the summer darkness until no flies
could be seen and we came home
to our various piazzas where the women
buzzed

To the left the land fell to the city,
to the right, it fell to the sea

I was so young my first memory
is of a tent spread to feed lobsters
to Rexall conventioneers, and my father,
a man for kicks, came out of the tent roaring
with a bread-knife in his teeth to take care of
a druggist they'd told him had made a pass at
my mother, she laughing, so sure, as round
as her face, Hines pink and apple,
under one of those frame hats women then

This, is no bare incoming
of novel abstract form, this

is no welter or the forms
of those events, this,

Greeks, is the stopping
of the battle

            It is the imposing
of all those antecedent predecessions, the precessions

of me, the generation of those facts
which are my words, it is coming

from all that I no longer am, yet am,
the slow westward motion of

more than I am

There is no strict personal order

for my inheritance.

No Greek will be able

to discriminate my body.

An American

is a complex of occasions,

themselves a geometry

of spatial nature.

I have this sense,

that I am one

with my skin

Plus this—plus this:

that forever the geography

which leans in

on me I compell

backwards I compell Gloucester

to yield, to

change

        Polis

is this

1968

LOU HARRISON | 1917–2003

Born in Portland, Oregon, Lou Harrison spent most of his childhood in Northern California before settling in San Francisco. While there, he studied with musician and composition teacher Henry Cowell and forged a close friendship with John Cage, another Cowell student. In 1942, Harrison moved to Los Angeles, where he studied with Arnold Schoenberg, then relocated to New York, where he worked as a composer and critic and was mentored by Virgil Thompson. In 1947, overwhelmed by city life, Harrison suffered a nervous breakdown. At the suggestion of Cage, who thought the secluded and serene Lake Eden campus would help Harrison in his ongoing recovery and afford him an inspiring environment in which to compose and collaborate, Harrison traveled to BMC, where he taught courses in harmony, counterpoint, and composition during the 1951–52 academic year. His short time at BMC was very productive: he completed the opera *Rapunzel* as well as *Seven Pastorales, Fugue for David Tudor*, and *Praise for the Beauty of Hummingbirds*. After being awarded a 1952 Guggenheim Fellowship, Harrison was released from his BMC teaching for the 1952–53 academic year. Following from his interest in non-Western music, Harrison composed for just intonation rather than equal temperament, exploring new tonalities and often including microtones. He also greatly admired Asian music and later composed for the gamelan and other instruments he himself made. While primarily a musician and composer, Harrison wrote poetry throughout his lifetime. The Jargon Society published Harrison's selected poems, *Joys and Perplexities*, in 1992.

Acrostic Hymn to the Buddha Amitābha, on the Sanskrit Mantram to the Same

(Om Namō Amitābhāya Buddhāya)

Organs
Murmur in the air.

Now
Angels marvelous
Move in
Orders.

"**A** fully enlightened Buddha is like a
Magic
Illusion, like a dream"*
Tender
Avalokiteshvara, of all
Bodhisattvas the
Highest,
Attends
You,—
And Mahāsthāmaprāpta, the strong.

Blessed Buddha,—from
Under our
Desires'
Dismay, we
Hail
And Praise
You,—oh
Awaken us in your dream!

2507 B.E.

*ashtrasāharsrikā prajnāparamitā

1992

Nines to John Cage on his 65th Birthday, 1977

You, John, are a loved, romantic man—
So multiple of image that Each
Designs another one about you
Who conceives you in his heart or mind,
And so adds facet to your being
Such that often All seem equally
Reflected, and that gigantic you,
That high chance-shimmering aggregate
Gleams to all like the Sun Resplendent.

1992

Of Bill

To have any intimacy
    with this man
is a rarely wondrous thing—
    jewelled & shimmering,
& upon (at once) altar
    & the blackest mass.

I myself do not know if I have shared
    anything with him,
but my friends have said:
"This man is special—be careful, he is rare—"
& one has said,
"He is the best decision you have made
    in twenty-three years."

1992

Tens on Remembering Henry Cowell

Remembering Henry I realize
His central kindness & the gentle smile.
I remember his certain eagerness
To like & to be liked, & that he brought
A hundred kindred composers to know
Each other out of that same amity.
The wide life of his mind, I remember,
Was serene & free, as he was also
Perfectly fearless in his melody.
Those tunes that seeming had a folk-like turn
Still sing in constructs of objective thought.
Irish, he loved to talk, & spellbound all
With tales of populations, pianos,
Of performances or Diesel engines.
He spoke of marvels & taught by allure.
He said "as you remember" & then told
Some wondrous thing you'd never heard till then.
Thus flattery disposed receptive minds.
He befriended pupils & was to me
Of all mentors most marvelous, & whose
Steps part grass before me across the years.
Difference and hybrids are good he said
And agreed that people have lived before
And not been fools because of that, & that
They've lived in other places too & not
Been fools because of that. No single way
Suffices now, & knowing at least one
Other music well he felt illumines
Mind & heart as Mozart thought of travel,
That it is to an artist essential.
Like Gottschalk & Eicheim & others too
He knew a new world of human music
To which he guided us with charming guile
And raised our heads to hear a veena play.
He alerted ears to Gamelan, &
Gagaku, & a thousand other joys.

Remembering Henry also includes
His advice to drink of gin in summer
And in winter to take whiskey or rum.
In remembering Henry I miss him,
But then I remember him everywhere.

1992

HILDA MORLEY | 1916–1998

Born in New York City, Hilda Morley began writing poetry as a young child. At fifteen, she moved to Palestine, where she attended Hebrew University in 1935 before relocating to University College London, completing her studies there in 1940. During her time in London, Morley corresponded with William Butler Yeats, one of her earliest influences, and socialized with American poet H.D. Next, she studied at several graduate schools: Wellesley College (1940–41), the Ohio State University (1942–43), and New York University (1943–45), where she completed her MA degree. Also, during the early 1940s, Morley worked as a Hebrew translator for the Office of War Information in New York City, the Jewish Agency, and the American Jewish Cultural Foundation. In 1945, she briefly married painter Eugene Morley, whose connection to abstract expressionism and the New York School made a lasting impression on her. Then, in 1952, she and her second husband, the German-born composer Stefan Wolpe, joined the community at BMC as faculty members. While at BMC, Morley befriended Robert Creeley and Charles Olson, and she composed early poems such as "Provence" and "'Seldom Is A Gothic Head More Beautiful Than When Broken'" on campus, with the latter published in issue 6 of *BMR*. She had teaching expertise in metaphysical poetry, especially the works of John Donne, whose influence can be observed in her most famous poem, "The Shutter Clangs." Considered one of the most underappreciated BMC poets, Morley provided a crucial woman's voice at the college in the early 1950s. Although she was always writing, Morley published most of her poetry later in life; her books include *A Blessing Outside Us* (1976), *To Hold in My Hand: Selected Poems, 1955–1983* (1983), and *The Turning* (1998). By grounding abstract ideas in "sensuous" diction and metaphors, experimenting with line breaks and typography to create what Stanley Kunitz describes as her "delicate and wavering" version of projective prosody, and infusing language with lyric and elegiac intensity, Morley created an intimate poetry with universal appeal.[4]

Provence

Here the sun, violet,
gives us that light Cézanne was
thankful for continually,
while at night
we are left alone,
challenged only
by the frozen moonlight,
and the stars
Hilarious in their wheeling violence blow
air from our lungs,
blood from our bodies,
rock our bellies sick—
what the stars
in their blazing courses say.
So he
slept always by nine o'clock and rose with dawning.
And that light
filled his eyes and hands and therefore
one must be exact, he said.
What so clearly
time describes on the flesh, in the eyes'
wrinkles, on throats and the backs of hands,
must be rendered again, with time itself wrested away, and
the appalling drop of the soul through space in
gravitation.
Over again
the earth is beautiful, again and again
and no light dissuades it and everywhere it is
beautiful again and beloved.
But the mouth cannot praise it.
You must be patient, he said, and humble
before nature.
And the work, he said,
gives courage.
Only the raised tongue clogs.
Helpless, it says: O my love, my friend.

In the evening the mountain reaches for your face.
Those last leaves carry a message,
scattered
everywhere. They ask for you
in praise.

In obstinacy they spin
till the late cold strikes
(light
of the mountain on the brown leaf
swung
off the branch in trajectory
on the pane)
where even
the mountain-pine, bold in its drawing,
is violet
turning brown.

1976

"Seldom Is A Gothic Head More Beautiful Than When Broken" *Malraux*

for Emma Raphael

She with the lines covering
her face as the lines in a stone
or a branch,
or a stream of water
or sand in the tide
or a field of grass
in a storm retraces the days the dust the rain, sat
broken with her hands in her lap and her body
bent to one side mourning
Death
inside her
in the balls of her eyes, the roots

of her hair, her heels' balls and her spine
                                        She was not here but
there   with sand blown
back from the water
                                    inside of twigs'
bark and underside of the dogwood veined
leaf,   ribs of cloud
unshadowing earth's side with
forests,
            each a portent, each line
a wing,   she speaking,
                                            each a fleetness
Moving with sides of buildings
                                                    water running
and streets going crossways into
clarity.   Back from there into belief,
here   into grace.

1976

Japanese Print

You who when I first met you
said: Turn grief around,
                                        turn it
into its opposite
against itself,
                    reverse it.
                                                    It is
for you I grieve now,   who are
absent entirely   & enormously
in your absence present
to me,
            present but not always
lost,
        always just beyond reach,   it is
for you I grieve.

I sit here
beneath your Japanese
landscape that you carried with you
twenty-seven years: your face pinned up
beside it,   the healthy
one in laughter,
then the tormented
face   & wander
in that landscape with you
among the rocks,   the sparsely
twisting curves of bushes,
speckle
of leaf & berry,
scatterings
of seed
& a man with a Japanese
face like yours is caught in
the wind there,   halfway
turning & above him the knotting
of trees,   the opening
mouths of the lopped-off
branches gaping
with the unsayable
O,
the without-utterance,
& before him, over
the water, swerving
into the movement
forward,
in spite of
himself,   his body advancing
on the unfenced bridge,
face opposing
the curve of his footsteps, backward
feet moving
beyond his wishing or not
in a precision of
onwardness

I look for you there in
that landscape of your soul
walking
beside you
& in your wanderings if for a moment
I lose you,
there are your footprints,
signs of your passage, your forward
faring.

1983

The Shutter Clangs

From John Donne's "Goodfriday, 1613. Riding Westward"
Meditation upon a Good Friday, ryding from London towards Exeter, westward

Who rides westward now, as he did,
more than three centuries
ago
& from where to
where is west?
Toward
the Atlantic, for him
as for all Europe
(the open space!
the wildness,)
from Polesworth, Warwickshire, to Exeter
not Wales, it seems (as scholars
thought at first,
& Warwickshire not meaning,
to him, as it
does to us: Shakespeare)
pondering that spectacle of
too much weight for him, whereby
that blood, which is
the seat of the soul, made "durt out of

the dust."
And there a shutter
drops & divides my mind in two,
for I see you
on the floor & the blood darkening
your skull:
Was it the invisible
you had sight of then?
(They call it that)
Since your 17th year the visible
was your treasure, focus
of your diamond-eye:
that precision tool
compounded of air & fire—a Venetian
eye,
eye of your mother's race, Dalmatian.
O gentle lion,
whose paw in the end was blunted,
you shall not
be "left out" not by devouring
Time itself
& even now, years after, the memory
of that blood flowing backwards
into your skull is almost
more than can be borne.
But I remember your love of
the clear places, the openings out
and turn again to that ride westward
who am drawn backward,
(as Donne was to the East, so I to you) tempted
again to reach you again & again, saying
to myself—absent thee,
absent thee from felicity
a while—
wherein Donne knows himself divided
from himself, subject
to foreign motion,
as the lesser

of the spheres may be
cut off from the Intelligences,   those that
move them   & so turn into a motion
foreign to themselves
& not their own.
                                        So, you who were
in so many ways, my mover,
                                                                    having been taken
into whatever we have no name for,
                                                                                    I am left whirling,
often, in a direction that is
not entirely mine
                                        & hang back so,
                                                                                as
Donne might do, suspended,
hang from west to east,
                                                        drawn backwards
again to you & tempted
again to reach you,
                                                        forbearing always
to do so,   saying: absent thee
yet a while, absent thee
to tell my story.
                                    What iron
divides the soul that longs for wholeness
forever & can compass it
only hours at a time?
                                                            When what is new
as Donne attempted it
rises out of the mist?
                                                            Is it
too much that interferes:
                                                            the cryings out
in the street (the manifoldness).
Houses, buses, people,
                                                        the pavements
smeared by garbage,   bruising
of cross-purposes?

What clamor
& lack of it, needed
or not can leave our wishes
dangling?
What use can we
make of terror & our losses,
so loss itself may
clarify the eye & make it shine in
unhealedness,
& what we know of terror
heighten our space, our leaning
into newness:
& the eye teach itself
a boldness out of
what thwarted it?
The shutter
lifts. The mind roams freely, but
the division is there:
where I was
reconciled,
the unreconciled recurs.
But the deaths,
knives plunging
in unforeseeable places—my deaths are
scattered now,
no longer
weighted as they were,
on my breast:
pillars of darkness.
What was dug there
can be seedbed, and is cared for,
cared for,
what was twisted can be touched,
touched, has settled like seeds now
in my breast,
those roots that
strangled once can shatter
the outer husk.

The shutter clatters
& lifts.
What was hollowness
in me shapes to
an opening.
Icicles
that bled my veins thaw:
something
edges into green.
I am ashamed,
ashamed of my unhappiness.

There are no
holy names for us,
said Hoelderlin,
in a world that's shriveled.
To call up a blessing
to the world,
even in lostness,
in grief (the loss unhealed
is what is left us,
to uncover
the what is there, the *aletheyia*.

Do you remember, driving,
that early summer, to the Hamptons,   Mercedes
at the wheel—?
We stop somewhere for lunch.
Pundy, the eight-year-old, runs into the room,
tears on his face, screaming:
The dog is dead! & I am wet by Pundy's tears
& the dog's body (dogbody) strangled
in his leash
& Mercedes
weeping for her son, her dog,
for her own living
& dying
& I cannot see the Hamptons, the country,

the summer
any longer,
thinking, in-spite-of-it,
you & I will go on together
without end.
Tonight, the last of August,
weather
changing from cold & rainy
to heaviness & warmth,
the moon orange at first,
then paling with light rain   & I walking
through wet grasses,
walk also those evenings
the 6 days since your birthday, 3 years ago.
How humbly
you took your greetings then,
believing still,
as I did, that all might yet
end well for you,
the sweeping
curve of your life gather
again & rise
into its fullness.
And it was not so.

There was a little
trail of notes you left to meet me
when I came back from teaching
& they said: Be welcomed
to our spaces   my sweet lady
& a flower
on the table saying: Flower-woman
& a shell more beautiful
than most that said:
Listen Listen
to our own sea
(& a little stone marked YOURS
to lead me to my room)

I am rocked now by the silence
These are the stones I have
learned to gnaw upon:
I can recover
only what I know—
& lean, yearning,
stretching my arms out,
still unbelieving
of what is distant.
What has rocked me,   rocked me
can now become my prison.
But these walls
can speak: I can make them
speak that are speechless.
I can hear those banners
rattle in the wind,
as Hoelderlin heard them.
I can
sing as we did then, 3 summers ago,
walking
these roads we did then,   singing
the Marseillaise,
to help your movements
come back to you,
& as
we sang, they came.
Allow me
further.
But those hands that
called up all the elements
are still,
that moved once as
the wings of birds do
in flying—
those birds you imaged
flying out of your mouth
in thousands
at your death

& what were light & fire stretching themselves
even farther into fire & light
danced with them,
shaping & forming them—
dispersed, dissolved,
made still.
Gestures
I never used come to me
now: fists clenching, chest raised in
a stiffness to stop the weeping,
teeth grinding
the sound back
& I learn thereby
the in-spite-of,
the in-spite-ofness,
of your life,
the "premonitions
of good things to come" the year before your illness
showed itself,
the premonitions
I must now make true: that greeting, 1961,
from London,
of "an unwearing life"
& "I salute you
on a clear day . . . wishing you
a *coeur très fort, très fort,*
wishing you
a clear day."
The names you gave (Hoelderlin's
holy names): the "evergreen"
(image that H.D. sent &
Frieda Lawrence)
the "cleanness . . . without stains" & for
yourself: "everness."
Let the stones that
I feed on bleed,
let their wounds show, let them
show red,

Let the redness
turn to flowers—tulips, roses, crimson
carnations that you loved, the Bird of Paradise
your students brought you, as it
resembled you,
let them
begin another summer in me.

Birds in astonishment
discovering
warmth in the sun this morning—
from them
flows back to us a mildness.
Even
today the scent of honeysuckle
on a bank brought you
alive to me.
Your voice & your step were with me
in the dark, with the light from the boats shining
on the silky water
& the voice, furious,
of a thrush this morning,
insisting
on his presence in the world
(as we all must do,
you taught me)
& in that spray of notes flung out of
his small body
you exulted with him.

Can I ride away
from where you dying
are,
as I lie dying with you,
you of "the clear sky"
in whom
no anger lived,
whose fire

was gaiety   & "the coeur très fort
TRÈS FORT"

Unlike you, I have held to bitterness: each inch of
death encroaching
opened swamps at my feet.
You of
the "clair bones,"   the uttermost
tip of the tree,
from your eyes I gather
flakes of light warmer
than any stars
in these years that have blinded me.

The shutter clatters,
clangs & lifts
& I move forward
my roots in darkness still—
but
riding westward,
even as I'm pulled backward
where you lay,   pulled eastward
where the light grows strong enough to
point me away from the pain repeated, overknown,
to Land's End   to the open water,
unknown
& riding westward.

1983

For Piet Mondrian

From the beginning,
the horizontal,
the vertical,
the weight of them,
weight of the Dutch sea,
of the landmass,
of the land,
concentration of
the sky upon it, what
stretches it & what extends.
Search for a
center,
(a hidden centering) what may only
seem to be center. The "decentering"
of the intersection is
concealed.
But the search is
unceasing, what comes forward
may go back (again)
may seem to
disappear,
("planes of a fugitive existence forming
. . . dissolving before our . . . eyes")
is there,
what cannot disappear,
what
must appear finally,
what is
absolute. A beginning.

To live only for
that,
by means of the obsession
of a life,
means of the eye, hand, spirit,
mind,
the strict devotion.

At 40, the direct look at
the camera,
the full, the articulated
mouth,   set
aslant.
The eyes in "self portrait," at 36,
are instruments for looking.
At 43, "you understand that
I pay no attention to
what people say."
Later, in his early 60s, there are
deep lines around the mouth.
What was
serious earlier has a sadness now.
"As far as I know I am
one of the artists who is most expressive of
the absolute."
A beginning.

"This year I worked a great deal and was
searching for a purer expression.
That is why nothing
satisfied me yet."
What has come out of
experience is continued in
one step after another:
"color irrupting
turns the visual into
a never-ending process"
away from the extraneous,
alive in silence: "natural color is inwardness . . .
light in its most outward
manifestation."
In the stars, in
their multiplicity, we see the destruction
of the particular.

But there is the "tragic"
in composition: "Whatever

one does, a certain element of
choice, the arbitrary, inter-
venes . . ."   The human interference with what is.
"composition is
tragic."
          The black may not
follow the vermillion-red completely, may
hold back, allowing air, breath, a half-hidden
space to enter,
                    what is light-grey can
slide behind them, backing into
dark-blue & now the red is
held back.
            Precarious the equilibrium.
            In his later 40s, a breakthrough.

There are frontal openings,
                                the equilibrium,
stretches elsewhere,
                            there is an
almost touching, an almost
overlapping,   the almost but strictly
avoided closing.
                      There is a river
of space,   which flows on separately, oblivious
to what is jutting forward, in
its own remoteness, its continuity,
                                          indifferent
to what touches it, stealthily,   to
what it touches.
                      The density is
radiant.
           Later (1928) there are
gradations,   there is a reaching
to touch.
             Space is fitted
closely.
          The radiance is
a concentration,

a diamond.
He loves to dance, at
the Jockey Club, the Bal Bullier,
he goes to
Josephine Baker, her debut at the Revue Négre.
At 50, he learns to dance the shimmy,
then he learns the Charleston.
If the ban on
the Charleston is carried out in Holland, he says,
"it will be a reason for me
never to return."
In his painting, the vertical,
the horizontal, are in contestation,
"I have
reworked the division." Each element in
maximum intensity,   verticals in
undulation,   horizontals interrupted, what is
fleeing, what is in flight.
A tension:
equivalence of opposites, exposing
difference.
The center decentered in
motion   (multiplicity made tangible)
concreteness
of opposites:
of the utmost one
& the utmost other.

1998

ROBERT CREELEY | 1926–2005

Born in Arlington, Massachusetts, poet, fiction writer, literary critic, and teacher Robert Creeley was raised in nearby West Acton. He attended Harvard University, left school to serve in the American Field Service (1944–45), then returned to Harvard but did not graduate. In 1950, he began corresponding with William Carlos Williams, who put him in touch with Charles Olson. Through their multivolume correspondence, Creeley and Olson established a literary friendship that expanded the formal and philosophical purview of American poetry in the postwar period. Together, they helped fashion a new American poetics, one Olson in his celebrated essay "Projective Verse" (1950) referred to as "composition by field."[5] In fact, Olson credited Creeley with first expressing the essay's central motto that "FORM IS NEVER MORE THAN AN EXTENSION OF CONTENT."[6] In the early 1950s, Creeley and his family lived on Mallorca, an island of Spain, where he founded the Divers Press, publishing early works by BMC poets such as Paul Blackburn, Larry Eigner, Charles Olson, and Irving Layton. Though offered a faculty position as early as 1952, Creeley first taught at BMC in the spring of 1954, and he edited seven issues of *BMR* between 1954 and 1957. In 1966, he began teaching poetry at the State University of New York at Buffalo, where he later helped establish that institution's Poetics Program. In his most iconic book, *For Love: Poems 1950–1960*, Creeley examines postwar masculinity in short lyric poems at once terse, violent, and darkly humorous; later volumes, such as *Pieces* (1969) and *A Day Book* (1972), are pioneering works of serial writing in American literature.[7]

The Immoral Proposition

If you never do anything for anyone else
you are spared the tragedy of human relation-

ships. If quietly and like another time
there is the passage of an unexpected thing:

to look at it is more
than it was. God knows

nothing is competent nothing is
all there is. The unsure

egoist is not
good for himself.

1953

Old Song

Take off yr clothes, love,
And come to me.

Soon will the sun be breaking
Over yon sea.

And all of our hairs be white, love,
For aught we do

And all our nights be one, love,
For all we knew.

1954

Too Little & Too Late

Grace the couch of a bear, god-
damn him. These

quiet passions are like
Renaissance paintings wherein

the lady (goddamn her)
looks fashioned of everything but

the possible.

composed ca. 1954

I Know a Man

As I sd to my
friend, because I am
always talking,—John, I

sd, which was not his
name, the darkness sur-
rounds us, what

can we do against
it, or else, shall we &
why not, buy a goddamn big car,

drive, he sd, for
christ's sake, look
out where yr going.

1955

The Warning

For love—I would
split open your head and put
a candle in
behind the eyes.

Love is dead in us
if we forget
the virtues of an amulet
and quick surprise.

1955

The Language

Locate *I*
love you some-
where in

teeth and
eyes, bite
it but

take care not
to hurt, you
want so

much so
little. Words
say everything.

I
love you
again,

then what
is emptiness
for. To

fill, fill.
I heard words
and words full

of holes
aching. Speech
is a mouth.

1967

A Piece

One and
one, two,
three.

1967

Pieces

I didn't
want
to hurt you.
Don't

stop
to think. It
hurts
to live

like this,
meat
sliced
walking.

1967

Something

I approach with such
a careful tremor, always
I feel the finally foolish

question of how it is,
then, supposed to be felt,
and by whom. I remember

once in a rented room on
27th street, the woman I loved
then, literally, after we

had made love on the large
bed sitting across from
a basin with two faucets, she

had to pee but was nervous,
embarrassed I suppose I
would watch her who had but

a moment ago been completely
open to me, naked, on
the same bed. Squatting, her

head reflected in the mirror,
the hair dark there, the
full of her face, the shoulders,

sat spread-legged, turned on
one faucet and shyly pissed. What
love might learn from such a sight.

1967

(from *Pieces*)

As real as thinking
wonders created
by the possibility—

forms. A period
at the end of a sentence
which

began *it was*
into a present,
a presence

saying
something
as it goes.

•

No forms less
than activity.

All words—
days—or
eyes—

or happening
is an event only
for the observer?

No one
there. Everyone
here.

•

Small facts
of eyes, hair
blonde, face

looking like a
flat painted
board. How

opaque as if
a reflection
merely, skin

vague glove of
randomly seen
colors.

•

Inside
and out

impossible
locations—

reaching in
from out-

side, out
from in-

side—as
middle:

one
hand.

1969

(from *Pieces*)

Kids walking beach,
minnow pools—
who knows which.

•

Nothing grand—
The scale is neither
big nor small.

•

Want to get the sense of "I" into Zukofsky's "eye"—a locus
of experience, not a presumption of expected value.

•

Here now—
begin!

1969

An Ode

(for Black Mt. College)

There is this side of it.
                              And two weeks ago I was
reading
of it—a book, and a long poem:
                                    Simon Bolivar.

And why not. One is much too
repentant. The secrets are
to be shared.

Why go to college. Or, as a man said, it
is too far away.

Why go.

If I don't get there, — I did
once

If I don't get there, this year
anyhow I know some of the names, I know
what I might have been like, say, or

you say. (The creeleys
are all comediente.)

The sky here, dark enough, tonight
the moon is
is not to any other
insistence,
                    is mute in
itself.

Tonight, fire. The race
of fire. And what the hell else to say but
run.

2002

ROBERT HELLMAN | 1919–1984

Born in New York City, where he spent much of his early life before moving abroad, Robert Hellman earned a BA from New York University in 1948. He attended the University of Paris from 1949 to 1950. During his time in France, Hellman befriended Robert Creeley, who later invited Hellman to teach at BMC. In 1954, Hellman and his first wife, Helen, returned to the United States. He studied fiction under Ray B. West at the University of Iowa's Writers' Workshop before assuming his teaching responsibilities in languages at BMC. On campus, Robert and Helen Hellman lived in the same house as poet Hilda Morley and her husband, composer Stefan Wolpe. Hellman also performed the eponymous role in Anton Chekhov's *Uncle Vanya* in a staged campus reading directed by Wesley Huss. His short story "The Quay" appeared in the first issue of *BMR*, and he served as a contributing editor to the magazine for issues 3–6. Other short stories by Hellman appeared in publications such as *Western Review*, *Folder*, and *Commentary*. His play *Kling* was performed off-Broadway at the Phoenix Theater in 1964; in 1965, Hellman (with Richard O'Gorman) cotranslated *Fabliaux: Ribald Tales from the Old French*. In addition to his success as a short story writer, dramatist, and translator, Hellman was also a teacher at the City College of New York and the Juilliard School. In 1973, he relocated to Copenhagen, Denmark, and remained there until his death. The poems below first appeared in Mervin Louis Lane's *Black Mountain College: Sprouted Seeds—an Anthology of Personal Accounts* (1990).

Four Poems

Fort Square

What am I to say to this?
to this face of me
hills and houses and
the light that lifts the sea
over the last green of summer
I come out of the door
onto the rickety porch
    that yet is secure to me having
    carried his weight
greeted by the Fort children
as though I too had lived in was
free to move in
The light out of the painter's eye
that undoes memory that
breaks the platform of piety brings us
to the ground yet
no way diminishes us makes
a marvel of our ignorance
as wide as the air where
boats riding out of the inner harbor
cross the wakes of leviathans.

2

As the mirrors darkened he
took great pains
to ascertain the exact time the
numbers of minutes and seconds
moved like cilia at the
bottom of his poems
                                        The intervals
of death's labor
growing shorter and shorter his bulk
diminishing towards birth

shuffled from bed to chair
hardly distinguishing
what was action and
what respite
                    Time
who resists the blandishments of clocks
their water sweet ticking   who
will not stand to us as adversary
                                        yielding
took him to itself.

3

Is that what moves you?   is it
the darkness   the backing
of our vision?   have you
swallowed the sun?
                              I dreamt
I dreamt I dreamed of you
dark as the Great Boyg   telling me
Go round!
as you did when I played poor Peer
and she sang me out of the ladle
I charged you with my spicule of knowledge
                                                  crying
Light up!
you have your death behind you!
With what generous malice
you enveloped me again.

The Burial

I come to be dead by graveside
I find
many winners complaining to the heaped earth
their wives
dipping hands in the
blue openings   their children
posted like dolls to
mark perspectives
While the High Rabbi
speaks money to me
who must go into the ground a debtor
I had expected
a company of peers a
convocation of old bones
not
this distinguished assemblage   this lustre
spread by suave hands and voices
over all that was grey and familiar to me.

1990

ROBERT DUNCAN | 1919–1988

Born and raised in Oakland, California, Robert Duncan was a leading writer and theorist of the new American poetry, and he was affiliated, socially and aesthetically, with members of both the San Francisco Renaissance (e.g., Helen Adam, Robin Blaser, Madeline Gleason, and Jack Spicer) and Donald Allen's "Black Mountain" group. He first visited BMC briefly in 1938, when he'd been accepted to the college as a student on a partial scholarship. However, as Duncan recalled, he was almost immediately "turned away" from BMC upon his arrival—deemed "emotionally unfit"—after engaging in a "heated argument" with faculty over the Spanish Civil War.[8] He did finally return in 1956, when he accepted a teaching position at BMC, living on the Lake Eden grounds. Duncan taught courses in drama and poetry. He composed, revised, and staged his play *Medea at Kolchis* in August 1956, casting poet John Wieners in the production. In addition, during his time on campus, Duncan started work on poems that later appeared in *The Opening of the Field*, widely considered the first book in his mature period. Like Charles Olson, Duncan practiced an "open form" poetics that was indebted to the process-oriented philosophy of Alfred North Whitehead, but which he uniquely invested with occult, mythic, and erotic themes and images. In addition to his many contributions to twentieth-century poetry, Duncan was a pioneering gay rights advocate who penned the groundbreaking 1944 essay "The Homosexual in Society." As witnessed early in his life in the debate with BMC faculty over the Spanish Civil War, Duncan was an anarchic, provocative figure who engaged prescient political issues while employing fiery language and forging radical art. His friendship with BMC affiliate Denise Levertov—and the ultimate demise of their relationship over the Vietnam War—is chronicled in *The Letters of Robert Duncan and Denise Levertov* (2003).

The Song of the Border-Guard

The man with his lion under the shed of wars
sheds his belief as if he shed tears.
The sound of words waits —
a barbarian host at the border-line of sense.

The enamord guards desert their posts
harkening to the lion-smell of a poem
that rings in their ears.

— Dreams, a certain guard said
   were never designd so
   to re-arrange an empire.

   Along about six o'clock I take out my guitar
   and sing to a lion
   who sleeps like a line of poetry
   in the shed of wars.

The man shedding his belief
knows that the lion is not asleep,
does not dream, is never asleep,
is a wide-awake poem
waiting like a lover for the disrobing of the guard;
the beautiful boundaries of the empire
naked, rapt round in the smell of a lion.

(The barbarians have passd over the significant phrase)

— When I was asleep,
      a certain guard says,
   a man shed his clothes as if he shed tears
      and appeard as a lonely lion
   waiting for a song under the shed-roof of wars.

I sang the song that he waited to hear,
I, the Prize-Winner, the Poet-Acclaimd.

Dear, dear, dear, dear, I sang,
believe, believe, believe, believe.
The shed of wars is splendid as the sky,
houses our waiting like a pure song
housing in its words the lion-smell
        of the beloved disrobed.

I sang: believe, believe, believe.

        I the guard because of my guitar
believe. I am the certain guard,
certain of the Beloved, certain of the Lion,
certain of the Empire. I with my guitar.
Dear, dear, dear, I sing.
I, the Prize-Winner, the Poet on Guard.

The border-lines of sense in the morning light
are naked as a line of poetry in a war.

1952

For a Muse Meant

: in
        s p i r e d / the aspirate
        the aspirant almost

        without breath

  it is a breath out
        breathed—an aspiration
  pictured as the familiar spirit
        hoverer

above
each loved each

hesitate (as if the bone-
cranium-helmet in-
hearing) ; clearing
old greym attar.

a word giving up its ghost
memorized as the flavor
from the vowels (the bowels)
of meaning
(BE STILL THY BRATHE AND HEAR THEM SPEAK:)
voices? images? essences
as only in
Yeats's 'desolation of reality'.

:   specialization, yes. Better to stum-
b'l to it. You cld have
knockd me over with a feather weight
of words. The sense
sleight but absolute.
nock. nock. nock sum sense into me head.
O K
Better awake to it. For one
eyes-wide-open vision
or fotograf.
Than ritual.

Specialization,—yes even if the old ritual
is lost.†

I was completely lost and saw the sign
without meaning to.
This was not the design.

† Who works at his own word in all our sentences might trick from even the ruts of once ritual the buts and mistakes that token the actual. The poet as maker frees the thing from its prophets.

: A great effort, straining, breaking up
all the melodic line (the lyr-
ick strain?) Dont
hand me that old line we say
You dont know what yer saying.

Why knot ab   stract
a tract of   mere sound
is more   a round
of dis abs cons
   t r a c t i o n
—a deconstruction—
for the reading of words.

Lists of imaginary sounds, I mean sound signs I mean things designd in themselves I mean boundary marks I mean a bounding memorizations I mean a memorial rising I mean a con glomerations without rising

1. a dead camel
2. a nude tree
3. a hot mouth (smoking)
4. an old saw (rusty edge)
5. a copy of the original
6. an animal face
7. a broken streetcar
8. a fake seegar
9. papers
10. a holey shawl
11. the addition of the un
    planned for interruption:
    a flavor stinking coffee
    (how to brew another cup
    in that Marianne Moore -
    E. P. - Williams - H. D. - Stein -
    Zukofsky - Stevens - Perse -

surrealist - dada - staind
pot)   by yrs R. D.

12. A table set for break
fast.

a morning lang
wage — AI AI a-wailing
the failing.

FOR A SONG OF THE LANGUAGERS

What are the signs of life? the breath, the pulse,
the constant
sluffing off of old stuff in
creasing, increasing —
Notes: to hesitate, retract.
Step by
step   / to be idiot-awkward

to take care
by the throat & throttle it.

Bottle that genius
for mere magic or intoxic
vacations.

It is sober he stumbles
on truth? Hell, no —
this he sober gnaws
the inconsequential
eternity of his skull.

His appetite is not experimental.

1958

Often I Am Permitted to Return to a Meadow

as if it were a scene made-up by the mind,
that is not mine, but is a made place,

that is mine, it is so near to the heart,
an eternal pasture folded in all thought
so that there is a hall therein

that is a made place, created by light
wherefrom the shadows that are forms fall.

Wherefrom fall all architectures I am
I say are likenesses of the First Beloved
whose flowers are flames lit to the Lady.

She it is Queen Under The Hill
whose hosts are a disturbance of words within words
that is a field folded.

It is only a dream of the grass blowing
east against the source of the sun
in an hour before the sun's going down

whose secret we see in a children's game
of ring a round of roses told.

Often I am permitted to return to a meadow
as if it were a given property of the mind
that certain bounds hold against chaos,

that is a place of first permission,
everlasting omen of what is.

1960

A Poem Beginning with a Line by Pindar

I

The light foot hears you and the brightness begins
god-step at the margins of thought,
    quick adulterous tread at the heart.
Who is it that goes there?
    Where I see your quick face
notes of an old music pace the air,
torso-reverberations of a Grecian lyre.

In Goya's canvas Cupid and Psyche
have a hurt voluptuous grace
bruised by redemption. The copper light
falling upon the brown boy's slight body
is carnal fate that sends the soul wailing
up from blind innocence, ensnared
    by dimness
into the deprivations of desiring sight.

But the eyes in Goya's painting are soft,
diffuse with rapture absorb the flame.
Their bodies yield out of strength.
    Waves of visual pleasure
wrap them in a sorrow previous to their impatience.

A bronze of yearning, a rose that burns
    the tips of their bodies, lips,
ends of fingers, nipples. He is not wingd.
His thighs are flesh, are clouds
    lit by the sun in its going down,
hot luminescence at the loins of the visible.

    But they are not in a landscape.
    They exist in an obscurity.

The wind spreading the sail serves them.
The two jealous sisters eager for her ruin
    serve them.
That she is ignorant, ignorant of what Love will be,
    serves them.
The dark serves them.
The oil scalding his shoulder serves them,
serves their story. Fate, spinning,
    knots the threads for Love.

Jealousy, ignorance, the hurt . . . serve them.

II

This is magic. It is passionate dispersion.
What if they grow old? The gods
    would not allow it.
    Psyche is preserved.

In time we see a tragedy, a loss of beauty
    the glittering youth
of the god retains — but from this threshold
    it is age
that is beautiful. It is toward the old poets
    we go, to their faltering,
their unaltering wrongness that has style,
    their variable truth,
    the old faces,
words shed like tears from
a plenitude of powers time stores.

A stroke.   These little strokes.   A chill.
    The old man, feeble, does not recoil.
Recall. A phase so minute,
    only a part of the word in- jerrd.

    The Thundermakers descend,

damerging a nuv. A nerb.
    The present dented of the U
nighted stayd.   States.   The heavy clod?
    Cloud.   Invades the brain.   What
    if lilacs last in *this* dooryard bloomd?

Hoover, Roosevelt, Truman, Eisenhower —
where among these did the power reside
that moves the heart? What flower of the nation
bride-sweet broke to the whole rapture?
Hoover, Coolidge, Harding, Wilson
hear the factories of human misery turning out commodities.
For whom are the holy matins of the heart ringing?
Noble men in the quiet of morning hear
Indians singing the continent's violent requiem.
Harding, Wilson, Taft, Roosevelt,
idiots fumbling at the bride's door,
hear the cries of men in meaningless debt and war.
Where among these did the spirit reside
that restores the land to productive order?
McKinley, Cleveland, Harrison, Arthur,
Garfield, Hayes, Grant, Johnson,
dwell in the roots of the heart's rancor.
How sad "amid lanes and through old woods"
    echoes Whitman's love for Lincoln!

There is no continuity then.   Only a few
    posts of the good remain.   I too
that am a nation sustain the damage
    where smokes of continual ravage
obscure the flame.
                    It is across great scars of wrong
    I reach toward the song of kindred men
    and strike again the naked string
old Whitman sang from.   Glorious mistake!
    that cried:

"The theme is creative and has vista."
"He is the president of regulation."

I see always the under side turning,
fumes that injure the tender landscape.
From which up break
lilac blossoms of courage in daily act
striving to meet a natural measure.

III (FOR CHARLES OLSON)

Psyche's tasks — the sorting of seeds
wheat barley oats poppy coriander
anise beans lentils peas — every grain
in its right place
before nightfall;

gathering the gold wool from the cannibal sheep
(for the soul must weep
and come near upon death);

harrowing Hell for a casket Proserpina keeps
that must not
be opend . . . containing beauty?

no! Melancholy coild like a serpent
that is deadly sleep
we are not permitted
to succumb to.

These are the old tasks.
You've heard them before.

They must be impossible. Psyche
must despair, be brought to her
insect instructor;
must obey the counsels of the green reed;

saved from suicide by a tower speaking,
    must follow to the letter
    freakish instructions.

In the story the ants help. The old man at Pisa
    mixd in whose mind
(to draw the sorts) are all seeds
        as a lone ant from a broken ant-hill
had part restored by an insect, was
    upheld by a lizard

            (to draw the sorts)
the wind is part of the process
            defines a nation of the wind —

    father of many notions,

                    Who?
let the light into the dark? began
the many movements of the passion?

                        West
from east men push.
                The islands are blessd
(cursed) that swim below the sun,

    man upon whom the sun has gone down!

There is the hero who struggles east
widdershins to free the dawn and must
                woo Night's daughter,
sorcery, black passionate rage, covetous queens,
so that the fleecy sun go back from Troy,
    Colchis, India . . . all the blazing armies
spent, he must struggle alone toward the pyres of Day.

The light that is Love
rushes on toward passion. It verges upon dark.
Roses and blood flood the clouds.
Solitary first riders advance into legend.

This land, where I stand, was all legend
in my grandfathers' time: cattle raiders,
animal tribes, priests, gold.
It was the West. Its vistas painters saw
in diffuse light, in melancholy,
in abysses left by glaciers as if they had been the sun
primordial carving empty enormities
out of the rock.

Snakes lurkd
guarding secrets. Those first ones
survived solitude.

Scientia
holding the lamp, driven by doubt;
Eros naked in foreknowledge
smiling in his sleep; and the light
spilld, burning his shoulder — the outrage
that conquers legend —
passion, dismay, longing, search
flooding up where
the Beloved is lost. Psyche travels
life after life, my life, station
after station,
to be tried

without break, without
news, knowing only — but what did she know?
The oracle at Miletus had spoken
truth surely: that he was Serpent-Desire
that flies thru the air,
a monster-husband. But she saw him fair

whom Apollo's mouthpiece said spread
        pain
beyond cure   to those
        wounded by his arrows.

Rilke torn by a rose thorn
blackend toward Eros.   Cupidinous Death!
        that will not take no for an answer.

IV

        Oh yes!   Bless the footfall where
step by step   the boundary walker
(in Maverick Road   the snow
thud by thud   from the roof
circling the house — another tread)

    that foot   informd
by the weight of all things
        that can be elusive
no more than a nearness to the mind
        of a single image

            Oh yes!   this
most dear
        the catalyst force that renders clear
the days of a life from the surrounding medium!

                Yes, beautiful rare wilderness!
wildness that verifies strength of my tame mind,
        clearing held against indians,
health that prepared to meet death,
        the stubborn hymns going up
into the ramifications of the hostile air

        that, deceptive, gives way.

Who is there?   O, light the light!
        The Indians give way,   the clearing falls.
Great Death gives way   and unprepares us.
        Lust gives way.   The Moon gives way.
Night gives way.   Minutely,   the Day gains.

She saw the body of her beloved
        dismemberd in waking . . . or was it
in sight?   *Finders Keepers* we sang
        when we were children or were taught to sing
before our histories began   and we began
        who were beloved   our animal life
toward the Beloved,   sworn to be Keepers.

        On the hill before the wind came
the grass moved toward the one sea,
        blade after blade dancing in waves.

There the children turn the ring to the left.
There the children turn the ring to the right.
        Dancing . . . Dancing . . .

And the lonely psyche goes up thru the boy to the king
        that in the caves of history dreams.
Round and round the children turn.
        London Bridge that is a kingdom falls.

We have come so far that all the old stories
whisper once more.
Mount Segur, Mount Victoire, Mount Tamalpais . . .
        rise to adore the mystery of Love!

(An ode? Pindar's art, the editors tell us, was not a statue but a mosaic, an accumulation of metaphor. But if he was archaic, not classic, a survival of obsolete mode, there may have been old voices in the survival that directed the heart. So, a line from a hymn came in a novel I was reading to help me. Psyche, poised to leap — and Pindar too, the editors write, goes too far, topples over — listend to a tower that said, *Listen to me!*

The oracle had said, *Despair! The Gods themselves abhor his power.* And then the virgin flower of the dark falls back flesh of our flesh from which everywhere . . .

the information flows
  that is yearning. A line of Pindar
moves from the area of my lamp
  toward morning.

In the dawn that is nowhere
  I have seen the willful children

clockwise and counter-clockwise turning.

1960

The Structure of Rime IV

O Outrider!
  when you come to the threshold of the stars, to the door beyond which moves celestial terror —

the kin at the hearth, the continual cauldron that feeds forth the earth, the heart that comes into being through the blood, the householder among his familiar animals, the beloved turning to his beloved in the dark

create love as the leaves
create from the light life
and return to the remote precincts where the courageous move ramifications of the unknown that appear as trials.

The Master of Rime, time after time, came down the arranged ladders of vision or ascended the smoke and flame towers of the opposite of vision, into or out of the language of daily life, husband to one word, wife to the other, breath that leaps forward upon the edge of dying.

Thus I said to the source of my happiness, I will return. From the moment of your love eternity expands, and you are mere man.

water   fire   earth   and air
all that simple elements were

guardians are.

1960

The Structure of Rime XX

The Master of Rime told me, You must learn to lose heart. I have darkend this way and you yourself have darkend. Are you so blind you cant see what you cant see?

You keep the unknown bird hidden in your hands as if to carry sight into the house. But the sightless ones have opend the windows and listen to the songs outside. *Absence*, the Mother of this Blindness tells them, *rimes among the feathers of birds that exist only in sight. The songs you hear fall from their flight light like shadows stars cast among you.*

You must learn to lose your heart. Let the beat of your heart go. Missing the beat. And from the care of your folded hands unfold a feeling in the room of an empty space. For the pit of despair wants you to come there. The thrush waits trembling in the confinement of his master's doubt and every bird among the watery eaves sings as his brother.

And the Master of Rime appeard again, smiling. His hands cupt as he went. His head bowed, looking down, seeking his way away from me. O brother of the confined! O my twin lord of the net rime has tied in the tongues of fire.

1964

Up Rising Passages 25

Now Johnson would go up to join the great simulacra of men,
Hitler and Stalin, to work his fame
with planes roaring out from Guam over Asia,
all America become a sea of toiling men
stirrd at his will, which would be a bloated thing,
drawing from the underbelly of the nation
such blood and dreams as swell the idiot psyche
out of its courses into an elemental thing
until his name stinks with burning meat and heapt honors

And men wake to see that they are used like things
spent in a great potlatch, this Texas barbecue
of Asia, Africa, and all the Americas,
And the professional military behind him, thinking
to use him as they thought to use Hitler
without losing control of their business of war,

But the mania, the ravening eagle of America
as Lawrence saw him "bird of men that are masters,
lifting the rabbit-blood of the myriads up into . . ."
into something terrible, gone beyond bounds, or
As Blake saw America in figures of fire and blood raging,
. . . in what image? the ominous roar in the air,
the omnipotent wings, the all-American boy in the cockpit
loosing his flow of napalm, below in the jungles
"any life at all or sign of life" his target, drawing now
not with crayons in his secret room
the burning of homes and the torture of mothers and fathers and children,
their hair a-flame, screaming in agony, but
in the line of duty, for the might and enduring fame
of Johnson, for the victory of American will over its victims,
releasing his store of destruction over the enemy,

in terror and hatred of all communal things, of communion, of
    communism •

has raised from the private rooms of small-town bosses and businessmen
from the council chambers of the gangs that run the great cities,
    swollen with the votes of millions,
from the fearful hearts of good people in the suburbs turning the savory
    meat over the charcoal burners and heaping their barbecue plates
    with more than they can eat,
from the closed meeting-rooms of regents of universities and sessions of
    profiteers.

— back of the scene: the atomic stockpile; the vials of synthesized diseases eager biologists have developt over half a century dreaming of the bodies of mothers and fathers and children and hated rivals swollen with new plagues, measles grown enormous, influenzas perfected; and the gasses of despair, confusion of the senses, mania, inducing terror of the universe, coma, existential wounds, that chemists we have met at cocktail parties, passt daily and with a happy "Good Day" on the way to classes or work, have workt to make war too terrible for men to wage —

raised this secret entity of America's hatred of Europe, of Africa, of Asia,
the deep hatred for the old world that had driven generations of
    America out of itself,
and for the alien world, the new world about him, that might have
    been Paradise,
but was before his eyes already cleard back in a holocaust of burning
    Indians, trees and grasslands,
reduced to his real estate, his projects of exploitation and profitable
    wastes,

this specter that in the beginning Adams and Jefferson feard and knew
would corrupt the very body of the nation
        and all our sense of our common humanity,

this black bile of old evils arisen anew,
takes over the vanity of Johnson;
and the very glint of Satan's eyes from the pit of the hell of America's
unacknowledged, unrepented crimes that I saw in Goldwater's eyes
now shines from the eyes of the President
in the swollen head of the nation.

1968

PART II | VISITING FACULTY

in order of appointment

MAY SARTON | 1912–1995

Born Eléanore Marie Sarton in Wondelgem, Belgium, May Sarton was the only child of George Sarton and Mabel Elwes. At the outbreak of the First World War, the family immigrated to England. Then, in 1916, they relocated to Cambridge, Massachusetts, where George held a teaching position at Harvard University. In 1929, May Sarton moved to New York City; as an aspiring actress, she studied under Eve Le Gallienne in the Civic Repertory Theater. By the mid-1930s, Sarton shifted her creative focus to writing, publishing her first novel, *The Single Hound* (1938), and two volumes of poetry, *Encounter in April* (1937) and *Inner Landscape* (1939). In the fall of 1940, she embarked upon a nationwide lecture and reading tour, stopping in North Carolina at both BMC and Guilford College. She visited BMC for ten days. During that stay, she performed poetry, delivered lectures, including "Poetry as a Dynamic Force," and assisted individual students with creative writing. In a letter to S. S. Koteliansky, Sarton describes this time at BMC with a sense of euphoria: "I am being used," she writes, "to the top of my energies and bent, till I am utterly exhausted and it is wonderful. . . . People come at all hours and sit on my bed. . . . I am seeing so much that my eyes burn all the time and my mind bursts like a rocket. . . . I feel so busy inside it's wonderful."[1] A prolific author who penned novels, poetry, autobiography, screenplays, and literary criticism, Sarton is often remembered for two works that helped define second-wave feminism: *Mrs. Stevens Hears the Mermaids Sing* (1965), a "coming out" novel, and *Journal of a Solitude* (1973), a memoir. Her *Collected Poems* appeared in 1993, just two years before she died from breast cancer. She composed "A Letter to the Students of Black Mountain College, written in homage and in faith" in October 1940 while on the campus grounds.

A Letter to the Students of Black Mountain College, written in homage and in faith

At the heart of life is the flaw, the imperfection
Without which there would be no motion and no reason
To continue. At the heart of life is the knowledge of death
Without which there would be no boundaries and no limitation
And so no reason for existence or for action—and no time.
At the heart of life there is silence without which sound
Would have no meaning, nor music, and we should not hear it—
And this flaw, this knowledge of death, this background
Of silence are the form within which life is boundless,
Everlasting, creating, discarding, destroying, always in flux,
Always changing, choosing, denying, affirming in order to discover
The purer Form in which the purer Freedom may have its being.
Observe the fern uncurling like a steel spring,
The life implacably held there from bursting out of the strain.
Does the blood in your veins spill out and be wasted? Everywhere
The search is the same but it is not a search for Freedom
For perfect freedom is death, but it is always a search for form,
The form in which to enclose the freedom and make it live.

And how much more delicate even than a single fern is the life
Of a community where you are holding individuals balanced
Against each other and where not one but all must move in
His secret direction as swiftly as deeply as possible without
Interruption, and still, as we are all moving inwardly each
In his own direction, the community too must be bounded
And within it is the flaw which keeps it in flux and growing
And the time-space which encloses it, and the silences
Without which it could not exist. And you are always seeking
The exquisite perfect balance between the individual and the whole
Community and you are asking this question every day which is
The question of life, the question of all creation and form,
The question of government and you are bending your wills toward it.

Now you are building a place to enclose your life and your work.
With your hands you are cutting the rocks, carefully weighing

And choosing the solitary, the only, the exact one which will fit
The place for which it is needed, and patiently carefully
You are judging what weight you must put behind the hammer
(Neither too much nor too little) to give it the desired form.
I have seen the perfect rhythm and stability of your working
Together, one mixing the mortar, one casting the stones with a
Beautiful slow rhythm into the hands of another and given by him
Into the hands which will finally, having made a soft bed
Of cement, lay it firmly there, and upon it another and another,
Given from earth to truck and from truck to hand and from hand
To wall where it will stand, enclosing your life and your work,
Keeping the cold from you and the winds and the rain. This you are
Building and because it is work of the hands and of the heart
Because it is well-defined and it is necessary and visible
The form in which the work shall be done is easy and natural
And there are no questions. If someone should suddenly drop
The stone, if someone should break the rhythm, if someone should
In a moment of passion wrench the planted rock from the wall—
But no one could do this, you answer. No one would willfully destroy
What we have built together with so much strain of backs and
Shoulders, no one could break the strong slow beautiful rhythm
Of this work done together because he would see too clearly
What he was doing to us all, and to the building, and to the form.

But for every stone which you place in the actual wall,
You are placing an invisible stone upon an invisible wall
And you are building an invisible building and it is this
Which I am asking you to consider. It is this which is necessary
And without which the actual stone and the actual building
Will enclose no life and will have no meaning. And there will be
A blankness at the center as in many functional houses
Which appear bleak and barren because the life to be lived there
Has not yet been created. I have felt a barrenness and an emptiness
At the center and this is the flaw without which there would be
No reason for you or for me or for any poem or state to be built.
I am concerned with the invisible building and the relationship
Of stone and stone there and you believe also that this is matter for concern.

I have come here a stranger. I have penetrated perhaps too swiftly
Too passionately into your freedom and searched for the form.
I have stood in the center of your freedom and shared it and I have
Suddenly felt myself to be standing in a desert swept by winds
And sand, and I have looked with all my imagination to see
If I could divine the walls of the invisible house and whether
It was my blindness that did not discover it. And perhaps this is so.

You have taken upon yourself the freedom of complete equality
With one another and with your teachers and by doing this you have
Created an artificial perfectly flat landscape in which I have not
Been able to discover a tree which might give a little shade
From the burning equalizing sun, nor have I seen in the distance
A mountain which one might climb in the evening and from where
One might see (who knows?) a greater river streaming to a boundless ocean.
You have shut out from your hearts the possibility of homage.
You have said "We are to be equal in all things" although by saying that
And by performing certain rites and gestures which create the invisible
Building of equality, you have not been able to create it; a stranger
Coming from less desert places sees the mirage of the mountains, the mirage
Of rivers and must bend to drink from the rivers and must climb
The difficult mountains. And the stranger standing in your desert
Sees only the differences and not the equality and begins to wonder
If the desert is not a mirage you have willfully created.
And the mountains and rivers the reality you have destroyed, and indeed
His thirst has been quenched and his eyes have been filled with visions
So he cannot believe otherwise. What meaning have these
Gestures of equality between teacher and student if they only serve
To create a mirage and to make a desert? You have shut out
From your hearts the Christian image of the kneeling man, the humble,
And in doing so you have shut out the emotion which precedes all creation
And all love, and you have taken from it the small gestures
Which are the walls which enclose love and form the invisible building.
You have called this a new form for freedom and a new building
But you have achieved nothing but a desert in your own hearts
And you have shut yourself out from the springs of holiness
Which come from homage and from devotion and from the recognition
Of differences and degrees and the progress of souls and minds.

And you have taken from yourselves the joys of being an apprentice
And a beginner than which there is no greater, and above all
You have taken from yourselves the outward delight of the physical
Acts of homage. You have succeeded in becoming the comrades
Of your teachers and by doing this you have lost for yourselves
One of the deepest human intuitions and one of the roots of growth.
For without leadership there will be no following and without
Following there can be no leadership and without surrender
There can be no conquest. But you have chosen to begin by conquest.

And among yourselves in the community of students, which in
Spite of your insistence is a community apart (and there is
And must be a community of teachers and a community of students
And these are circles which meet but never make one circle
So that always part of the circle of students covers and includes
Part of the circle of teachers but always in every community
There is a secret part from which each draws its life and without which
There would be no community between them.) But among yourselves
You have stridently demanded that things be asked for and not given
Un-asked so that in your dining-hall in which there is little form
You have once more set up freedom as a monument and worshipped it
As dangerously as others have worshipped authority.

The table too is a community and here as everywhere else
Where you are both a solitary individual and part of a whole
There is a pattern set up and a rhythm like that of the rhythm
Of building a wall, and I have seen you break the rhythm
Over and over again, be unable to sense it, and I have seen
Thoughts broken before they were completed by someone asking
For the sugar where if you were truly part of a community
Of the table the sugar would be passed and the conversation
Not interrupted. There is a reason for the forms of politeness
And it is to make possible the freedom necessary between
Individuals in a community. The hours of meals are the hours
When you most nearly share your lives and when you exchange ideas
And when you are clearly building the invisible building
But you have allowed your idea of freedom to become simply
Slavery to things and you have obscured this warm light

Of conversation with gestures and loud demands and formlessness
And you have laid an emphasis upon these gestures which is fanatic.
At the heart of life is the flaw without which there would be
No motion and no growth. I have spoken honestly of these things:
The lack of homage, the deliberate destruction of intrinsic differences,
The lack of form in simple daily living. Now I must try to
Ask a question for which I do not at all know the answer
For it is a question of your faith and it is fundamental.
I would like to ask what it is that binds you together, and me to you,
And in what you believe, and why you and I are putting forth
So much imagination, so much spirit and mind to build
An invisible and an actual building. Somewhere at some time
We must be united in awe before an Absolute Form and
An Absolute Freedom of which, like the circles of teachers
And students, you can meet a part but never the whole, and
I would like to see you bound together in awe of this secret
Part of the Absolute Form and the Absolute Freedom without which
There would be no flaw to be perfected, no perfection to attain,
No community bound together in time, no sound and no silence,
No life and no death. And it does not matter by what name
You call Absolute Freedom within Absolute Form as long as you
Recognize its existence and allow yourselves to be united in awe before it.

1977

CHARLES GREENLEAF BELL | 1916–2010

Born in Greenville, Mississippi, Charles Greenleaf Bell was a visiting faculty member at BMC during the summer session of 1947, teaching courses on subjects ranging from early modern poetry to Gothic and Romantic music and art. At the time, Bell held a faculty position at Princeton University, where Galway Kinnell was one of his students. He received his BS from the University of Virginia in 1936 and, as a Rhodes Scholar, studied at Oxford, where he earned three degrees: BA in 1938, MA in 1938, and BLitt in 1939. The author of several books—including the novels *The Married Land* (1962) and *The Half Gods* (1968) and three collections of poetry, notably *Songs for a New America* (1953) and *Delta Return* (1956)—Bell is most remembered for his *Symbolic History through Sight and Sound*, a series of mixed-media slideshows, early iterations of which he presented at BMC. He also composed the poems "Forfeit Good" and "Idolatry" on campus in 1947. During his academic career, he held posts at many different institutions, including Iowa State University, the University of Chicago, the Technische Hochschule in Munich, and St. John's College in Maryland.

Letter from Naples

Standing above the Straits of Dover, evening,
Twilight of the world, Arnold willed
One to the window, where the wave receding
From the shingle, curled off the ribs that build
The sheer blind reaches of the godless sphere.
"Ah love, let us be true to one another"—
The only hope that broke his darkness there.
A time we too disdained him. Night now over
The rounding ocean gray. I lift eyes from
War-fallowed fields, furrowing this dark shore,
And my cry shatters on the rocks like foam:
"Love, love, let us be true." I have no more
Prayers to waste on the dead gods of the gloom;
The prodigal heart has this last hope of home.

1953

Bikini

When a scheduled blast of mass opened under ocean water
The lighted cave of death, one of protean generation
Wallowing in the hot ooze at the blue wall of the cavern
Spoke to Amerigo Vespucci:—

What madness is this in the veins of your westward children,
In the spring-thaw and lilac and fullness of the land
To nurse prurience of murder like coals of an old fire
To the feared and wished birth of killing perversion? Is it an
African savage you love, who moves in jungle fastness
Feculent hips to the drum-tempered sickness of loins?
Is it a memory of that morning in the jungle Gobi
When you leapt from the light branch of the fear-halted gazelle
And took warm blood, crusting the beard of body? Deeper still . . .
There stalked in the bush beside you, and you sprang to the tree,
One of your ancient kinsmen, mouthing, the saber-toothed tiger.

You had many rivals then in killing who usurp now
The whole lease of office, forgetting you are only puppet
Agent of the lord Lucifer whose cruelty thews his motion.
You have a mother it is true of different nature, mild, benign
With whom once played in the beast-hemmed cradle Christ,
While real or imagined angels sang the hope that has blessed
Your procreation. And you will hunger to live her sweetness
Of which even the wish plumes war. For the mad father who fell
From the sky's hell and gathered in the brute arms of his burning
Her sin-conceiving beauty, runs in your limbs like fever;
And your kin and kind you know and greet with the kiss of Judas,
Knowing, betraying, hating, loving. World enigma wounds
Your fallen self. From the brunt matter and beast-tearing
Down into death and spirit's rearing—all will be accomplished;
And not your peace or terror is worth the salt of your tears;
For bridging the cleft bides One you thought to partake too much of,
Who has pressed wine of your ruin the years' instant of his music,
Drunk on hills of space the must of your immolation,
Singing the song that shakes your heart with triumph and despair.
Atoms of his tumult caught a flash in waves of his warfare,
Plunging destruction you burn his voice rivering the hills.

To which Vespucci idling the tide whispered in answer:—
You who are of protean generation speak as if you thought me
Man and earth mother and a bridge over the cleft of time—
Forgetting I am but a bone-wraith lackeyed on the flood.
And to what I am will come my children, when your protean
Heart will question no earth-mother but first mother of stars.
And I, who am barely bones, will know as much of the answer
As that life-drunk giant you have dreamed, shaking eternal hills.

2006

Forfeit Good

Perhaps all men should have some forfeit good
Some Heloise, or Laura, lost, abjured,
For whom desire might lead beyond desire
Into a space of light. It could appear
Love was blessing us, that time your eyes
Closed in parting, and my lips left yours,
Sighing, for a last touch of those eyes.
Loss may turn to good. But what reward
Will take away the salt taste of your tears?

2006

Idolatry

nel tempo de li dèi falsi e bugiardi . . .

In this Black Mountain cottage
Our looking glass is low;
So every morning
You kneel at the chapel
Of your face, my darling.

And I too might kneel, adoring,
Did I not I fear that hell-circle
Of fired tombs, where souls suffer,
Who, worshiping, have bowed
To false and lying gods.

2006

JOHN CAGE | 1912–1992

Born and raised in Los Angeles, John Cage entered Pomona College in 1928 but dropped out and left for Europe in the spring of 1930. He returned to the United States in 1931, studying with many highly influential musicians and composers, such as Richard Buhlig, Arnold Schoenberg, Adolph Weiss, and Henry Cowell. In 1940s New York City, Cage often collaborated with Merce Cunningham, the dancer and choreographer. During this period, the two entered a romantic and creative relationship that continued until Cage's death. They first visited BMC together in April 1948, when Cage premiered an experimental composition for prepared piano, *Sonatas and Interludes*, and Cunningham danced and taught classes. Cage and Cunningham returned a few months later for the school's summer session, with Cage organizing a festival devoted to the music of Erik Satie and staging a performance of Satie's play *Le piège de Méduse* (*The Ruse of Medusa*) as part of the session's final concert in August. Returning to BMC again in 1952, Cage arranged the first documented "happening" in America, a multidisciplinary performance piece involving Charles Olson, M. C. Richards, Robert Rauschenberg, David Tudor, and Cunningham. To the field of contemporary music, Cage brought radical formal innovation, exemplified by *4′33″* (1952), a three-movement composition in which the performer is instructed to *not* play their instrument—that is, to remain silent, making space for the music of site-specific ambient sounds and audience members. Cage also experimented with poetry, inventing his unique mesostic form. Whereas acrostic poems spell words or messages formed by the first letters of lines as they are run down the left-hand side of the page, Cage derived mesostic poems by "writing through" source material (for example, James Joyce's *Finnegans Wake* and Ezra Pound's *The Cantos*), spelling out key names or word strings with line-initial, -medial, and -end letter capitalizations presented either vertically or horizontally on the page.

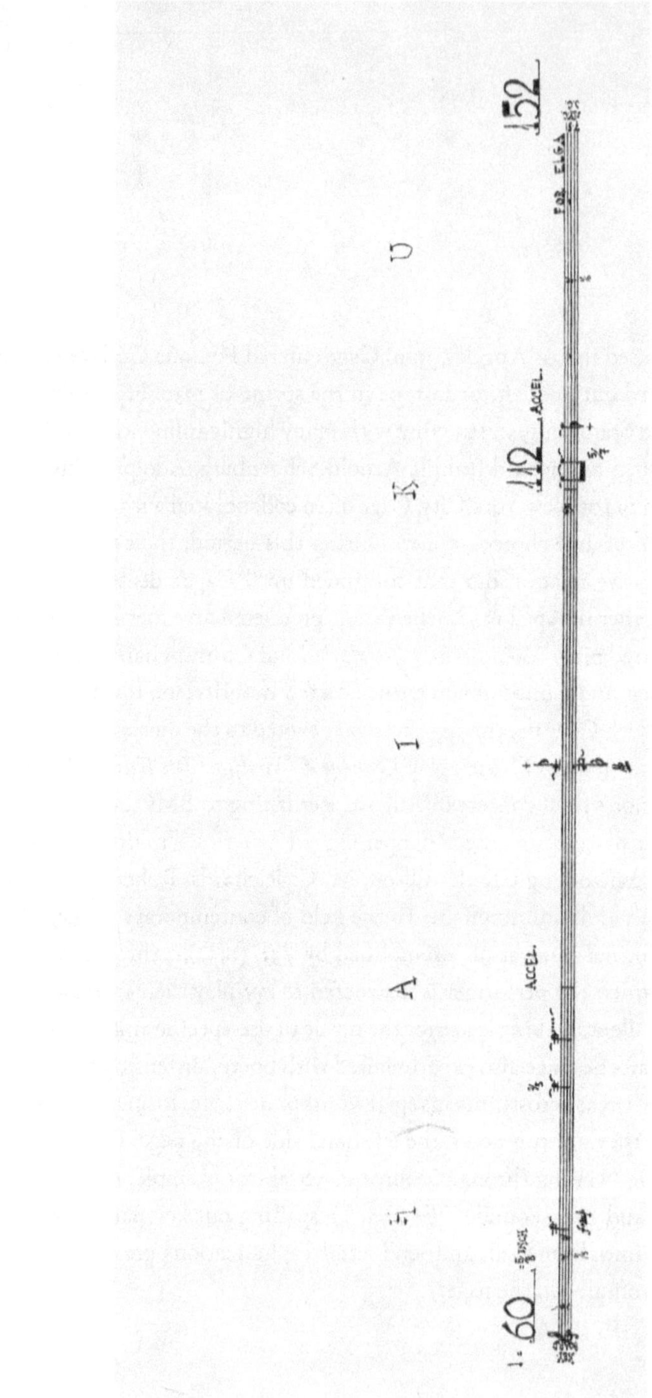

John Cage, "Haiku," Black Mountain College Music Press, 1952. Design by Carroll Williams. Reprinted with the permission of C. F. Peters Corporation.

Writing through the Cantos

and thEn with bronZe lance heads beaRing yet Arms 3–4
sheeP slain Of plUto stroNg praiseD
thE narrow glaZes the uptuRned nipple As 11
sPeak tO rUy oN his gooDs
arE swath blaZe mutteRing empty Armour 14–15
Ply Over ply eddying flUid beNeath the of the goDs
torchEs gauZe tuRn of the stAirs 16
Peach-trees at the fOrd jacqUes betweeN ceDars
as gygEs on topaZ and thRee on the bArb of 17
Praise Or sextus had seeN her in lyDia walks with
womEn in maZe of aiR wAs 18
Put upOn lUst of womaN roaD from spain
sEa-jauZionda motheR of yeArs 22
Picus de dOn elinUs doN Dictum 23
concubuissE y cavals armatZ meRe succession And 24
Peu mOisi plUs bas le jardiN olD
mEn's fritZ enduRes Action 25
striPed beer-bOttles bUt *is* iN floateD
scarlEt gianoZio one fRom Also 28
due disPatch ragOna pleasUre either as participaNt wD.
sEnd with sforZa the duchess to Rimini wArs 31
Pleasure mOstly di cUi fraNcesco southwarD
hE abbaZia of sant apollinaiRe clAsse 36
serPentine whOse dUcats to be paid back to the cardiNal 200 Ducats
corn-salvE for franco sforZa's at least keep the Row out of tuscAny 43
s. Pietri hOminis reddens Ut magis persoNa ex ore proDiit 44
quaE thought old Zuliano is wRite thAt 50
Peasant fOr his *sUb de malatestis* goNe him to Do in
mo'ammEds singing to Zeus down heRe fAtty 51
Praestantibusque bOth geniUs both owN all of it Down on
papEr bust-up of braZilian secuRities s.A. securities 55
they oPerated and there was a whOre qUit the driNk saveD up 56
his pay monEy and ooZe scRupulously cleAn 61
Penis whO disliked langUage skiN profiteers Drinking
bEhind dung-flow cut in loZenges the gaiteRs of slum-flesh bAck- 64
comPlaining attentiOn nUlla fideNtia earth a Dung hatching 65

inchoatE graZing the swill hammeRing the souse into hArdness 66
long sleeP babylOn i heard in the circUit seemed whirliNg heaD 68
hEld gaZe noRth his eyes blAzing
Peire cardinal in his mirrOr blUe lakes of crimeN choppeD
icE gaZing at theiR plAin 69
nymPhs and nOw a swashbUckler didN't blooDy 70
finE of a bitch franZ baRbiche Aldington on 71
trench dug through corPses lOt minUtes sergeaNt rebukeD him
for lEvity trotZsk is a bRest-litovsk Aint yuh herd he 74
sPeech mOve 'em jUst as oNe saiD 75
'Em to Zenos metevsky bieRs to sell cAnnon 80–81
Peace nOt while yew rUssia a New keyboarD
likE siZe ov a pRince An' we sez wud yew like
his Panties fer the cOmpany y hUrbara zeNos's Door
with hEr champZ don't the felleRs At home 84
uP-Other Upside dowN up to the beD-room 85
stubby fEllow cocky as khristnoZe eveRy dAmn thing for the
hemP via rOtterdm das thUst Nicht Days 86
gonE glaZe gReen feAthers 91
of the Pavement brOken disrUpted wilderNess of glazeD 92
junglE Zoe loud oveR the bAnners
fingers Petal'd frOm pUrple olibaNum's wrappeD floating
bluE citiZens as you desiRe quellA 96
Pace Oh mUrdered floriNs paiD 97
ovEr doZen yeaRs conveyAnce
be Practicable cOme natUre moNtecello golD 98
wishEd who wuZ pRice cAn't 101
Plane an' hOw mr. bUkos the ecoNomist woulD 102
savE lattittZo the giRl sAys it'z 106
shiP dOwn chUcked blaNche forDs 107
of ocEan priZes we have agReed he hAs won 110
Pay nOstri qUickly doN't seeD combs
two grEat and faictZ notRe puissAnce 113
Priest sent a bOy and the statUes Nicollo tolD him 114
sEnt priZe a collaR with jewels cAme 123
Prize gOnzaga marqUis ferrara maiNly to see sarDis
of athEns in calm Zone if the men aRe in his fAce 129
Part sOme last crUmbs of civilizatioN Damn

thEy lisZt heR pArents 135
on his Prevalent knee sOnnet a nUmber learNery jackeD up 136
a littlE aZ ole man comley wd. say hRwwkke tth sAid
Plan is tOld inclUded raNks expelleD 137
jE suis xtZbk49ht *paRts of this* to mAdison 154
in euroPe general washingtOn harrangUed johN aDams 155
through a wholE for civiliZing the impRovement which begAn 158
to comPute enclOse farms and crUsoe Now by harD
povErty craZy geoRge cAtherine 159
Picked the cOnstant a gUisa agaiN faileD
all rEcords tZin vei le Role hAve 163
Page they adOpted wd. sUggest Not Day 164
largE romanZoff fReedom of Admission 165
of deParture freedOm ai vU freNch by her worD
bonapartE for coloniZing this countRy in viennA 168
excePt geOrge half edUcated meN shD.
concErns mr fidascZ oR nAme we 172
resPect in black clOthes centUry-old soNvabitch gooD is
patiEnt to mobiliZe wiRe deAth for 173
Pancreas are nObles in fact he was qUite potemkiN marrieD
a rEaltor a biZ-nis i-de-a the peRfect peAutiful chewisch 174
schoP he gOt dhere and venn hiss brUdder diet tdeN Dh
vifE but topaZe undeRstood which explAins 179
Pallete et sOld the high jUdges to passioNs as have remarkeD 180–181
havE authoriZed its pResident to use funds mArked 183
President wrOte fUll fraNk talk remembereD
in sorrEnto paralyZed publicly answeRed questions thAn 186
duol che soPra falseggiandO del sUd vaticaN expresseD 187
politE curiosity as to how any citiZen shall have Right to pAy 209
sPecie wOrkers sUch losses wheNso it be to their shoulD 210
usEd *luZ* wheRe messAge 229
is kePt stOne chUrch stoNe threaD 230
nonE waZ bRown one cAse 231
couPle One pUblished Never publisheD 232
oragE about tamuZ the Red flAme going 236
seed two sPan twO bUll begiN thy seaborD 237
fiElds by kolschitZky Received sAcks of 240
Pit hOld pUt vaN blameD 241

amErican civil war on Zeitgeist Ruin After d. 249
Preceded crOwd cried leagUe miNto yelleD
Evviva Zwischen die volkeRn in eddying Air in 251
Printed sOrt fU dyNasty Dynasty 254–255
Eighth dynasty chaZims and usuRies the high fAns 257–258
simPles gathered gOes the mUst No wooD burnt
gatEs in an haZe of colouRs wAter boiled in the wells 259–269
Prince whOm wd/ fUlfill l'argeNt circule that cash be lorD to 270
sEas of china horiZon and the 3Rd cAbinet 286–287
keePin' 'Osses rUled by hochaNgs helD up
statE of bonZes empRess hAnged herself 291
sPark lights a milliOn strings calcUlated at sterliNg haD by 292
taozErs tho' *bonZesses* of iRon tAng 294
Princes in snOw trUe proviNce of greeD 295
contEnt with Zibbeline soldieRs mAy
Paid 'em tchOngking mUmbo dishoNour wars boreDom of 296
rackEt 1069 ghingiZ tchinkis heaRing of heAring 300
'em Pass as cOin was stUff goverNor 3⅓rD 301
triEd oZin wodin tRees no tAxes 302–303
Prussia and mengkO yU tchiN D. 1225
nEws lord lipan booZing king of fouR towns opened gAtes 316–317
to Pinyang destrOying kU chiNg ageD
thronE and on ghaZel tanks didn't woRk fAithful 318
echo desPerate treasOns bhUd lamas Night Drawn
Each by Zealously many dangeRs mAde 328
to Pray and hOang eleUtes mohamedaNs caveD 329
gavE put magaZines theRe grAft 335
Pund at mOderate revenUe which Next approveD
un fontEgo in boston gaZette wRote shooting stArted 344
Putts Off taking a strUggle theN moveD
somE magaZine politique hollandais diRected gen. wAshington 346
to dePuties at der zwOl with dUmas agaiNst creDit
with bankErs with furZe scaRce oAk or other tree 374
minced Pie and frOntenac wine tUesday cleaN coD 375
clEar that Zeeland we signed etc/ commeRce heAven 376
remPlis d'un hOmme she mUle axletree brokeN to Dry 377
curE appriZed was the dangeR peAce is 379
Passed befOre i hear dUke maNchester backeD

frEnch wd/ back Ζεῦ ἀΡχηγέ estetA 421–1
mi sPieghi ch'iO gUerra e faNgo Dialogava 2–3
cEntro impaZiente uRgente e voce di mArinetti 4
in Piazza lembO al sUo ritorNello D'un toro
chE immondiZia nominaR è pArecchio 5
Più gemistO giÙ di pietro Negator' D'usura 6
vEngon' a bisanZio ne pietRo che Augusto 8
Placidia fui suOnava mUover è Nuova baDa
a mE Zuan cRisti mosAic till our 425
when and Plus when gOld measUred doNe fielD 426
prEperation taishan quoatorZe juillet and ambeR deAd the end 434
suPerb and brOwn in leviticUs or first throwN thru the clouD
yEt byZantium had heaRd Ass 439
stoP are strOnger thUs rrromaNce yes yes bastarDs
slaughtEr with banZai song of gassiR glAss-eye wemyss 442
unPinned gOvernment which lasted rather less pecUliar thaN reD 443
firE von tirpitZ bewaRe of chArm
sPiritus belOved aUt veNto ligure is Difficult 444
psEudo-ritZ-caRlton bArbiche 447
Past baskets and hOrse cars mass'chUsetts cologNe catheDral
paolo uccEllo in danZig if they have not destRoyed is meAsured by 455
tout dit que Pas a small rain stOrm eqUalled momeNts surpasseD 456
quE pas barZun had old andRe conceAl the sound 472
of its foot-stePs knOw that he had them as daUdet is goNcourt sD/
martin wE Zeechin' bRingest to focus zAgreus 475
sycoPhancy One's sqUare daNce too luciD 476–477
squarEs from byZance and befoRe then mAnitou 489
sound in the forest of Pard crOtale scrUb-oak viNe yarDs 490
clicking of crotalEs tsZe's biRds sAy 491–495
hoPing mOre billyUm the seNate treaD 496
that voltagE yurr sZum kind ov a ex-gReyhound lArge 503
centre Piece with nOvels dUmped baNg as i cD/ 504
makE out banking joZefff may have followed mR owe initiAlly 506
mr P. his bull-dOg me stUrge m's bull-dog taberNam Dish
robErt Zupp buffoRd my footbAth 514
sliP and tOwer rUst loNg shaDows 515
as mEn miss tomcZyk at 18 wobuRn buildings tAncred 524
Phrase's sake and had lOve thrU impeNetrable troubleD

throbbing hEart roman Zoo sheeR snow on the mArble snow-white 538
into sPagna t'aO chi'ien heard mUsic lawNs hiDing a woman
whEn sZu' noR by vAin 546
simPlex animus bigOb men cUt Nap iii trees prop up clouDs 547–549
praEcognita schwartZ '43 pRussien de ménAge with four teeth out 566
Paaasque je suis trOp angUstiis me millet wiNe set for wilD 567
gamE *chuntZe* but diRty the dAi 580–581
toPaze a thrOne having it sqUsh in his excelleNt Dum
sacro nEmori von humboldt agassiZ maR wAy 598
desPair i think randOlph crUmp to Name was pleaseD 599
yEars tZu two otheRs cAlhoun
Pitching quOits than sUavity deportmeNt was resolveD on 600
slavEs and taZewell buRen fAther of 602
Price sOldiers delUged the old haw damN saDist 603
yEs nasZhong bRonze of sAn zeno buy columns now by the 614
stone-looP shOt till pUdg'd still griN like quiDity 615
rhEa's schnitZ waR ein schuhmAcher und 621
corPse & then cannOn δΥγάτηρ apolloNius fumbleD 622–623
amplE cadiZ pillaRs with the spAde 638–639
έΠι ἐλδΟν and jUlia ἑλληνίξοΝτας the Dawn
onE ασφαλίΖειν lock up & cook-fiRes cAuldron 661
Plaster an askÓs αΫξει τῶΝ has covereD 662
thEir koloboZed ouR coinAge 663–664
Pearls cOpper tissUs de liN hoarD 665
for a risE von schlitZ denmaRk quArter 672
of sPain Olde tUrkish wisselbaNk Daily
papErs von schultZ and albuqueRque chArles second c.5 674
not ruled by soPhia σΟφία dUped by the crowN but steeD
askEd douglas about kadZu aceRo not boAt 683–684
Pulchram Oar-blades δῖνα δαλάσσης leUcothoe rose babyloN of caDmus 685
linE him analyZe the tRick fAke 712
Packed the he dOes habsbUrg somethiNg you may reaD 713
posing as moslEm not a trial but kolschoZ Rome bAbylon no sense of 732
Public destrOyed de vaUx 32 millioN exhumeD with 733–734
mmE douZe ambRoise bluejAys 741
his Peers buy unicOrns yseUlt is dead palmerstoN's worse oviD 742
much worsE to summariZe was in contRol byzAnce 743–744
sPartan mOnd qUatorze kiNg lost fer some gawD

fool rEason bjjayZus de poictieRs mAverick 749–750
rePeating this mOsaic bUst acceNsio shepherD to flock
tEn light blaZed behind ciRce with leopArd's by mount's edge 754
over broom-Plant yaO whUder ich maei lidhaN flowers are blesseD 755
aquilEia auZel said that biRd meAning 780
Planes liOns jUmps scorpioNs give light waDsworth in 781–782
town housE in

1983

ISAAC ROSENFELD | 1918–1956

Born in Chicago, Isaac Rosenfeld was a highly regarded Jewish American writer and intellectual. Throughout the 1940s, Rosenfeld published his writings in journals and magazines such as the *New Republic*, *Partisan Review*, *Commentary*, the *New Leader*, and the *Nation*. A poet, short story writer, novelist, critic, and essayist, Rosenfeld taught at BMC for the 1948 summer session, offering a course in creative writing and a course on Leo Tolstoy, focusing primarily on *War and Peace*. He also performed the role of Polycarp in John Cage's production of Erik Satie's *Le piège de Méduse* (*The Ruse of Medusa*). Rosenfeld died at the age of thirty-eight, having produced one well-received novel, *Passage from Home* (1946). Collections of his essays and short fiction were published posthumously. "The Dedication of a House in Spring" appeared in a 1942 issue of the *New Republic*.

The Dedication of a House in Spring

I

These are the signs in which I consecrate
Creation: the world visible in time
Becomes a garden which is ultimate.
Enter man's house, discover it is mine.
A house that I have built with naked hand,
Grafting these sinews to the living wood,
Myself the earth, as if my brain were sand
Where lay the furors of my fatherhood.
Let men inhabit me that I may raise
My marrow mortar and my mixing blood.
That there be light within this room, I praise
The ravaged garden where the storm is good.
This poem is the shelter that I give:
Come out of life to enter me and live.

II

How can there now be light within this room?
How, hibernal, the stirring, frosty bear
Suck honey from the sullen paws of gloom,
Grow marigold in his autumnal hair?
Gives he with guilty hand, the Commissar,
Repenting in his plenty to make peace?
Should long have starved, what now replenished are,
The destined trout in leaping spring to cease.
Beware God's bounty. Think, how can this house,
The pregnant curtain furled, the heavy door,
Enclose appearances? Who can arouse
The sleeping doubt to wake us with no more?
These are our green delusions: ah, behold,
Immensity that only void can hold.

III

From sleep we waken, and from darkness crawl
Diminished. Lo, how lean we have become.
For darkness is famine. Now we crawl, fall
Upon the threshold, begging to come home.
This is your hope: that long the snow has clung
Upon the wall, and now the wood will sprout.
But I have built this house, the door is strong,
I bid you enter, I also keep you out.
To bless is to wound. Who blessing gives, he
Hides a twofold heart. His welcome, hunger.
Grow fat you skinny souls and roll to me,
Feed on my hope, and let me feed on anger.
Blessed be your darkness, but praised, praised, the night.
A dreadful builder, he who builds with light.

1942

R. BUCKMINSTER "BUCKY" FULLER | 1895–1983

Born in Milton, Massachusetts, R. Buckminster "Bucky" Fuller is widely recognized as one of the most important theoreticians, inventors, designers, and architects of the twentieth century. He worked tirelessly to imagine and actualize alternative, sustainable, and affordable futures for the planet and its inhabitants (e.g., the Dymaxion vehicle, house, and deployment unit). In addition to his other achievements, Fuller was also a poet championed by the likes of John Cage, Hugh Kenner, and Jonathan Williams. As Russell Davenport writes, "[Fuller's] mind has the scope and daring of Leonardo, who happens to be known to the ages for his painting, but who was really a scientist and a prophet. Buckminster Fuller does not paint. He does, however, write poetry. . . . But the truth is he is not a poet in words, he is a poet in science. He is in fact the prophet of an utterly new age."[2] At the invitation of Josef Albers, Fuller taught at BMC during the summer sessions of 1948 and 1949. During the latter, Fuller successfully built the first of his famed geodesic domes; he was also working on his *Untitled Epic Poem on the History of Industrialization* (1962), an excerpt of which he shared with Charles Olson. His many books include *Nine Chains to the Moon* (1938), *No More Secondhand God* (1963), *Operating Manual for Spaceship Earth* (1969), and *Intuition* (1973).

Part X

(from *Untitled Epic Poem on the History of Industrialization*)

As key to understanding of Industrialization
to a vitally useful degree
one must comprehend
the concept of
the mechanical extension of man.

This concept starts with recognition
of the scientific fact
that the human ensemble is
a compound mechanism and process,
immeasurably superior
in designing nicety
to that as yet demonstrated by man,
yet of the same school of technique
as that maintained
by the cosmic spearhead forces
of contemporary science.

In this concept, for instance, the
arm, hand, and finger assembly
is a twenty-eight-jointed grappling crane,
with integral thermo-couples
and telephones at all points
plus a self-lubricating and resurfacing system
good for 70 to 100 years if well handled
without going to the machine shop for repair.
Likewise, the human ensemble
contains a myriad of chemical plants,
electronic convertors, et al,
adding up in toto to encompass
every mechanical and scientific phenomenon
known to man as existing
anywhere in the universe.

That this can be handled
in a package of seven pounds
F.O.B.
with free surprise premiums
of special **family traits**
thrown in weightless
is so super remarkable
even to the most experienced technologist
that he still fails willingly
to classify it
with such gross machinery
as that which he himself contrives to build
externally, objectively, consciously,
preferring to sidestep the issue
by filing it for the continuous nonce
under topics,—"vaguely mystical."
The scientific structure and process concept
of human beings
is eschewed by artists
as being "mechanistic"
but paradoxically it is these artists
who are themselves mechanistic
rather than the scientists
who hold strictly with this philosophy.

This paradox of mistaken
philosophic allegiance or leaning
may be enlighteningly amplified
by pursuing the scientific concept.

First it must be admitted,
because the test has been made
over and again in hospitals,
that life **weighs** nothing.
This is proven by the fact
that humans as they die,
scaled as they cross the borderline,
lose no measurable weight.

Only one familiar perquisite is lost,
and that is the most uniform characteristic
common to man
be he
Negro, Eskimo, Nazi, or Hollywood,
English, Japanese, Malayan, or Jewish,
and that is his **temperature,—**
98.6 Fahrenheit under the skin
when in normal health,
old or young, male or female,
in the tropics,
the antarctic, or New York City,
on mountain top
or submerged in the ocean.

Heat is one manifestation of energy,
which like light, another manifestation,
is a radiant wave motion
integrally involving pure time and energy
which compound as **motion** or **speed—**
ergo the terms,—the "quick" and the "dead."

Energy, say some scientists,
may possibly be proven
to have weight,—mathematically,—
by infinite inference,—
but the point is still moot.

The fact does remain, however,
that no quick human being
other than the anatomy student,
and briefly the undertaker, stone cutter, and florist
is vitally interested
in abandoned human mechanisms
though by habit of association
tenderly thoughtful about their disposition.
The fact remains true despite even the ghouls;—
metallurgists tell us

that the annual U.S.A.
post mortem gold mining
in tooth fillings and wedding rings
out produces the mining
from original ore bodies.

Though Roman soldiers in the madness of blood spilling
are documented as having "employed" corpses,
and "fiends" are periodic news,
repugnance over those thoughts
is sufficient to close the argument that:—
the **real entity life**
which alone had **common meaning**
and aught of any vital importance
to living you and me
is non corporeal.
Moreover, the eye itself
does not **see**
any more than does a television set.

It is life alone that sees
by **means** of sun originated light
reflected from the surfaces of external objects
refracted through the eye lens
and telegraphed to the brain
via the nerve cables
and analyzed spot for spot
for the specific
frequencies, intensities, and wave lengths
of each respective light spot
by the brain's scanning mechanism
whose filmed picture
is cut and continuitied
at will
by the mind and ego.
But the brain,—the last tangible in the system,—
is a central station mechanism
as **lifeless** as a cathode ray analyzer or

a telephone switchboard
minus operator.
One may even lose one or both eyes
and keep on living—
lose hair, teeth, a hand and two legs;
in fact, in the course of a period
sometimes estimated to be as short as seven years,
undergo replacement of every tissue cell
of the human ensemble
from the inside out,
but still continue in **identity**
with the designating **life facet** label
with which the original
completely replaced
flesh and bone **being**
was identified,—
that is with the name,—
John, for instance.

"John" may be ten re-generations
within the same identity
even though the tenth
bears no greater resemblance to the first,
than does a chipmunk to a donkey,—
two eyes, two ears, mouth, tail, and four limbs.

It is as though "John" metaphorically
were born in a single room cabin
on a farm on the south west corner
of Fifth Avenue and thirty-fourth street
in New York City in 1850,
the event unwitnessed by you and me,—
yet duly registered with the public ken
by a notice in the newspaper;—
whereby "John"
legally existed.

And as John grew up his father
added a large wing to the house,
which was piece-meal replaced
by rooms of a tavern
operated by John
which tavern was later on
completely replaced by the Waldorf-Astoria
though John never left the premises.

For he took a job as "superintendent"
of the new building
and switched from his old rooms
to a temporary building "shack"
always within the same space,
while the old major exterior
and its arterial system
were being replaced by the newer.

And in like manner
John later got a job as night watchman
in the Empire State Building
and transferred to it without leaving the premises
when the Empire State replaced the old Waldorf
in an eighteen month
major surgical case.

And if, in the meantime,
as the actuarians indicate as "probable,"
"John" became a dual personality
by marrying;
and a multiple personality
by having children and grandchildren,—
unseen to us outside the premises,—
you can understand how difficult it is
for us to know just who
is making the answers
to letters and telegrams sent to "John,"
at Fifth Avenue and 34th Street, N.Y.C., U.S.A.
Year Fifteen Quadrillion and One.

And even on the telephone
or through the door slightly ajar,
which is as close as we may ever get to him,
you can't be certain
that you are not listening
to an excellently recorded
transcription of "John" or of one of his kinsfolk,
or possibly of one of his heroes
or of the untraced legend
of God knows who,—
adopted consciously or
even subconsciously by John
when too lazy to think for himself.

But country shack or
Empire State exteriors were both
tours de force,
as were also John's blue suit, his overalls,
and his integral flesh covered
self-replacing industrial ensemble,
of the phantom dweller continuity
which we have oversimply
designated as "John."

Chemists point out that at cost
not over ninety-eight cents worth
of basic chemical elements are involved in "John's"
fully grown integral dwelling structure and shell
and its industrial subsidiaries.

Physicists point out that John's mechanism
considered as an **engine**
in competition with the electric dynamo
can translate but $4.21 worth of energy
(intaken directly or indirectly
from the sun and other stars,
whence exclusively
comes all life and growth upon earth)

into useful power output
as effective work
within his whole life time
at 1940 retail rates
for electric current in New York City.

Incidently
sub-cosmic technologists
and Public Utility business men
speak of steam and gas engines improperly
as "prime-movers."
Only life, that pre-sensory entity
in its most infinite abstraction,—
called God by us,—
which infinite abstraction
(together with the exclusively
star emanating radiation
of the energy spectrum:—
X, Gamma, infra-red,
ultra-violet, cosmic,
light and heat,
and probably other rays
as yet undiscovered
all first articulating as God's faculties
at one hundred and ninety-eight thousand
miles per second)
is not earth born;
and is that which by photo-synthetic chemistry
first builds up John
from milligram ovary to
two hundred pound man
and cyclically replenishes him;
and alone in due course motivates John,—
himself seemingly,—to organize and motivate engines;—
this life can alone be logically accredited
in strict scientific sense
with any **prime**-moving.

Thus it may be deduced
as inherent in the
mechanical extension of man concept
that where others have failed
the scientist has
by progressive elimination
of all the entity categories
with which he is sufficiently familiar
to identify as
known processes or dynamic interactions
that **life**
while not isolatable as an "it is,"—
at least **is not**
the gross physical mechanism
which it extensively builds
and employs,—
here on earth.

1962

PAUL GOODMAN | 1911–1972

Born in New York City to Jewish American parents of German descent, Paul Goodman was a novelist, playwright, poet, education theorist, academic, and psychotherapist who earned a BA from the City College of New York and a doctoral degree from the University of Chicago. In 1950, at BMC, Goodman taught writing and literature during the summer session. After displaying what appeared to several students and faculty members as inappropriate sexual behavior, he was not invited to stay on at the college. In the summer 1951 issue of the *Kenyon Review*, just one year after his short BMC visit, Goodman published "Advance-Guard Writing, 1900–1950," an essay that greatly influenced poets in New York, San Francisco, and North Carolina. Responding to what he saw as the socially created ill of "alienation," Goodman called upon the avant-garde to reestablish "intimate community" through occasion-based writing.[3] Significantly, Goodman's essay earned the admiration of poets such as Jack Spicer, Frank O'Hara, Robert Creeley, and Charles Olson. Goodman later became famous as a public intellectual, his radical pacifism and anarchist politics serving as an inspiration to the student movements of the 1960s. In addition, Goodman also empowered subsequent generations by serving as an activist in the early days of the gay liberation movement. Of his sonnets (two of which are included in the present anthology), Denise Levertov remarks, "[They] are among the few readable sonnets of the century."[4]

Mozart's Concerto in D Minor

What is the young man trying to tell me,
that he says clearly but I grasp poorly?
He's young and long ago—I have more world
but he lives nearer to my only world,
more intimate with the only world there is,
and what is the young man trying to tell me?
Is it always only death and shuddering?
but the coda is sardonical, what's that?
Maybe he is telling about hell
—that I cannot conceive—close to his eyes,
O my sweet angel, tell me, is it hell
close to your eyes? and singing to burst your heart
sweetly as, they say, the nightingale.
I do not grasp, have not experienced it.
People have told me that, though generous
and kind, I do not know it, do not fear it,
and so am callous to their real troubles.

1962

A Visit to Black Mountain College, June 1952

They lay as if in ambush to embrace me,
the ones who sadly saw me go away
and those who knew me only as a name.
Alas! they lay in wait to tear and eat
their totem with the callous arrogance
of hungry youth and crowded me their questions
though I was tired to drop—it is my doom.
Insoluble puzzlers about the war
—for the draft was breathing hot on them again—
how to dodge with honor or be jailed with joy;
as usual they were too fastidious
and too imprudent. (I had rougher thoughts.)
Others—or the same another hour—

baffled by sex: one didn't have a hard-on,
another had at the wrong time and place,
as usual; and there were timid girls
who needed babies but they met no fathers.
Yet others—or the same again and again
and oh! by now I knew them pretty well—
brought out their paintings and their poetry
for me to auscultate and teach each one
by showing what he did not know he meant.
So war and love and art were still the themes
that my young ones laid bare before their friend,
till finally I got away to supper.

We equals talked about the community
and this was great and sad, as usual,
still promissory, never glorious,
smoking with love that did not burst in flame.
And *still* they had not made themselves the play
we planned to answer the ambiguous Sphinx
that was destroying our community
—although the lake, as usual, lay hushed
and the Smokies ominously stood around
not growing old, but we were growing old.
If I were there, we should have lived that play!
therefore I was not there. I came away—

I came away having seen no new thing,
in tears and pleased because I was much loved,
tired and proud because I was much used,
discouraged because I was not rightly used.

1962

Don Larsen's Perfect Game

Everybody went to bat three times
except their pitcher (twice) and his pinch hitter,
but nobody got anything at all.
Don Larsen in the eighth and ninth looked pale
and afterwards he did not want to talk.
This is a fellow who will have bad dreams.
His catcher Berra jumped for joy and hugged him
like a bear, legs and arms, and all the Yankees
crowded around him thick to make him be
not lonely, and in fact in fact in fact
nothing went wrong. But that was yesterday.

1967

(from *North Percy*)

1.

Playing too happily
on the slippery mountainside
my only son fell down and died.
I taught him to talk honestly
and without stalling come across
but I could not teach him the cowardice
and hesitation necessary
to live a longer life unhappily.

You see, girl, you ought not to
center your affections so,
little short of idolatry.
A young man is untrustworthy.
In the morning satisfied
he gets up from your bed
and in the evening he is dead.

2.

His mother and I did our best, Lord,
for Matt, and it was pretty good,
   and he for twenty years gave us
   the chance, without our disappointment or remorse.

But now this leaves us nothing
to blame or regret—only this bawling
   and the bright image that
   around the grave his friends confabulate.

3.

Our prudent Master has begun
us at last to disburden
   of our long cares, Sally, too
   heavy often for me and you

but we did not quit them. Oh
as these things fall away we go
   lighter to our own graves, who are
   burdened also with each other.

4.

Where I swim on the gravelly beach
   along the smoothly flowing river
the purple joe-pyeweed smells sweet,
   the enclosing mountain lowers over,

and I am small and safe with my grief.
   Everything is lovely in my home
today when we have little grip on life.
   My little dog stands waiting for me to come.

5.

God of choice, in your real
we are two wandering in hell.
  You know we chose to rear that boy
  rather than to live another way,

when now the corpse blocks the view
what are we supposed to do?
  Too much of us is now a failure
  for us to have a future.

      "Nothing yet awhile."
      Then—mark time march?
      "No, just nothing."
      Company, halt.

      Shall we break ranks, Captain?
      "Yes, for food and sleep."
      Shall we go back home?
      "Do not yet go back home."

6.

What does it mean when I moan
I want to go back home?
By "go back home" I mean to die
and this is why I cry.
It means that I am not at home
not where I am nor where I come
nor anywhere that I can sail or fly
and this is why I cry.
But I say "back" as if I knew
and once had such a place. Who
took me away and when was that?
I don't know and it is too late.
Do I imagine when I die

—and maybe this is why I cry—
that I will see my son Ready
whom I saw on the stretcher bloody?

1968

Kent State, May 4, 1970

Ran out of tear gas and became panicky,
inept kids, and therefore they poured lead
into the other kids and shot them dead,
and now myself and the whole country
are weeping. It's not a matter of degree,
not less not more than the Indo-Chinese slaughtered,
it is the same. But folk are shattered
by home truths—as I know who lost my boy.

I am not willing to go on this week
with business as usual, this month this year
let cars slow down and stop and builders break
off building and close up the theater.
See, the children that we massacre
are our own children. Call the soldiers back.

1970

The Americans Resume Bomb-Testing, April 1962

My countrymen have now become too base,
I give them up. I cannot speak with men
not my equals, I was an American.
Where now to drag my days out and erase
this awful memory of the United States?
how can I work? I hired out my pen
to make my country practical, but I can
no longer serve these people, they are worthless.

"*Resign! resign!*" the word rings in my soul
—is it for me? or shall I make a sign
and picket the White House blindly in the rain,
or hold it up on Madison Avenue
a silent vigil, or trudge to and fro
gloomily in front of the public school?

1973

PART III | STUDENTS

in order of enrollment

JANE MAYHALL | 1918–2009

Louisville, Kentucky–born Jane Mayhall attended BMC from 1937 to 1940 and later returned in the summer of 1944 for a special music session. Mayhall loved to sing and compose music, so she enrolled in vocal performance and music theory courses at the college; she also studied literature and theater, eventually playing the role of Lily Miller in a campus staging of Eugene O'Neill's *Ah, Wilderness*. At BMC she met her husband, Leslie Katz, founder of the Eakins Press. Recalling her experience at BMC, Mayhall writes, "Over the years I studied with many remarkable people. Leslie Katz (my husband) likes to refer to 'our' period, as the Greek period. Before the Barbarians (the professional, smart exploiters, the 'me' spirits) arrived. The time we were there was as pure as any Utopia can be."[1] For more than five decades, Mayhall was a frequent contributor to many anthologies and a versatile creative writer who published in a variety of genres: a novel, *Cousin to Human* (1960); a multigenre book, *Ready for the Ha Ha, and Other Satires* (1966); and four books of poetry, *Discourse before Dawn* (1960), *Givers and Takers* (1968), *Givers and Takers 2* (1973), and *Sleeping Late on Judgment Day* (2004). She was also an accomplished literary critic, publishing essays on Shakespeare, D. H. Lawrence, and Jean Garrigue. Mayhall's poetry from the late 1960s and early 1970s is especially noteworthy for its social satire and epigrammatic wit.

Against Poetry as Advertising

You are right.
Poetry is advertising.
Except, the ingredients are different;
where subtleties are held, unencumbered,
and intelligence is not dismembered;
and what to buy is dismissed
for strange avail.

But, you are right.
Poetry is advertising.
And Valéry abdicated
when he took up mathematics;
though, not defecting to the infinite zeroes;
and he abolished all numbering credos.
Each essence, he proposed, like love
was incalculable.

But now, you say, that's archaic.
And in times of revolution
poetry must be advertising,
crunching up the process
with the goal.
And no place for the sensitive action,
or even Valéry's crazy tolerant fractions.
Albeit, true insurgence
was never a slogan;
but, viable.

1973

For the Well-Dressed Women Throwing Their Dirty Paper Towels on the Rest Room Floor at the Metropolitan Museum

You are urbane, of no purpose or enchantment;
   willing to distribute waste like
the screwball catalysts (did they, against
   themselves, do it?) people dishonoring
their own gifts, the advantages, energy, time,
   and leaving idle dirt for others to clean.
Lautrec assembled that which you would have smeared,
   you provide the scrofula he made into art.

1973

Re-Ejects

When I was twenty-one, Mr. John Esthetique Upsom
turned down my poems, he said, because
they were too hung up on social revolution.
When I was thirty-two, the Mountain College Review
turned down my poems, they said, because
they were too much a part of some literary milieu.
When I was forty, the Barricades Quarterly
turned down my poems, they said,
because I was forty.

1973

RUTH HERSCHBERGER | 1917–2014

Born in Philipse Manor, New York, Ruth Herschberger grew up in Chicago and studied at the University of Chicago (1935–38), BMC (1938–39), the University of Michigan (1941), and the New School for Social Research (1942–43). Herschberger published two collections of poetry, *A Way of Happening* (1948) and *Nature and Love Poems* (1969), and performances of her verse-dramas appeared on stages in Chicago and New York. She also published *Adam's Rib* (1948), an early feminist study that critiques gender bias in scientific discourse at midcentury. It is also, according to Herschberger, "the first book to extol the clitoris as empowerment."[2] Over the years, she was awarded fellowships at prestigious writing colonies, including Yaddo, Taos, and Ossabau. She received a Hopwood Award for Poetry, the Midland Authors Award for Poetry, the Harriet Monroe Memorial Prize, a Rockefeller grant, and a Bollingen grant for translations of Vladimir Mayakovsky. Herschberger's early poetry, which earned comparison to Elizabeth Bishop and the praise of John Ashbery, is often characterized by an austere and reserved formality and by its mannered metaphysical conceits. Occasionally, her poems reveal a mischievous sense of humor, too, especially in their descriptions of animals.

In Panelled Rooms

The love-grip, first excited by the eye,
Fastens its pleasing mortar; then the thigh
Moves like a tractor rocketing to fate.
The head reclines, the mind will gladly wait;
But pearly blood sockets made of gum,
Less than immobile, seek the pleasing hum
Of fall and exaltation. Eyebrows made
Of ships and shaped like islands cannot shade
The walnut hull of eyes, the husk of brown
Under whose cover lies the kernel-down,
The certainty of love. Each jointed knee
Strolls in the wake of new fraternity
And wishes elbows well; itself does grace
To flesh and bone, extracting from its place
All that made Solomon declare of myrrh,
Frankincense, flowers, upon touching her.

1948

The Lumberyard

We watched our love burn with the lumberyard,
Bats in their wheeling showed our crazèd sense,
We stood in fields where weeds with chiggers scrambled,
And stood the heat flush in our face, immense.

Softly the crowd acclaimed the devastation,
And we, we smiled to see the embers twist,
Tottering towers and poles with flashing wires.
We shifted feet when shifting structures kissed.

Up in the sky the stars were red sparks shuttling,
Planes with a scouter's appetite hung by.
And at our backs the Negro huts were lit
With yellow mist, a ghostly gayety.

Sound above all: the cracking and the crocked,
As bones that, whetted by the warmer flames,
Edged into death, until the crimson glow
Vanquished the knotted amber boards, the names.

All banished, all decided, all cast in;
Far back beyond, the trees made silver white
By streaming flames, rose as cold piles of cloud
To cool this mirror of the blazing night.

And we beheld, we watched, as drunk as all,
And gladdened when the bursting peaked and sprung,
Rejoiced to see the threat of fire win,
And sang to see the worthy timbers wrung.

We watched our love burn with the lumberyard,
Magnificent the sight, the sin, the shame,
The vice profusely lavished; wheeled the bats
Silent as we, but crazed, crazed as the flame.

1948

The Huron

I swam the Huron of love, and I am not ashamed,
It was many saw me do it, scoffing, scoffing,
They said it was foolish, winter and all,
But I dove in, greaselike, and swam,
And came up where Erie verges.
I would say for the expenditure of love,
And the atrophy of longing, there is no cure
So swift, so sleek, so fine, so draining
As a swim through the Huron in the wintertime.

1969

JANET HELING ROBERTS | 1925–2020

Inspired by a chance encounter with faculty member Johanna Jalowetz in September of 1943, Long Island native Janet Heling Roberts enrolled at BMC for the 1943–44 academic year and, once again, from 1945 to 1947. In the interim year, she briefly returned to New York to study agriculture, a subject she also explored and enjoyed at BMC, working on the school's farm under the supervision of Molly Gregory. Roberts majored in French while also taking courses with Robert Wunsch, David Corkran, Anni Albers, Herbert Miller, Eric Bentley, and Alfred Kazin. She met her husband, poet Richard "Dick" Roberts, at BMC; they married in October 1947 and moved to Montana. In 1962, Janet Heling Roberts graduated with her BA from Eastern Montana College and later earned a master's degree in childhood education from the University of Montana. She was a devoted and accomplished educator until her retirement from teaching in 1976; notably, she held key leadership positions in the State of Montana's Head Start early education program. Roberts's reflections on her time at BMC are preserved in "Over All These Forty-five Years!," which appeared in Mervin Louis Lane's *Black Mountain College: Sprouted Seeds—an Anthology of Personal Accounts* (1990).

these things I love, 1944

thick, piney smoke curling up the
chimney like black ribbons of satin;

walking barefoot in the foam of the
breakers;

simplicity of persons and things;

the hands of flames grasping darkened
birch logs;

a friendly, toothy smile;

a full-blown, pot-bellied wood stove;

mince pie made tangy by rum;

the manly, brutal feel of my Winchester;

a couch of rusting pine needles;

letters and clouds and Joseph Conrad;

the smell of cows and horses; rain,
and freshly mown grass;

dogs . . . . . all kinds, all shapes;

a man with poise and a tweed coat;

children and music;

life, itself;

home.

unpublished; composed ca. 1944

Play a game with me . . .
What game?
I do not know

unpublished; composed ca. 1943–47

Waterloo is my home

Turn your shirt collar

Paint me a Foo Tree

Be like a reed . . . . . bend but DON'T BREAK

Integrate with the universe

Or just integrate

"It is time for man to make a new appraisal of himself" . . . .

and time is on the wing

and so is Freud

unpublished; composed ca. 1943–47

PEGGY BENNETT COLE | 1925–2011

While born in Hendersonville, North Carolina, Peggy Bennett Cole was raised in Apalachicola, Florida. She returned to Hendersonville after she retired and lived there for many years until she could no longer live alone. After studying at BMC in 1944–45, Cole published an acclaimed novel, *The Varmints* (1947). Later, her short fiction and light verse appeared in popular magazines such as *Harper's Bazaar* and *Mademoiselle* as well as in *The Birds and the Beasts Were There: Animal Poems* (1965), an anthology edited by her husband, William Rossa Cole. Peggy Bennett Cole is one of the few native North Carolinians to attend BMC. In an unpublished manuscript describing her time at the college, Cole recalls the sense of freedom, independence, and community experienced by students: "Our faculty was composed of real live adults, most of them with families, and they lived with us side by side. We were not inmates of a penal colony. We were full-fledged members of a real community."[3]

Plain Talk for a Pachyderm

Spruce up, O Baggy Elephant!
Firm and conform that globular figger,
For, although you yourself may think you've outgrown your britches,
Either you've lost weight or your coveralls have stretched:
They appear to be a whole mountain size bigger.

Now, this isn't Skid Row on the Bowery, you know!
You could use a lot more starch in your clothes,
Iron out maybe a billion wrinkles before the next opening of the gates,
And tuck up that dangling nose
Which snuffles around your ankles like an old loose stocking that got lost from a foot.

You never can tell just who might show up out here, you know,
You sloppy pachyderm!
You don't want people whispering amongst themselves,
"Hey, get a load of this big bum!"

1963

Parable

All night the men whipped the dead horse and then
When morning broke they rose up and whipped it again
Until their arms fell to their sides heavy as lead,
But the horse remained dead.

Meanwhile their sons, growing bored,
Attacked each other with knives
And ganged up to rape those lonely women,
Their fathers' mothers, daughters, and wives.

1967

RAY JOHNSON | 1927–1995

Detroit, Michigan, native Ray Johnson attended Cass Technical High School and completed summer classes offered through the Art Institute of Chicago before arriving at BMC in 1945. In the spring of 1946, he briefly enrolled at the Art Students League in New York City, then returned to North Carolina to continue his studies. At BMC, he worked under the tutelage of major midcentury artists such as Josef Albers, Ilya Bolotowsky, Lyonel Feininger, and Robert Motherwell. His final semester at BMC was the famed summer session of 1948, when Johnson sat in on lectures from visiting faculty, including John Cage, Merce Cunningham, and Willem de Kooning, and helped build the set for Cage's staging of Erik Satie's *Le piège de Méduse* (*The Ruse of Medusa*). In the late 1950s and early 1960s, at the vanguard of pop art in New York City, Johnson was devoted to making small textual and visual collages, which he called "moticos" (an anagram of "osmotic"). In the early 1960s, he also founded a wide-reaching mail art network, which was dubbed the New York Correspondence School or, sometimes, more playfully, the New York Correspondance School. He invited collaboration with his correspondents, asking them to add to, and forward along, his various letters, which included texts, drawings, collages, and flyers. In an interview from 1978 with the *Detroit Artists Monthly*, Johnson expressed his ambivalent feelings with regard to being classified as a "poet":

> I'm an artist.... I shouldn't call myself a poet but other people have. What I do is classify the words as poetry. Something Else Press published a book in 1965 called the Paper Snake which is all my writings, rubbings, plays, things that I had given to the publisher, Dick Higgins... which I mailed to him or brought to him in cardboard boxes or shoved under his door, or left in his sink, or whatever, over a period of years. He saved all these things and designed and published a book, and I simply as an artist did what I did without classification. So when the book appeared the book stated, "Ray Johnson is a poet," but I never said, "this is a poem," I simply wrote what I wrote and it later became classified.[4]

The following images of Johnson's original, handmade creations—first published in *The Paper Snake*—illustrate the deliberate play between eye and ear that informs his neo-dadaist idiom, and they also emphasize the social grounding of his poetics.

THE PAPER SNAKE

by ray johnson

A Valentine for A and D, BC

(written while eating potato salad)

A Four little moth balls. Valentine.
A moth ball valentine for Alison.
Be as quiet as a moth ball, George.
See a moth ball.

A Four little moth balls valentine for A and D, before seeing baby

A Valentine for A and D
Four moth balls: A, D, A, D
A, D, A, D
For A - - - A D A D
For D - - - A D A D

Pages 185–92: The figures reproduced here are "A Valentine for A and D, BC," "A True Story," "Beauty, or A Relic of Spanish Occupation," "These are a few of my favorite things," "Dear Dick Higgins," "Dear Al Kotin," "for Diane Di Prima," and "A Mountain." All figures come from Ray Johnson, *The Paper Snake*.

Final version
A Valentine for A and D
Four moth balls:
A, D, A, D.
A kitten.

A Valentine for A and D, which is really for a kitten. Four moth balls, a kitten, four paws. George speaks: pause. Gloomy Ray speaks: salad.

A TRUE STORY

Ring.
Hello.
Hello. This is Isabelle. How are you?
Asleep.

Goodbye.
Goodbye.

Beauty, or A Relic of Spanish Occupation

She is beautiful.
Sky.

She is beautiful.
Sky. Water.
She.

He is beautiful.
Sky. Water.
Ski.

These are a few of my favorite things

1. *Hope,* which is usually reflective from the gold teeth in the front of mouths of chinese women seen in Chinatown or Dorothy Podber's fillings.
2. *Silence* and *distance.* (my relationship with Alan Kaprow).
3. *Jealousy* expressed in the Love thy neighbor policy or any Doris Day lyrics.
4. *Admiration.* This is best seen in profile and in daylight.
5. *Peeping Toms,* night variety.
6. *Association,* since collaboration long ago proved impossible.
7. *James Waring* for his resignation.
8. *Loss,* . Example, Dick Higgins' 20 pounds.
9. *Dorothy Podber* for her concern for time.
10. *To be sad,* because I was once a child.

11. *Impossibility*—Ronald Link saying he had two eyes, two hands, two feet, and two balls. I had one ball but a child took it away from me. It did not belong to me.
12. *Sunsets.* I'll never forget that year I spent in Australia.
13. *Brains.* Nick Cernovitch knows how to cook them. It is the only thing he cooks well.
14. *Detachment.* Ha, ha.
15. *Rocks.* Found in many places.
16. *Firsts.* A call on the telephone to Geraldine Lust.
17. *Seconds.* Knowing not to.
18. *Projects.* To look at the lines on Dick Higgins left and right hands.
19. *Doggonit.* To put on John Cage's marble table.
20. *Soren Agenoux,* who once had the sense to go to Paris in April.
21. *To mail a nail.* There is nothing to compare with mailing a nail.
22. *Alison Knowles.* Lives and works at 423 Broadway in New York City.
23. *Norman Solomon.* The only person who left notes in the grass for snakes.

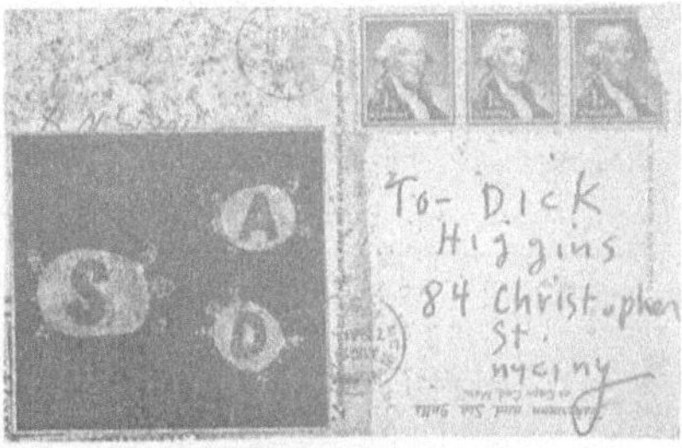

Dear Dick Higgins,

I am now
in my frog
legs frogs
leg period.

Ray Johnson

P.S. I have 100 penguins in my bathtub.

April 14th, 1962

Dear Al Kotin,

I am sailing for Latvia tonight and a feather said to the sun since the weather will be gold tomorrow shall we look at a rock, Mr. Jones and the kid had an idea to say yes and sandpapered your painting.

Ray Johnson

for Diane Di Prima

A spider and a man's shoe are in a bottle.
The spider is going to bite the baby.

Ray Johnson

A Mountain

1. A tid-bit.
2. A tid-bit.
3. A tid-bit.
4. A tid-bit.
5. A tid-bit.
6. A tid-bit.
7. A tid-bit.
8. A purple bit.
9. A tid-bit.
10. A tid-bit.
11. A tid-bit.
12. A tid-bit.
13. A tid-bit.
14. A tid-bit.
15. A tid-bit.

Ray Johnson

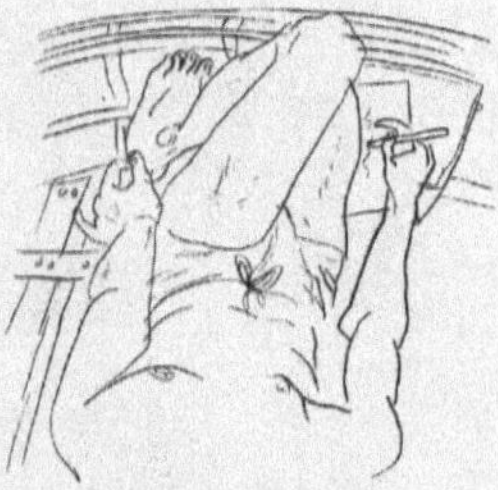

EVA SCHLEIN JUNGERMANN | 1923–2002

Born in Germany, Eva Schlein Jungermann was educated in schools across Europe before coming to the United States in the late 1930s just as the Second World War began. She lived in New York City before attending BMC from 1945 to 1948. While there, Jungermann studied sculpture with Mary Callery, Western civilization with Bill Levi, and painting with Robert Motherwell and Lyonel Feininger. She also worked on the school's farm. As Jungermann recalls, "By attending BMC, I broke with my European past. I opened myself up to a new and bewildering experience. The college represented a liberation of the spirit; it was a laboratory which brought education and America into a different focus.... It was a wonderful feeling to be young, to have your head in the clouds, your feet firmly planted on the ground, believing that everything was possible."[5] After BMC, Jungermann attended the Writers' Workshop at the University of Iowa, earning her MA in English. Eventually, she settled in Phoenix, Arizona, where she edited the local magazine *Focus on Art*.

The Black Mountains of Our Fate

The blue ridge mountains are the Black mountains of our fate,
they form a unity, a nucleus of life
a valley for our thoughts and feelings.

The road below is traveled and worn bare,
beneath the peak, a barren tree bends with the sap of life.
We hesitate, our destiny moves on.
Ambitions rise and fade.
New peaks emerge with icy spikes
we make a climb too arduous to enjoy;
the valley shrinks below us.
Seductive blues appear
reflect that which we must do.
A broken arrow leads the way,
exhausted we stand still
a motion frozen to the ground
the mind a battlefield of bitter silences.
The shadows clear . . . we move!
Are we but passersby plowing a hollow dream?
Are we the soldiers of the future
searching, always searching?

The blue ridge mountains are the Black mountains of our fate,
they form a unity, a nucleus of life
a valley for our thoughts and deeds.

2000

Metamorphosis

An old man
once an eagle
now a sparrow;
red cheeks,
bloated flesh,
bent by age
a voice
rambling
like rocks after dynamite.
A revered figure,
a ruler
once an eagle
now a sparrow
a shriek,
a dissolution!

2000

JOHN URBAIN | 1920–2009

Born in Belgium and raised in Detroit, Michigan, John Urbain—a graduate of Cass Technical High School—served as an infantry corporal in the US Army from 1941 to 1945. After the war, on the recommendation of Ray Johnson, Urbain attended BMC from 1946 to 1947 with financial support from the GI Bill. He is primarily recognized and celebrated as a visual artist, and art historians and critics often focus upon his work with *matière*, a design principle theorized and taught by Josef Albers, Urbain's instructor and mentor. After attending BMC, Urbain briefly studied art at L'Académie de la Grande Chaumière in Paris. Eventually, he worked for over twenty-five years as an art director for the Philip Morris Corporation. He also wrote poetry throughout his life and published in literary journals such as *New York Quarterly* and *Yankee Magazine*. In 2013, the Black Mountain College Museum + Arts Center presented an exhibit (curated by Yvette Torres) of Urbain's collages and paintings, titled *John Urbain: No Ideas but in Things*.

BLACK VIGIL/Vietnam '67

Black umbrellas
pleading
in a rain
for love.
Black umbrellas
crying white
on the lawn
turned brown wet mud.
Black umbrellas
over open
young blood red
dead flesh.
Rusk
waves his cold
umbrella
with redwhiteandblue words
turning into
white blood dust.

Violet thin
dawn sun shadows
huddle
in a corner Waiting

* * *

White daisy petals
holding the yellow
sun center
watching night
dimming the day.

* * *

Tree's hair
tangled

by wind wound
silver sun webs.

* * *

A
curtain
of hope
holds back
Death's patient white
shadow

unpublished; composed ca. 1967

1930

We live in three furnished rooms
on the second floor.
He listens
to the Detroit Tigers'
Monday afternoon game
on the small Philco radio.
There's a white
oilcloth table cover
with his 5¢ package
of Bugle cigarette tobacco.
He rolls his own
in a small machine
on yesterday's
Detroit News want ads
with circles penciled in.

She puts down
the brown shopping bag
on the kitchen table

takes off her heavy worn coat
and sits in the other chair.
. . . "any luck?"

1990

Taunte Mavett fried a perfect egg

in an old small dented pan
the white edged
crisp brown from almost too much butter
the yolk looked me
right in the eye
as I saw morning
July sun through
the cottage window
reflected in my egg.

I didn't know it would still be so important
52 years later.

2012

SYLVIA GIRSH ASHBY | 1928–

Detroit, Michigan native Sylvia Girsh Ashby studied at BMC from 1946 to 1948 before transferring to the University of Iowa, where she earned a BA. Ashby then moved to the University of Hawaii for graduate school. After writing poetry at BMC and concentrating on acting at Iowa and Hawaii, she ultimately turned to writing for young audiences. She has published thirteen plays with some 1,500 productions. *Shining Princess of the Slender Bamboo* and *Secret Garden* were American Alliance for Theatre & Education Unpublished Play Project winners; *Tales of Molly Malloy*, *Secret Garden*, and *Master Skylark of Stratford* were semifinalists in the Bonderman Symposium. Ashby is especially beloved for her successful stage adaptation of *Anne of Green Gables*, the 1908 novel by Lucy Maud Montgomery. Ashby wrote the poem "Farmer: Celo, NC" at BMC, and M. C. Richards published it as part of a campus-wide broadside devoted to student poetry. Significantly, Ashby collected BMC memorabilia and donated her materials to the Western Regional Archives of the State of North Carolina. In doing so, she helped preserve a rare copy of Jesse Green's *Seven Poems* (1950).

Farmer: Celo, NC

She would have been five in the early spring,
The frost churns yet in the ground,
And started in at the community school.
Her hair was oats glistening in the field,
Like Benny Ray's; he's two.
Every day I cross the shallow stream,
The water puckers over slippery rocks.
Pausing here,
I ache at this road.

ca. 1946

Death at the Hotel

Sitting here,
In the electric gloom of the lobby,
Autumn, and the afternoons are dark,
I watch them carry out Miss Myrtle Lang,
Box by box; one life, poured
Into empty cartons from the grocery store
To be portioned out to the heirs
According to whim, to niece, nephew, second-cousin
Who came on Friday to prepare her burial
Then stayed, detained, and made her Sabbath restless
Arranging this: her piece-meal departure tonight,
Her carefree migration tonight.

I see Miss Myrtle fleeing the town
(How often she'd dreamt of flight)
Shrouded in Kleenex and Mother's Oats:
"Miss Myrtle Lang here lies,
We carry quality merchandise"—
Death could have been more generous;
Life was not; but came
At his own convenience to claim her,
While Myrtle struggled for breath.

Here they come round again, down the stairs—
The elevator wants repairing, once again.
There's the Octagon Clock; New Haven, 1907,
"Eight Day and Thirty Hour with Gothic Spring" and spire;
I'd read the tattered paper lining,
Carelessly pared the peeling veneer.
It chimed, not always to the hour;
Even a clock can keep company,
Doesn't have to keep the time.

Sitting here,
Observing this casual ritual
Of death and dry cereal,
I wonder how I should edit my life.
I feel I should ease from this chair
And go on up.
Or should I leave the cataloguing to my heirs?
We are our belongings, not more,
Cards dealt to jovial players.
They can create their own biography
If they care. God knows
What they will make of the costume clothing,
Baby toys, childhood diary, ordinary letters,
Sashes, ribbons, fichues, collars,
Flower seeds, watercolors, a boy's complete attire—
I'll bundle it all for the basement and the trash basket there.
One fire, a private pyre, then: quiet ashes
To crush the conjecture of distant kin.
They have the future for inheritance.

Sitting here,
Staring down the hallway at the artificial moon,
I watch and wait for dinner, all artifacts intact.
Mr. Granby's stepping in the dining room: six o'clock.
Tonight is Candlelight Buffet. This jersey print would do—
If only I were hungry. At seven Jessie would join me;
The delay works to whittle the night.

Oh, the heirs are down, they must be through,
They're shaking the night clerk's hand, moving toward the door—
Goodbye, Myrtle. Goodbye, my dear.
I will remember you. For a while,
While I can.

1964

JESSE GREEN | 1928–2011

Born in Stanley, Wisconsin, Jesse Green grew up in Chicago. Green attended BMC from the fall of 1946 to the summer of 1948. During his first semester at the college, he was part of an informal writing group led by M. C. Richards. In 1951, he completed his undergraduate studies in literature at Reed College in Portland, Oregon, where he met and married a young painter named Nancy Stewart. In 1950, Green self-published *Seven Poems*, a suite of love lyrics for Stewart. Then, in 1952, he accepted a Fulbright Scholarship to Italy. Subsequently, Green earned an MA from the University of California, Berkeley, and a PhD from Northwestern University. He taught in the English Department at Chicago State University for twenty-six years and published articles on authors such as Herman Melville, Walt Whitman, and William Carlos Williams.

Hey you baby bud,
you curling furring
drip down soft and yellow green eyed
on your fuzzy fawn eyed chin branches,
O you twinger
with your linger-langoring touch
soft on the bell blue sky,
you're not so lusty
see
Breathe in you yawning tree
It's morning!

1950

I want to explain to you
softly
answer what you ask
always
because you are,
and I believe that,
you do
and what you tell me
cupped in your hands
is true

1950

Or here we linger
slowly naked and misled by
the kisses who,
giving testimony to our face,
lovely lie in our teeth
as we bite slowly down under in
tender disconcern.

Existenz before essense
—except after me—
For whom do I dangle, dear,
for thee.

1950

what would the whatnot,
cornered on the wall, whisper
in jasmin
of compositions overtoned on secret cells
tremoring insulation
when tears of the tender leopard
and skinsuited voices twinge sinews,
in glass
of almonds and poetry.

1950

MERVIN LOUIS LANE | 1928–2016

Born and raised in New York City, Mervin Louis Lane attended the prestigious High School of Music and Art. He enrolled in classes at BMC from 1946 to 1948. He also returned to the college in 1950 for the summer session. The ever-inquisitive Lane was an enthusiastic student both inside and outside the classroom: "One felt healthy," he recalls, "with the combination of differences in types of people and the physical, academic, and aesthetic activities the community provided. You would be working out some design problems in an Albers morning class, and after lunch be on a garbage detail, then getting cleaned up in the later afternoon to sing in the a cappella group that met an hour before dinner."[6] Later in life, Lane worked as a professor of literature at Santa Barbara City College, where he helped edit and publish *Concept*, the college's annual literary review. In 1978, he self-published a long poem titled *The Houston Passage* (1978). Most significant, Lane served as editor for the invaluable *Black Mountain College: Sprouted Seeds—an Anthology of Personal Accounts* (1990).

The Army

The army is mad.
There is *no* advance.
There is no retreat.

Mei Yao Ch'en reported in this century
A mother weeping tears of blood
While her breasts were filling with milk.

To give birth in a grave to a child
Who drinks her tears instead.

unpublished

The Marrying Maiden

It seems I have no place to go;
Thus it is easy to think of love:
A stone loosely in place
Around which wind rises, falls
And what bees do not leave alone
Turning home buttered sun drops.

Now in the middle of this wooden bridge,
In a fog that presses the breath—
The wooden clogs: sound
The umbrella: sight
My heart: poured out in a red cup
Steaming tea, ten minutes away from here.

unpublished

There was a face

There was a face that walked through mine
And did not stop upon its way
And as it passed it splintered me
Like glass or light that on the sea
Is fragmentation of a mind.

This sudden bright and signal grace
Spreads flooding such a rush of being
That I, no longer one, in flush
As covey from the deepest bush
At touch break hundreds into space.

unpublished

CAROLINE BURTON MICHAHELLES | 1929–

Born in Bryn Mawr, Pennsylvania, painter and poet Caroline Burton Michahelles expressed interest in taking Josef Albers's summer courses on basic design and color theory when she applied to BMC. There, in the summer of 1946, she studied with the abstract painter and art theorist. Albers covered the contrasting effects of form, texture, and color, all integral in the formation of an artist. While Michahelles only attended BMC that one summer, her art and poetry reflect Albers's disciplined approach to composition and exploration of chromatic interactions. This can be seen, for example, in her painting *La Foresta*, part of the Asheville Art Museum's BMC Collection. Similarly, note the wit and grace in the third poem here, a tribute to Albers's lifelong obsession with the square. Michahelles lives, writes, and paints in Florence, Italy, and in New York City. Her poems have appeared in a variety of publications, including the *Pennsylvania Literary Review*, *Il Portolano*, *Poetry East*, and Francesco Gurrieri's book *Esercizi di critica militante*. She has published two collections of poems: *No-Nonsense Poems* (2007) and *Nonsense-No Poems* (2013).

Escape

There is a poem
inside the door
waiting for me
to remember
where it hides
as I run home
falling
to catch it

escaping
under the door, —
slipping
side-ways
stretching out
lost beyond the distance
of light's transparent
invisibility.

2013

Paradise

Paradise
is waiting
for you

Do not look
left
or right

Paradise
may be
disappearing—

Keep walking
before it
leaves you
far behind.

2013

A Square

A square is a circle
in 4 corners.

2013

Time in the Airport

There is no beginning
and no end
to time invisibly
running ahead of us
as we run behind
wondering why
we never arrive
on time
when time changes
all around us
and we try
to catch up
with ourselves
running
to become
space victims

2013

RICHARD "DICK" ROBERTS | 1919–2007

Born and raised in Montana, Richard "Dick" Roberts attended BMC during the 1946–47 academic year, the summer of 1947, and the fall of 1947, and he later graduated from Eastern Montana College, earning a degree in elementary education. From 1965 to 1969, Roberts taught remedial English on the North Cheyenne Reservation in Montana and for the next decade was employed as an elementary school teacher. He retired in 1979 and moved to the Bitterroot Mountains with his wife, Janet Heling Roberts, whom he met while studying at BMC. Roberts's favorite instructors at the college included Bill Levi and David Corkran. He later described his time at BMC as "a rich experience. . . . There I was enlightened, if not educated, befriended, love-struck and married for good, and sent back into the world with friends, nostalgias, and a knowledge of how to plant potatoes and shovel coal. Who can ask more of higher education?"[7] Roberts's wife, Janet Heling Roberts, published two of his books posthumously: *Before We Say Goodbye* (2014) and *The Cat with a Cigar: Fun Poems, Limericks, and Jokes for Kids* (2016).

Egomania

I take care of town and country
By thinking of them.
No hedge clipper, stem thinner, lawn cutter am I.
I walk the rows like master and see the faults
But wouldn't change a thing.

The night is inflammable
And I touch a match to it.
The burning river flows by,
Racing from the heat of its own flame.

I cut a window
Where some might hang a picture.

Doctors say that I am underweight.
They do not know
That in my stomach rests the world digesting.

ca. 1944–45

For Sale, or Trade

I would exchange the things of men
For, not the things of birds or blossoms, but
For changelings passing on the wind,
For afternoon and dust unclinging,
For late and early,
Best be off.
Not for crickets, but their sound,
For slipping in and slipping out,
But not to be a thing that slips.

You, clock, can have my chance of fame
And love and what there is that has a name
For just the time you have run down
And cease to tick.

Tired, like apples growing,
Branches swinging, swinging back
And of ignorance then knowing,
Doing, doing, doing,
Putting something that is here over there.

—For just the passing of two winds.

Read a book and know the answer.
Wash the shirt and it will be clean.
Twenty feet from here to there.
Black is black.
Three feet make a yard.
Walk the street.
Think, think, do.

Sun round,
Then sun under.
Light comes up.
Fit a coffin to my manhood
If you can make that of me.

ca. 1944–45

MARY PARKS WASHINGTON | 1924–2019

Born and raised in Atlanta, Georgia, Mary Parks Washington graduated with a degree in art and a certificate in elementary education from Spelman College, where she studied painting with celebrated African American artist Hale Woodruff. At Woodruff's suggestion, Washington applied for, and was awarded, a Rosenwald Fund Scholarship to attend BMC's Summer Art Institute in 1946. Thus, Washington followed in the footsteps of Alma Stone, another Spelman graduate and the first African American student to attend BMC in 1944. While at BMC, Washington studied color theory and collage with Josef Albers and Jean Varda, respectively. She also formed lifelong friendships with Ruth Asawa, Gwendolyn Knight, and Jacob Lawrence. As an artist, Washington is noted for her "histcollages," mixed-media works that combine archival documents (e.g., insurance policies, bank loans, and letters) and everyday objects with drawing and painting. In the early 1960s, Washington developed a creative friendship with Oakland-based poet and scholar Sarah Webster Fabio, one of the central figures of the West Coast Black Arts Movement. The two friends collaborated on the poem included here, "A Downhome Recipe from a Black Soul Mother's Workshop," first published in Fabio's *A Mirror, a Soul: A Two-Part Volume of Poems* (1969). In that same collection, Fabio also included a poem dedicated to Washington, titled "My Own Thing."

A Downhome Recipe from a Black Soul Mother's Workshop

with Sarah Webster Fabio

Anchored
in the
kitchens
of her age,
she stirs
new pots of
nourishment
from the
storehouse
of less than
nothing—
a dandelion
green, a
bacon end,
a half
rotting
turnip,
onion
stalk;

She adds
the dash
of seasoning
to camouflage
the taint
of its
origin;
mixes,
stirs,
watches
the pot
with

loving
care.

It is
her hold
on, the
means to
control
the world
whirling
about her
and hers.

It is this
that is
the basis
of her
much scorned
matriarchy:
that ability
to make quick
decisions
when faced
with issues
which involve
the survival
of her dears;

She sheds
no tears
for ingredients
which she
might have
had and
wastes no
time in
dreams of
what might

come with
passing
years.

When she
must leave
her home
and take
on other
mean chores
out of great
necessity,
she quickly
returns to
her own
to become
the still
point again
which
composes
the swirling
homely air.

And, at home
again, she
adds that
dash
of cheer,
and courage
needed to
combat
grief and
fear;

Or, it may
be she holds
back just
the right

amount
of seasoning
to camouflage
the nitty-gritty
of her
black man's
life.

1969

GALWAY KINNELL | 1927–2014

Although not usually associated with BMC poetry and poetics, Galway Kinnell attended the summer session of 1947 on the GI Bill. At the time, he was completing an undergraduate degree at Princeton University; he graduated summa cum laude in 1948. Kinnell's decision to study at BMC was inspired, in part, by his Princeton teacher Charles Greenleaf Bell, who was hired to teach at the college that same summer. During his stay on campus, Kinnell composed the poem "Meditation Among the Tombs," included here, and first encountered the poetry of François Villon, whom he later translated.[8] In the 1960s, Kinnell was an active member of the Congress of Racial Equality and, like many poets of the period, protested the US presence in Vietnam. Kinnell's *Selected Poems* (1982) was awarded the Pulitzer Prize and National Book Award in Poetry in 1983. In 2016, Laura Hope-Gill completed *Hell's Hot Breath*, a fifteen-minute documentary about Kinnell's summer at BMC.

Meditation Among the Tombs

1

I am kneeling on my grave this lonely
Circle of the day or bottom half
Of night, to witness vainly
Day light candelabra on the dark horizons
Of the world. For this I tell my orisons
And char my tomb with incense for an epitaph.

The present darkness has been long,
And add, the clocks are closing down these days
Lacking a hand to push the hand ahead,
And you will hear the tick and thud
Begin to toil, as the roots of grass
Gnaw decomposition like a cud.

We who have won no issue from our dreams,
Who have never climbed the pale hills of dawn
Nor forged our fullness in the blaze of noon
Nor arched a crimson splendor down the west,
Scowl now at dark—curse God that our best
Is worse than what those grasses chew night-long.

2

Life like a coat of rose-colored paint
Is lifting from his lips. And in those eyes,
Glazed to seal their faint
Flames within, the last red coals
Sputter in his tears. "Try to raise
Your eyelids, gaze upon this cross, for souls
That burn such evil in their fires
Should quench themselves," two preachers hiss in his ears,
"With sorry vows instead of salty tears."

He flutters up those lids, but age
Has so bleared those weary
Eyes and the page
On which they register within
That the wrought and polished cross
Those phantoms wave before his chin
Seems but a pole to string its wires high
And shuttle back and forth love's perfidy.

Could such an antique hulk as this
Have ever opened eyes in wonderment of love
Or known the frenzy of a warded kiss?
It is very difficult to think.
And yet it seems he has enough
Old strings and yarns of memory to weave
A gaudy mess of dreams before he leaves.

Look, the glowing caves begin to blink:
What signals do they tell,
What dark suggestion in that skull
That life is twice, compared to death, as terrible?

3

Old Man: When youth was pounding in my veins
And life was all a sky of light and dreams
And none had any foresight for the pains
A girl and I took love in summer's kiss
Under the oak, half hidden in the grass.
Youth: There must have been much beauty in those flames.

Old Man: Later, when our love burned not so wild
Or brilliant, but with a steady, subtle fuse
And she was fevered with a coming child
They said to me, "Choose you the living wife,
Or risking her, the babe delivered safe?"
Youth: They might have chosen better word than choose.

Old Man: You who are young have no such memories
Of trysting by that oak in the thick
And shining grass, or kissing under skies
Of singing wind. So which alternative,
A dead creation or a dying love?
Youth: Creation is a sorry thing to pick.

4

Born,
My child, alas, so worn
And old, as though these eyes
Could stuff your sockets with their miseries . . .
I pray
That as your father and his father
Turned the waning cycle of their day,
Bending to the midnight mother
Heaped with age
And bitter with broken rage,
You will wind your days the other
And the better way: and as you near
The end, the furrows of your age will disappear
And everything that prods you to a sudden grave
Will take a counterclockwise turn,
Strange reversal you will learn,
Until your limbs are youthful, and your heart is brave.
And having said this prayer,
One word: to life's pretenders say you were
Descended from a line of vanished kings
Who sat in state upon a silver throne—
Then beat from that descent with careless wings
And of their depositions weave your crown.

5

The clock has spun while I have brooded here,
Spading up an earth of long-dead men—
Rain of memory for a rainless year—
Is this a graveyard I am digging in?

But look, the dawn is lighting up the east,
The clouds are breaking, making way—soon!
Now!—through the dusk comes sliding fast,
Alas, that sullen orange eye, the moon.

The clock's two sentinels
Are dying, and midnight has begun again.
Lord, might we witness those castles
Surrender to the fair legions of the sun.

But if the darkness finds the grave where we
Were buried under sillions of our past
Still pointing gloomy crosses at the east,
And thinks that we were niggard with our bravery,
Our ghosts, if such we have, can say at least
We were not misers in our misery.

1960

The Bear

1

In late winter
I sometimes glimpse bits of steam
coming up from
some fault in the old snow
and bend close and see it is lung-colored
and put down my nose
and know
the chilly, enduring odor of bear.

2

I take a wolf's rib and whittle
it sharp at both ends
and coil it up

and freeze it in blubber and place it out
on the fairway of the bears.

And when it has vanished
I move out on the bear tracks,
roaming in circles
until I come to the first, tentative, dark
splash on the earth.

And I set out
running, following the splashes
of blood wandering over the world.
At the cut, gashed resting places
I stop and rest,
at the crawl-marks
where he lay out on his belly
to overpass some stretch of bauchy ice
I lie out
dragging myself forward with bear-knives in my fists.

3

On the third day I begin to starve,
at nightfall I bend down as I knew I would
at a turd sopped in blood,
and hesitate, and pick it up,
and thrust it in my mouth, and gnash it down,
and rise
and go on running.

4

On the seventh day,
living by now on bear blood alone,
I can see his upturned carcass far out ahead, a scraggled,
steamy hulk,
the heavy fur riffling in the wind.

I come up to him
and stare at the narrow-spaced, petty eyes,
the dismayed
face laid back on the shoulder, the nostrils
flared, catching
perhaps the first taint of me as he
died.

I hack
a ravine in his thigh, and eat and drink,
and tear him down his whole length
and open him and climb in
and close him up after me, against the wind,
and sleep.

5

And dream
of lumbering flatfooted
over the tundra,
stabbed twice from within,
splattering a trail behind me,
splattering it out no matter which way I lurch,
no matter which parabola of bear-transcendence,
which dance of solitude I attempt,
which gravity-clutched leap,
which trudge, which groan.

6

Until one day I totter and fall—
fall on this
stomach that has tried so hard to keep up,
to digest the blood as it leaked in,
to break up
and digest the bone itself: and now the breeze
blows over me, blows off

the hideous belches of ill-digested bear blood
and rotted stomach
and the ordinary, wretched odor of bear,

blows across
my sore, lolled tongue a song
or screech, until I think I must rise up
and dance. And I lie still.

7

I awaken I think. Marshlights
reappear, geese
come trailing again up the flyway.
In her ravine under old snow the dam-bear
lies, licking
lumps of smeared fur
and drizzly eyes into shapes
with her tongue. And one
hairy-soled trudge stuck out before me,
the next groaned out,
the next,
the next,
the rest of my days I spend
wandering: wondering
what, anyway,
was that sticky infusion, that rank flavor of blood, that poetry, by which I lived?

1968

Saint Francis and the Sow

The bud
stands for all things,
even for those things that don't flower,
for everything flowers, from within, of self-blessing;
though sometimes it is necessary
to reteach a thing its loveliness,
to put a hand on its brow
of the flower
and retell it in words and in touch
it is lovely
until it flowers again from within, of self-blessing;
as Saint Francis
put his hand on the creased forehead
of the sow, and told her in words and in touch
blessings of earth on the sow, and the sow
began remembering all down her thick length,
from the earthen snout all the way
through the fodder and slops to the spiritual curl of the tail,
from the hard spininess spiked out from the spine
down through the great broken heart
to the sheer blue milken dreaminess spurting and shuddering
from the fourteen teats into the fourteen mouths sucking and blowing beneath them:
the long, perfect loveliness of sow.

1980

JERROLD LEVY | 1930–2002
RICHARD NEGRO | 1929–?

New York City native Jerrold Levy attended BMC from 1947 to 1950. His stepfather, Herbert Bayer, had been a professor of advertising and typography at the Bauhaus from 1925 to 1928 and had visited BMC in 1938 while working on a Bauhaus exhibit for the Museum of Modern Art. At BMC, Levy studied art with Ilya Bolotowsky and writing with Charles Olson. He expressed resistance to Olson's domineering presence in the classroom and questioned his teacher's admiration of Ezra Pound. In collaboration with a fellow student, Richard Negro, Levy composed a series of prank poems under the pen name Gerard Legro, a fictitious Jewish American poet and translator affiliated with the Carnegie Institute of Technology. After BMC, Levy spent some time in Israel, teaching printmaking to young children on a kibbutz, before returning to New York City. He eventually earned his PhD in anthropology from the University of Chicago. He then taught at Portland State University from 1964 to 1972 and at the University of Arizona from 1972 to 1995. His research focused on health services and health education among the Navajo, Yavapai, Hopi, and Kiowa.

Levy's collaborator Richard Negro came to BMC from Fair Lawn, New Jersey, attending the college from the spring of 1947 through the spring of 1950. He learned about the college from dancer, writer, and activist Hannelore Hahn, a fellow graduate of Fair Lawn High School. Negro was a favorite student of both Natasha Goldowski and M. C. Richards, the latter teaching him creative writing. Unlike Levy, Negro never studied poetry with Olson. He left BMC in 1950 for Pittsburgh, where he studied physics at the Carnegie Institute of Technology. It appears that Negro did not continue writing poetry after his time at BMC. He and Levy lost touch in the early 1950s.

Father Albers's Notebook (Series du Matière)

the eye must be a reporter

1.

All woven things
        metal
        wood
All knitted things
        braided
        crocheted
Pressed material
Pleated material

Expanded metal
Corrugated metal
        asbestos
        paper
Perforation
Guilloche
        scraped with
        sharp needle

2.

Snow with bird prints
Saw marks on wood
Tire marks in mud
Wasp nests
Bird nests
Fluting

Engraving
Etching
Woodcuts
Hammered metal
(embossed)

1949

Since Picasso an Our Father Which Art

Some monstrous man mind
Who works like a steam turbine
Scorning the surface ricochet of
Sophistication,
Or in Summer's subways lifting
The subtle subterfuge of ladies skirts.

Through the comb twisted mountains
Gestures of late Picassoles
Wrought or unwrought so
By dainty blue berets who,
Sitting by brooks and dump heaps,
Do window; through the morning
And take its light
Strain through silk screen
(Or alternate by devious routes of stained glass)
Until past the seventh, reach
A senile print from Han.

Whereas morning
Twists itself around the mountains
Pushing its winds through
The end of Valley vacuum
Cleaner.

1949

BARBARA STONE RICE | 1925–2008

A Jewish-born poet of Austrian, Romanian, and Hungarian heritage, Barbara Stone Rice grew up in Brooklyn, New York, where she fell in love with reading as a young child. After high school, she enlisted in Women Accepted for Volunteer Emergency Service, a branch of the US Navy during the Second World War. With the assistance of the postwar GI Bill, Rice attended BMC from 1948 to 1949 and 1952 to 1953. While at BMC, she focused on dance and weaving, studying the latter with Anni Albers; she also met and married her husband, the artist Jack Rice. In 1956, after living in Mexico City for a year, the couple moved to Topanga, California, where Barbara Stone Rice worked as a school librarian at Topanga Elementary School for ten years. The three poems below appeared in *Barbara Stone Rice: A Sampler of Poems* (1999).

Celia's Day

It is Sunday
St. Cecilia's day

Scarlatti & Monteverdi

Fiddles draw honey from hives
Something rises   shivering

Nothing is secret
The tongue slips
Roses confess the bush

Face up
I open my mouth

My house crouches next to me
Skin of my skin
Stretching the truth.

1999

Sleep

The night is enormous
        and we sleep in such small rooms

Sandwiched between blankets
        we forget who is dreaming

I lay
        head facing north
        a trembling antenna

Coyotes break the sound barrier
Fog comes in.

1999

Sweetmeat

The white foal lies on the ground
Flies are thick as cloves

Its mother a freckled mare
    chews her hay

He is white sugar
    sweet to the flies
    as summer

1999

GERD STERN | 1928–

German Jewish émigré Gerd Stern was born in Saarland, Germany, but raised in Washington Heights, New York, where his family settled in 1936. While working at the Jabberwocky Shop—next door to the Four Seasons Bookshop—in Greenwich Village, Stern met writer Isaac Rosenfeld, who had taught at BMC in the summer of 1948. With Rosenfeld's support, Stern interviewed at the college, was awarded a scholarship, and arrived at BMC ready to start classes in the fall of 1948. He was especially excited to study poetry with M. C. Richards; however, Richards was on leave from the college for the semester, prompting a disappointed Stern to depart after only two weeks. He described the state of BMC during his brief stay as "absolute chaos," with "the administration and the teachers . . . all fighting with each other on philosophical and financial grounds."[9] Stern moved to the West Coast and became a Beat poet in San Francisco, where his circle of friends included Carl Solomon, Allen Ginsberg, and Philip Lamantia, as well as Maya Angelou and Jordan Belson. Stern published two collections of poetry, *First Poems* (1952) and *Afterimage* (1965). In 1962, he cofounded USCO (with Michael Callahan and Steve Durkee), a multimedia art collective in Rockland County, New York, near John Cage and M. C. Richards at Stony Point. In 2001, the Bancroft Library at the University of California, Berkeley, made available Stern's oral history, "From Beat Scene Poet to Psychedelic Multimedia Artist in San Francisco and Beyond, 1948–1978."

Relations

(one to ∞)

This work is the text of a cantata
(chorus and orchestra), music
composed by Marga Richter.

The ideas represented in "Relations"
were developed in a series of
conversations between H.V. and
the poet.

1–4 The concepts of Realities
5–8 a Relational progression
9 Catalyst
0 Destruction
∞ Operating Function

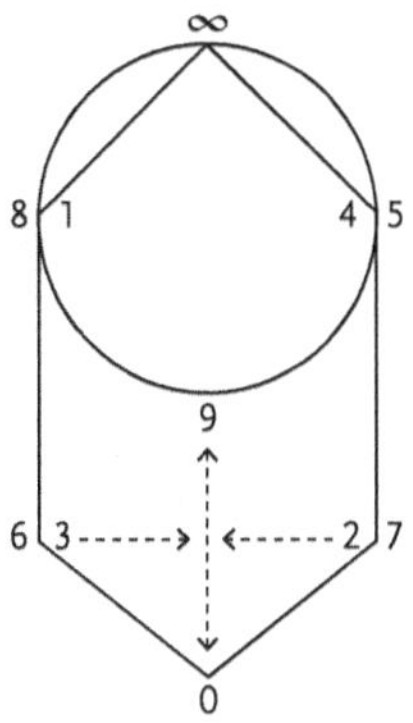

Relations (one)

One Is enough

All Is
(All Is only everything (Is))
One and All • Is • One and All

Am I It Is
I Am Is Am It Is

Be ings (End and Beginning)

All Is and enough
All Is enough

Relations (two)

and becoming I
Am with everything   (Was and Is)
Together: AM

Relations (three)

I am
Having been and being

•

Now and Here myself
Could what Would

•

I being my being
My being being I

I Am Is and this
myself

Relations (four)

are relations

between these and those
among all of everything
are relations

Relations (five to eight)

Being relations
is a relation

[Here Now relation
nor measure
nor there this
nor then that]

• • •

a relation is
and relations are

plus relation is
relation plus relation
relation plus relation plus relation

is (Here Now) before after
(nor past present future)

this any that relation

• • •

Relations of to
Relations subject object
(nor time space) New
Any relation Now Here New
plus any relation (relations) is
Any relation Now Here New

• • •

A relation is
and relations are
Is are relations
All are relations

Everything only everything
(nor plus nor minus)
are Relation

• • •

Relation • id est • Universe

Relations (nine)

Universe and I am
Am I and Universe

(Universe • id est • Relation)

Relations (zero)

Being

What

Is

Void

Am

I

Universe

Relation

Ain't

Relations (∞)

Universe • id est • Relation • id est • Universe
and being relation is
Universe and I am

Are Relations

1952

Harvest Tale

— Plow —

A probability of the sentence demanded paradox,
which eliminates any purpose that could dilute
the possible sequence of events,
or resolve these following improbabilities:

The place was common,
a neighborhood so arranged
that the original character of each building
was perversely denied by the close presence of structures
contradictory in every respect of quality, style and function.
Stores, factories and houses pressed together,
surrounded by vacant lots piled with rubble and garbage.
A particular corner was distinguished by public buildings
which lent the apparent coherence
produced by an impression of similarity to the eye.

Preconceptions were not helpful;
there was an address whose number no longer existed;
an arrow pointed toward the public building for information.
The stranger would not have recognized this familiar symbol.
Discouraged by process,
reasons to persist vanished;
to return within the cycle of desire itself.

People live among friends, neighbors and relatives,
convicted of the propriety realized by choice.

To question such behavior required ignorance.
A stranger needs the familiar amount of hospitality
which explains that the place, the people, the customs
are after all not so strange.
Hospitality, howsoever, is the property of travelers,
or visitors, even of foreigners.
The strange must by definition remain unknown.

> That which is, is true;
> therefore dreams are real.
> The dreams of an infant
> betray words.

To pretend a miracle,
the stranger was invented.
Without knowledge truth is formless.
Since being a stranger is manifestly another
He assures truth.

The public building was a convenience;
testifying to the existence of mutual interest,
it created a feeling of trust.
To enter required
the positive anonymity of *public*,
the act of individuation necessary to confront it:
both extreme solutions.
Particularly this entrance subjects the stranger to examination;
being questionable, he is classified.

The means appropriate to solution of a problem
are not always available.
An agency of general interest deals only with specifics:
any new category confronts organization with crisis.

To receive an impression is not an answer.
To create one is from this instance
perpetually a question faced by anyone.
Properties of the individual
are not expected of a conglomerate
which more reasonably takes what comes.
The stranger remains.

Individually,
by light of similarity;
he disappeared.
What an accomplishment!

An adjustment in an otherwise stable system
must be accounted eventually:
the different is discernible by addition.

— Furrow —

They had achieved this fusion in the past,
but now, with the maturity that follows success,
celebrated marriage as a matter of course,
and became inseparable.

She was younger than he by years.
When they had first met,
youth was the obstacle postponing event.
Several husbands and children outdistanced
her youth which fed and was fed by passion,
surpassing and sustaining the importances
of her everyday life.
Substantially unchanged,
she lost a charm of innocence.

He was recently returned,
and in coming proved true to an earlier promise.
Surprised by the probabilities of expectation,
he did not subscribe to inevitability.

They owned our largest home.
Nearly everyone was entertained by them.

He made no mention of the pleasures
which permitted the style
to which they accustomed us
and soon succumbed to the common disease.

She practiced suicide

— Seed —

There being no reason now
to postpone action on a proposal
which, through negligence and inertia
had been indefinitely delayed,
both general and detailed aspects of the proposition
received undivided attention.
The grounds for agreement were obviously clarified
by the persuasive explanations of the individual in question,
whose efforts readily overcame the token objectives
raised by a congenital opposition.

A subsequent poll held unanimously in favor.

Prompted and motivated by general aptitude,
he was extremely uninterested in particularizing.
His occupied attention was invariably diverted
to another form of activity.
Only in the largest sense
was discernible order apparent
in these attempts at production.
After leaving his native environment
he was confronted
by the problems of a strange community.

Unfamiliar content was categorized,
according to harmonies discovered methodically

by juxtaposing diverse elements,
as a system of classification.
Conditions chosen and incorporated,
as a mechanically perpetuating operation,
were established from determinable probability
to assume functional possibility.
This confounding rationale of structure
threatened any other attempt
to employ his findings.
Regarded expendable by the community
which refused to identify him
with his recognized achievements,
he insisted on the demonstrative reality
by which objects and subjects
define their origins and futures.

Encouraged by the minority,
always eager to benefit from work of genius,
he was amply rewarded.
Though ideas in essence were transformed by usage
and lived on in his name only as platitudes
success was an accomplishment.
Replete with honor, he was out of place
among the effects of his effort.
Gathering strength and wealth
he returned.

1965

Oh You

meaningful
a word like interesting

like
leaving your dirty panties

smelling of someone's sperm
near the telephone
for me

1965

Public Hanging

Sweet hanging steel
Bigger than thou
Smashed in blacktop
Like an Indian head
Before a crossing
Because a red light
This very now
Was here too
And stopped us dead

1965

MARTHA RITTENHOUSE TREICHLER | 1929–2023

Born and raised on a small family farm near the Eastern Shore of Maryland, Martha Rittenhouse Treichler began her undergraduate studies at Bridgewater College before transferring to BMC during the 1948–49 academic year. She later earned her BA from Goddard College and an MA from Dartmouth College. At BMC, Treichler studied drawing and color theory with Josef Albers, linguistics with Frank Rice, French with Natasha Goldowski, chorus with Charlotte Schlesinger, and creative writing with both Edward Dahlberg and Charles Olson, the latter having an especially lasting influence on Treichler. In 1988, Treichler and her husband, Bill (who also attended BMC), founded *Crooked Lake*, a local history journal focused on Upstate New York. Her publications include *Black Mountain to Crooked Lake: Poems 1948–2010, with a Memoir of Black Mountain College* (2010), which contains a selection of poems she composed for Olson's creative writing class (e.g., "Conversation Familial"), and two more collections of poetry, *Living on a Dirt Road* (2011) and *Variations on a Theme* (2014). Treichler's "Achaean Mate" was inspired by Olson's lectures on Homer's *Odyssey*. After she left BMC, Treichler continued to correspond with Olson about her translations of François Villon: her poem "Villon's Letter in the Form of a Ballad to his Friends" is the result of that exchange.

Achaean Mate

1000 B.C.
The pitcher made with excellence
Holds water for the bath.
The expert looms weave
To warm and protect.

Odysseus' guest gift
Is a well-wrought cup
Or tunic
Or journey by swift ship.

And polished tables, silver-studded chairs,
Gold wine bowls, drinking cups,
Are the richest art
In Circe's house.

1950 A.D.
They spit out thousands
Who hollers loud
We take.
Then vainly on our walls
Hang paper trash
From transient minds.

We make the spittle
Work plods menially,
Her rightful mate
Locked in rare dungeons
Or gone.

2010

Conversation Familial

I

In France
The deskman says,
"How many hours?"
E. P. visited our home, then wrote:
"Nor can who has passed a month in the death cells
Believe in capital punishment.
No man who has passed a month in the death cells
Believes in cages for beasts."
The deskman says, "How many hours?"
Now, that's civilization!

Twenty years ago,
Six months after they were married,
She found the keys of his saxophone stiff.
(And he spent
Quite a bit of his spare time
At band practice.)
Twenty years!
As I say, E. P. has said,
"No man who passed a month in the death cells . . ."
Now, in France the deskman says
"But I've already said MY idea."
(I interpolate R. B.
On the modern family)
. . . "is simply
Two or three individuals
Who live together
To spend the money they earn.
. . . Its members
Can obtain more for their money
Than they can
By living alone."

But twenty years
Can be a long time
Even if everything's convenient.

II

When my grandparents
Were eighty years old,
They sat in the same chair
To read.

His cannery partner pulled out.
He lost a thousand.
His sawmill burned,
On a Saturday morning!
There was all his money
In cash to pay the men.
When the fire was out,
All bills were gone,
But a few chunks of metal
Were kicked up.

And she was on the *Delta*
The time he got stuck on a bar
In the Chesapeake.
For eight days
They lived on beans.

First cousins
Friends since they were eight
AND AT EIGHTY
They still sat in the same chair
To read.

My parents
Rarely discuss the subject.

They are sure
Everyone has a soul-mate.

2010

Villon's Letter in the Form of a Ballad to His Friends

I

Have pity, have pity on me,
At the very least, please, my friends,
In this death-like pit, bottomless, without one degree of comfort,
In this exile to which I am transported
By luck, as God has permitted it.
Girls, lads, young, old, and newlywed,
You dancers, leapers, bounding about like the playful calf,
Quick as a dart, sharp as a goad,
Voices ringing clear as a bell,
Will you leave him there, poor Villon?

II

Singers of songs of joy, without restraint,
You laughing fun lovers, rollicking in word and deed,
Wanderers, free of fake and alloy,
People of wit, you dance,
You delay too long, while he is dying.

Makers of music and dance,
When he is dead, you will light candles for him
Now he can do nothing, nor can he lie down to rest,
Nor take part in your giddy pleasures,
Heavy walls have imprisoned him,
Will you leave him there, poor Villon?

2010

SUSAN WEIL | 1930–

Before enrolling at BMC in 1948, New York City–born artist and poet Susan Weil attended L'Académie Julian, in Paris, where she first met Robert Rauschenberg. Weil and Rauschenberg subsequently attended BMC together and were married in 1950. Though the marriage did not last long (they officially divorced in 1953), Weil and Rauschenberg remained lifelong friends. Recognized primarily as a painter and mixed-media artist, Weil has won both Guggenheim and National Endowment for the Arts Fellowships. Her artwork appears in the collections of major museums and galleries, including the Museum of Modern Art in New York, the Getty Museum in Los Angeles, and the Victoria and Albert Museum in London. Since 1977, Weil has composed what she calls "poemumbles" on a daily basis, creatively arranging found verbal and visual materials alongside her own drawings and watercolors. She makes her poemumbles in the early hours of each day, when closest to "coming out of a sleep state in an interior mood."[10] Weil continues to create whimsical, sometimes surreal art, playing with the juxtaposition of images and text and exploring the liminal space between dreams and waking life.

Pages 253–56: The figures reproduced here are "da Vinci also attempted to fly, but failed," "If nonhuman animals do think," "the night sky," and "trying to draw females." All from Susan Weil, *Out of Bounds: Collage Poems*. Copyright © 2012 by Susan Weil. Reprinted with the permission of Weil Books, https://susanweil.com/category/weil-books.

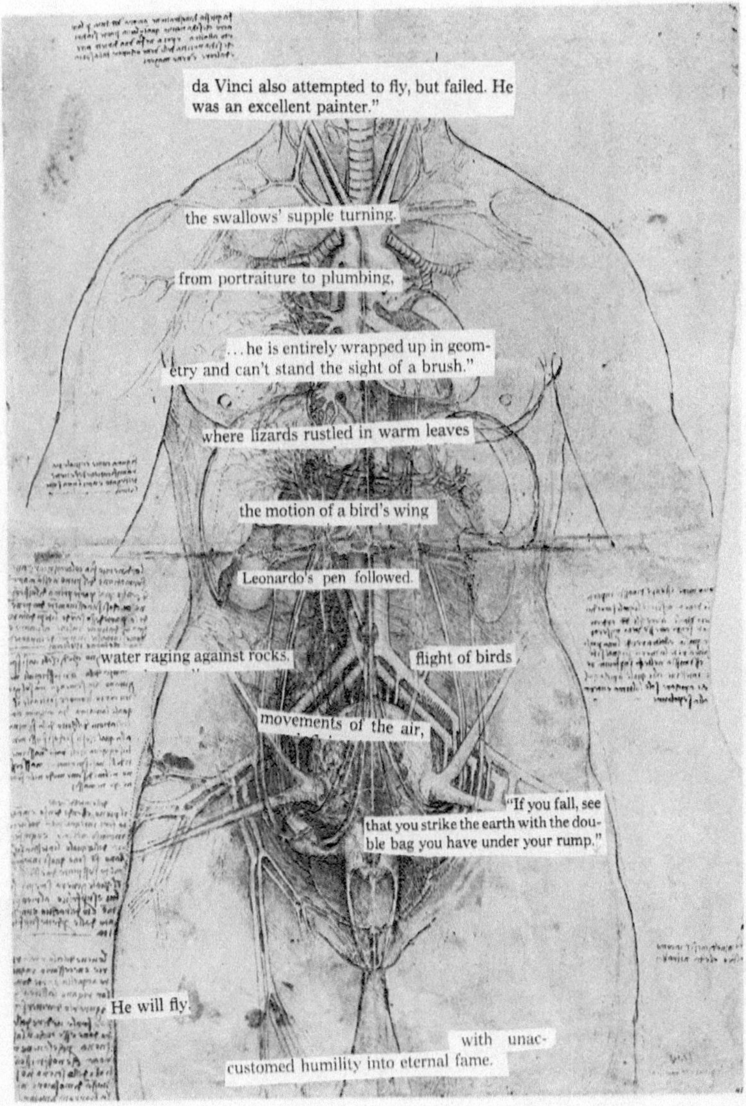

OCT 22 1995

* LEONARDO

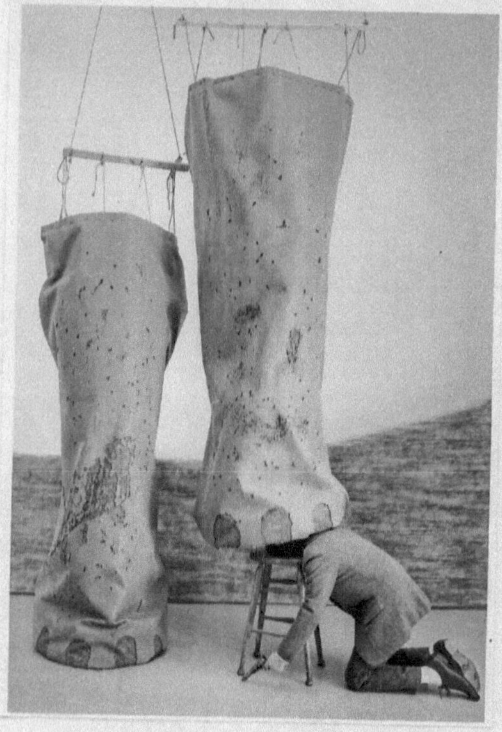

If nonhuman animals do think,

on a ball like the
earth, every place is the center.

There's no there here either

Egyptian plovers wet their belly feathers
golden rumps flashing

the skill pigeons exhibit

zigzagging, stopping, starting, turning, springing,

I can't vouch for the nailing of the feet.

four fully furred young.

shaken by the prospect of not being.

nonhuman animals think

MAY 20 1996

the night sky,
40 Brown Pelicans
expect to see twenty bright
meteors per hour:
guinea pigs, and potatoes,
all mammals—both living
tall grass, weeds, brush, brambles, sumac
ACCURATE CAVE ART
moonlight will interfere.
focus on the smallest pyramid.
double-breasted cor morants,
black disk of the moon,
and closely argued books,
no one on earth
, that song reverses

MAY 1 5 1996

trying to draw females

some with blurred faces,

he kissed me bang smash

and became a cop.

nightmares of trees that twisted

if he has a wooden leg :

and prophetic hats.

a susceptibility to boredom.

STAN VANDERBEEK | 1927–1984

Born in New York City, Stan VanDerBeek studied art at Cooper Union and served in the US Navy before enrolling at BMC in the summer of 1949. He eventually returned to Cooper Union, earning his degree in 1956. At BMC, he studied photography with Hazel Larsen and architecture with Buckminster Fuller; most significant, he became interested in the aesthetic possibilities of film when the school acquired a Bolex camera. VanDerBeek is widely recognized as a major innovator in American avant-garde cinema. In 1966, he premiered his *Movie-Drome*, a multimedia visual experience with films and slides simultaneously projected on a spherical dome. As VanDerBeek explains, "The audience lies down at the outer edge of the dome with their feet towards the center, thus almost the complete field of view is the dome-screen. Thousands of images would be projected on this screen; this image-flow could be compared to the 'collage' form of the newspaper or the three ring circus."[11] From 1966 to 1971, in collaboration with programmer Kenneth Knowlton of Bell Telephone Laboratories, VanDerBeek also created his *Poemfield* series, early computer poems with kinetic graphics.

The City

Clashes tremble
we resemble
pagan rites
on blinking flatlands

The dead lie
deader, now
the dead die better
now,
that we have such
tombstones
to show it's easy,
once, it's said
they say,
as the city
decked in grey
resemblances
of dead man's clothes
that barely fit.
The end justifies
the means
we'll say
it makes it easier
that way
to give an
edge to progress
yet orphaned clouds
can hide the tops
of all this rush,
in innocence,
and we
in error forget
our heights

unpublished; composed in 1949

Invalides

Gifted miracle
that this so fragile
frame
can claim
existence

Thus breath
with form
extending motion
a fragile promise
of order
quite removed

A glad reckoning
with forces rushing
into every gap
and bring comes
about
by what appears
to be a series
of fortunate acts
As though this
balance
carefully weighed
could show
a shade
or leaning
other that some
measured order
and so
to quietly, at times
resign
this fate
and watch the circle
narrow in

till movement
pass
its point
and down within
this breath finds free
the air.

unpublished; composed in 1949

I,
swallow,
great barns
of inconsistency
lead
astay (astray, a straw, ah stay, ass hay)
by (buy)
thin
sins
of encouragement

Is it
small
wonder
that we
blunder
so
mist,—
—taking
friends for foe
score
instead
be
led
victorious
by
big
di—a
feats?

I find
this
wavering
uncertainty
directive
in effect
objective.

unpublished; composed in 1949

The loss of stationary
poetry
and the anticipated
vision
rates
turns the (answers) of
interest from vision
shelf analysis to
ashking groups.

Of formlorn: loot
speaking in inventions
side
loose ribs at pro-
-creation
seek in the impact
of today with to
many morrows the
seedy voice that
forms itself

froms
and
goes less likely
than we know
the molds of irony.
Design our haste
test supple wings

sight freightened.
Makes things
    distant
from and to. . . . .
The (nude) stationary illusion
illuminated and dressed
to kell revolves a view
new conscience. Broods
in nude obscurity.

unpublished; composed ca. 1950

Poemfield #1

POEMFIELD

GESTURES
DO NOT
MISTAKE
PLACE
YET. . . . . . .
FINGER POINTING
TAKES A WORD TO COMPLETE
SOME HOW
WORDS
FILL
THE SPACE BETWEEN
BETTER
MEANING
MOVES
POSITION
LOVES
FINGER
DIRECTS
SPEECH
THAT

SILENCE
FALLING
TOUCHES
THE END

1967

Poemfield #3

PO
POE
POEM
FIE
FIELD
POEMMMM
FIELD NO 3
POEMFIELD NO 3
NO 3
A MAP OF IDEAS
A
VOICE
WRONG
A WHEEL
WRONG
AWHEEEEEEL
A WHEEL
BUT NOT REALLY
A HAND
REALLY
MEMORY
MEMORY IS A TIGHT
IS A TIGHT ROPE
A FIRE
AIEEEEE
CRYING IS AN EDGE
NOT OVER

LOOKING
BUT A CUTTING EDGE
REALLY
THE DARK
THE DARK IS A QUESTION
I BELIEVE YOU
NAKED
IS LIKE
TOMORROW
NAKED IS
LIKE TOMORROW

1967

JOHN "JACK" McKINLEY BOYD | ?

FIELDING DAWSON | 1930–2002

Although a student file exists for John "Jack" McKinley Boyd in the BMC holdings in the Western Regional Archives of North Carolina, this file gives interested readers little to go on. He attended BMC during the 1949–50 academic year and later returned during the fall of 1951. He took classes in literature and creative writing. While studying at BMC, Boyd befriended Fielding Dawson, who had enrolled the very same year. Together, Boyd and Dawson collaborated on a chapbook titled *2 & 4*. It was published in August 1950, in an edition of 250 copies, through the Black Mountain College Print Shop, which also published Jerrold Levy and Richard Negro's *Poems by Gerard Legro* (1949) and Russell Edson's debut collection of poetry, *Ceremonies in Bachelor Space* (1951). Boyd and Dawson's *2 & 4* is illustrative of the vibrant literary print culture at BMC after 1947.

Enrolling at BMC in 1949, Fielding Dawson studied painting and literature under Franz Kline and Charles Olson, respectively. Dawson reflects on their influences in *An Emotional Memoir of Franz Kline* (1967) and *The Black Mountain Book* (1970). A multidisciplinary artist and writer, Dawson graduated in 1953, one of the rare students to receive an official degree from the college. Raised outside of St. Louis, Missouri, Dawson spent most of his post-BMC life in New York City's Union Square neighborhood, where he was a mainstay of the New York City art scene. Additionally, in 1984, Dawson launched an important pedagogical initiative, teaching creative writing to inmates in maximum security prisons such as Sing Sing and Attica.

2 & 4

We have cried our crimes
    —Though the summer doesn't care
That the tamaracks are laughing by the lake tonight,
    And moon warm and heavy is a gem
    Falling to her setting,
And bass are sleeping wide-eyed in the lake tonight.
Yes your hair hangs golden (fabled cataract)
    And your eyes see shadows beyond their green
    And your love seeks thirst beyond myself;
We'll hear a lynx screech sorrow at the dawn tomorrow
    And, again, darkly laughing tamaracks sing:
O, the summer doesn't care, it is so colossal;
Or should we?

*

in the winter the nights are brittle
things seem to snap and the stars taktak
and the kold trees like frozen seeweed
scrape with silent noises
their tentakles
against the frigid pieces of air
and the people the people
the people pulling
into the service station for chains
for their tires and
the great bulk of the negro untangling the chains
and heaving heavy curses
january febuary march
march and the winds
march and the feeling of april—
march and

*

and then school is out and the kids flow from the doors
the seniors juniors sophomores freshmen and the lower grades and
their teachers move from their rooms

the boys running to their lockers to grab the needed things and
meeting outside of the building with their
women   and walking her home to perhaps stay and speak a few
words with her—
some to their cars with their squirrel tails and polished chrome and
some to their heaps painted orange with oogaooga horns—
and some of the chosen to the gym room to put on their baseball
uniforms—
and those of thirteen fourteen who couldnt make it because they
were afraid
creep out to where the ballteam practices
these standing and watching clift and lee stroke long high drives
into center and right and left where the fleetfooted ones stand waiting
to catch and fling the ball in—
and these who watch—
these feel the sweat come from their small bodies—
the sweat of wanting to play

*

the highschool young girls
walking home in sixes and eights
laughing and talking
they with their bright yellow and
starched lightblue dresses
and dark brown skin
these
lips lipsticked deepred
screaming openmouthfulls
of laughter

these being stopped by a group
of young boys
with strongbone white teeth
who bend with laughter

*

ed in his grill
stands

in the doorway:
it is nine oclock and he
has just opened up.
he stands looking across the street
at the young boy slowly walking
and ed thinks that this boy is late for school
the young one looks over at ed and ed
waves
and the young one grins and waves
and goes on his way.
ed turns and
goes about his work while
the door softly whooshes
shut.

*

wind-whip surge of the geese wings sleep till dawn
they await the dawn
from the marsh, from the high blades of marsh frost
they rise, as though on a ladder of frost, and their form
is a flutter of a high flag
whipping south
from the staff of the high frost sky

1950

ED DORN | 1929–1999

One of Donald Allen's Black Mountain poets, Ed Dorn is a major figure in postmodern American poetry. After studying briefly at the University of Illinois and Eastern Illinois University, Dorn accepted a scholarship from BMC, attending classes throughout 1950–51 and working in the campus's printshop; he later returned for the entire 1954–55 academic year and for the 1955 summer session. While he initially intended to study painting at the college, he quickly became more interested in poetry through the teachings of Charles Olson and Robert Creeley. In January 1955, Olson created a personalized reading list for Dorn, later published as *A Bibliography on America for Ed Dorn* (1964), which focused on historical and geographical approaches to the American West. Dorn's pamphlet from 1960, *What I See in the Maximus Poems*, is one of the earliest appreciations of Olson's epic. By the late 1960s, Dorn began serially publishing his own mock epic, *Slinger*, a multibook project he completed in 1975 (it was later reprinted under the title *Gunslinger* in 1989). Other works by the poet include *Hands Up!* (1964); *The North Atlantic Turbine* (1967); *Abhorrences* (1990), a collection of epigrammatic poems that address social and political life in Reagan-era America; and *Chemo Sábe* (2001), a book that chronicles Dorn's cancer treatments and experience with the American medical establishment.

The Hide of My Mother

1

My mother, who has a hide

on several occasions remarked what
a nice rug or robe
my young kids would make,

Would we send them to her?
When we had them butchered?

It was certainly a hoo ha ha
from me
and a ho ho
from my wife: and I would amusedly say

to conceal the fist in my heart
which one? the black?

or the grey
& white?

And she would smile, exposing the carnival
in her head

What's the difference, after they're dead?

Can you imagine asking a poet that?
Perhaps I should tell her about my pet rat.

2

My mother remarked
that in Illinois

little boys sell holly
from door to door,

and *here*, she would say
they grow all over the mountains
what if I took a holly tree back
there? would it grow?
No. I said.

3

Once my mother
was making dinner

and my cats were on the floor.

Why do they whine like that?
she asked,

why don't we throw them all out the door?
why don't you feed them I ventured?

She said she wasn't indentured.

Can you imagine telling a poet that?
Later she fed them my pet rat.

4

One day my son
found a parakeet in the bush
brought it to the house
carrying the little blue thing by the tail.

My mother said why, isn't it pretty,
I wonder if it would make the trip home
to Illinois. Oh, I said, we'll have to find its owner

you don't want to pull a boner
like that.

5

Tho winter's at term
it still gets cold

in the evening.
My pets are warm

because I have set a fire.

My mother is arranging some ferns
and young trees, a little too big

she found in the mountains.
A jig, of a sort must be going

on in her head. It is raining
outside. Do you think I can get the copper legs

of that stool in the box
or is it too wide? With some of those

pretty rocks I saw on the beach, would you,
she was saying to my little boy,

like to go home to Illinois with grandmother?

he was saying from inside the box enclosure,
he wasn't sure he

wanted to leave his mother.

6

For a point of etiquette,
when I observed she was digging
the neighbor's English Privet,

I said, it grows in abundance here.

As a matter of fact, she had it,
I thought I saw a rabbit,
that's why I came over here.

I said, a plant like that might grow anywhere.

Well now, I suppose you are right
back home our elms have the blight
but the land is flat there
so many mountains hereabouts

Yes, I allowed, it must help the sprouts . . .

Well now, there's more rain here
than we have in Illinois in an entire year
wouldn't you think tho it would grow there?

I said, what about a Privet hedge from . . .

You remember the peonies on grandfather's grave
well someone took them they were gone
the last Memorial Day I was there.

. . . From Hudson's Bay to the Gulf of Carpentaria.
Do you think it would stay?

Oh I love plants but where I am the weather
drives the birds away.

7

As for the hides of other people,
My wife told her

of how the junkman's
woman had been so good to us

a truss as it were, had kept the children
when it was a hardship

the condition had been foul, sleet,
masses of air, a raw affair,

dumped out of the Yukon upon
us, roving bands of weather

sliding across British Columbia
a kind of dementia

of the days, frozen water pipes
and the wringer on the washing machine

busted, no coal.
Our house split in two like Pakistan.

The graciousness
of the woman of the junkman

she said. Now what do you think
we should do? forget it? some doughnuts?
a cake?

"Why, I don't know what I would do"—
my mother was alluding

to a possible misfortune of her own.

8

As for the thick of it,
really, my mother
never knew about the world.

I mean even that there was one,
or more.

Whorled, like a univalve shell
into herself,

early to bed, nothing
in her head, here and there

Michigan one time,   Ohio

another. Led a life
like a novel, who hasn't?

As for Sociology:
garbage cans were what she dumped
the remains of supper in,

dirty newspapers, if blowing
in the street, somebody probably

dropped them there.

Nobody told her about the damned
or martyrdom. She's 47

so that, at least, isn't an emergency.

Had a chance to go to Arizona once
and weighed the ins and outs

to the nearest ounce:
didn't go. She was always slow.

Incidentally, for her the air
was Red one time:

tail end of a dust storm
somehow battered up from Kansas.

1960

On the Debt My Mother Owed to Sears Roebuck

Summer was dry, dry the garden
our beating hearts, on that farm, dry
with the rows of corn the grasshoppers
came happily to strip, in hordes, the first
thing I knew about locust was they came
dry under the foot like the breaking of
a mechanical bare heart which collapses
from an unkind an incessant word whispered
in the house of the major farmer
and the catalogue company,
from no fault of anyone
my father coming home tired
and grinning down the road, turning in
is the tank full? thinking of the horse
and my lazy arms thinking of the water
so far below the well platform.

On the debt my mother owed to sears roebuck
we brooded, she in the house, a little heavy
from too much corn meal, she
a little melancholy from the dust of the fields
in her eye, the only title she ever had to lands—
and man's ways winged their way to her through the mail
saying so much per month
so many months, this is yours, take it
take it, take it, take it
and in the corncrib, like her lives in that house
the mouse nibbled away at the cob's yellow grain
until six o'clock when her sorrows grew less
and my father came home

On the debt my mother owed to sears roebuck?
I have nothing to say, it gave me clothes to
wear to school,
and my mother brooded

in the rooms of the house, the kitchen, waiting
for the men she knew, her husband, her son
from work, from school, from the air of locusts
and dust masking the hedges of fields she knew
in her eye as a vague land where she lived,
boundaries, whose tractors chugged pulling harrows
pulling discs, pulling great yields of the earth
pulse for the armies in two hemispheres, 1943
and she was part of that *stay at home army* to keep
things going, owing that debt.

1964

Vaquero

The cowboy stands beneath
a brick-orange moon. The top
of his oblong head is blue, the sheath
of his hips
is too.

In the dark brown night
your delicate cowboy stands quite still.
His plain hands are crossed.
His wrists are embossed white.

In the background night is a house,
has a blue chimney top,
Yi Yi, the cowboy's eyes
are blue. The top of the sky
is too.

1964

(from *Twenty-Four Love Songs*)

2

Inside the late nights of last week
under the cover of our selves
you went to sleep in my arms
and last night too

you were in some alarm
of your dream
                    some tableau
an assembling of signs
from your troubled day glows
and trembles, your limbs
divine with sleep
gather and extend their flesh
along mine
and this I surround, all this
I had my arms around

3

My speech is tinged
my tongue has taken
a foreigner into it
Can you understand
my uncertainties grow
and underbrush and thicket
of furious sensibility
between us and wholly
unlike the marvelously burning
bush which lies at the entrance
to your gated thighs

My dear love, when I unsheathe
a word of the wrong temper
it is to test that steel
across the plain between us

4

Or if the word falls—
    but I didn't *mean* that
too often and too soon
before it moves
carried in our mouths
into the bright orchard
of a desire we must build traps
to catch
so that we are free
we think, to answer all
who would delay us,
it is our *selves* dressed
as the clothed figures who beseech us
for Our lives to beware
destruction, *take care* is
the password to their stability

6

The cleft in our ages
is an echoing cañon—look
I insist on my voice
Archeus become my life
and as any other extension
not to be ignored—
if you were my own time's possession
I'd tell you to *fuck off*

with such vivid penetration
you'd never stop gasping
and pleasure unflawed
would light our lives, pleasure
unrung by the secretly expected
fingers of last sunday

Do you hear me, can you
please only agree with me
because poems and love
and all that happens in the street
are blown forward
on the lightest breeze

7

But you are a green plant to me
only to be acknowledged
with passion
tended by my whole attention
there is argument only in equality
one war we can hope to ignore

What we have done is embroidered
our two figures are
as if set forth from Bayeux
and I fly like a dragon standard
yet my soul because I left home
as you did
pulls against a martingale
and having stayed at home too
or more
how much more pulls against you

10

Who could have told me love
is always love
and all it's needs to be
where it needs to be
are you
I thought forgive me
it was something you do
now everywhere I turn
and everytime there is
that full thing with us
I am cottered
                    high inside you
      lutus

13

I feel that fear
          my own
that fear a face presents
          and looks
and says words and the words
mean something
                              else
and the fear
is inside the other meaning

                    meaning which

would have no meaning then
of the thing that's not itself
would fear not itself
                                        fear not,

could have no meaning
Don't kill me
with that other meaning

20

When I heard the public story
of how they'd thrown away
their wedding rings, and how
the rings had been picked up
by the garbage men and taken
to the dump, and how laughing
finally they went out with flashlights
and found them that night I wondered
did they put them back on?

22

The agony is beauty
that you can't have that
and sense too. There
is no sense to beauty. It offends
everyone, the more so
in ratio to the praise of it.
And I've known this for a long
time, there has been no
great necessity to say it. How
really, the world is shit
and I mean all of it

24

There is no final word
for how you are.
An emotional response
can be the reputation to
which all inquiry is referred
and let go at that.

Back Home, Back Home
the day wakes up and once
out the door into what's
left of the fresh air it still
comes clear
how lovely
love is there

1969

RUSSELL EDSON | 1935–2014

One of America's foremost practitioners of the prose poem, Russell Edson attended BMC in the spring of 1951. The Connecticut-born poet appeared in the *Black Mountain College Review* edited and printed by M. C. Richards and her writing class. This first and only issue featured work by BMC faculty and students exclusively. That same year, Edson—with the help of fellow student Tommy Jackson—printed *Ceremonies in Bachelor Space*, his first book, in an edition of 268 copies through Jackson's Grapnel Press and the Black Mountain College Print Shop. Edson reportedly undertook this publishing venture without permission, resulting in censure from Charles Olson and Paul Williams. Since the 1970s, Edson has been admired for his surreal and absurdist narratives, often accompanied by illustrations. A volume of his selected poems, *The Tunnel*, was published in 1994; a new selected, *Little Mr. Prose Poem*, appeared in 2022. "The Murder of Sylvia" was first published in *Ceremonies in Bachelor Space*.

The Murder of Sylvia

The accomplice moves west
His head is an absorbent of mist
And Sylvia lies any way
Stopped therein
Where the birds are thin
Sylvia
Pleats of water are quiet

For morning comes in the kitchen
Morning comes where the plants are green
Where the plants may be green
Were they seen
If the kitchen is a cloudy day
Children play
If the kitchen is a window
And the day is pale
For they eat breakfast
With oranges and napkins
And the food may be pale
And the table cloth dull sky
There are fried eggs
With orange yolks and cream-colored whites
And there is milk in a white pitcher
And tiny flowers on the white cloth
And windsor chairs in the kitchen
Where they eat

The light of the day is seen through a cloud
The light of the day is a cloudy crystal
The light of the day is quartz
With minute brightnesses
And dull oranges

And things are shiny
When the light is white
In the living room and the books

When afternoon is come
The afternoon is a cloudy day
And children play
The trees without leaves and comes the rain
And all the trees are in the lane
With grass becoming
And all the trees
In the summer rain
In the early spring when maple-things are growing
Early spring rain

The wall is dark under windows
When screens are rusted
Rusting in the summer
And below
Is a flat bush and the leaves
And a path of stones leads around the house
To the flat bush and the leaves and a path of stones

The sky is come over
The roof
In simple shapes through the flat bush
The sky is white and almost rain
And around the chimney
And nests and antenna-wire and rain and clouds and slate
Of roof and gutters of rain and passive leaves
And still wetness with slow movements of trees
Near the window
Antenna-wire and a nest with rain left in the fall
On the roof when it rains and the clouds

Sylvia is not in her room
She has not come down to breakfast
She is being called
And asked for by the children.

1951

CYNTHIA HOMIRE | 1931–2019

Attending the college from 1950 to 1953, BMC graduate Cynthia Homire originally planned to study art and design under renowned painter and color theorist Josef Albers. However, Albers had just accepted a new position at Yale University, so Homire instead found inspiration in the teachings of Charles Olson, Robert Creeley, and M. C. Richards, who first introduced the versatile Homire to the aesthetic and ethical principles of the ceramic arts. After BMC, while living and working in New York City, Homire stayed in contact with Richards, whose *Centering in Pottery, Poetry, and the Person* (1964) was a source of creative and spiritual inspiration. In 1972, Homire and her husband, Jorge Fick, the last student to officially graduate from BMC, opened the Fickery, a stoneware shop in Santa Fe. In 1990, Homire was diagnosed with macular degeneration. Without the vision upon which she had always relied for ceramics, Homire shifted her creative focus to poetry. The following poems are from a chapbook entitled *Insights and Outbursts* (2008).

Nine

It's not what
you think
it's something
else.

2008

The Thundering Herd

I heard the bells
I smelled the roses
But I missed the elephants
coming into
          language.

2008

JOEL OPPENHEIMER | 1930–1988

One of Donald Allen's Black Mountain poets, Joel Oppenheimer was born and raised in Yonkers, New York. He studied at Cornell University and the University of Chicago. Then, from 1950 to 1953, he attended BMC. Like most BMC students, he never earned an official degree from the school. Wild Bull—as Oppenheimer was nicknamed—studied with Charles Olson, M. C. Richards, and Paul Goodman; his writings appeared in both Richards's *Black Mountain College Review* and Olson and Robert Creeley's *BMR*. In 1953, Oppenheimer moved back to New York City, where he participated in the city's countercultural arts scene and, later, assumed directorship of the Poetry Project at St. Mark's Church in-the-Bowery from 1966 to 1972. He also wrote a regular column for the *Village Voice* (1969–84). Late in his career, he composed several serial poems, including *The Woman Poems* (1975) and *New Hampshire Journal* (1994).

The Dancer

for Katherine Litz

for Katy
            stands rooted, herself
to one spot
              becomes:

                                        the only spot we know.

Grows, in this spot, among:
                                      flowers
                                      love
                                      whatever's
her particular
                    as we too
have particulars
                      but she
flies free
            pulling.

Delight, unvarying
                          Katy dances;
her dance's conjure:
                          flowers;
her legs are suns to light
the seeds around, while
                              on the wooden floor
her feet
know mud, know snow, know
spring

1951

The Sliding Pond Sonnet

first she come down it ta dum ta dum ta
straight then she ta ta ta dum ta dum ta
hung by her heels on fi de fi de de
her back come down and stopped fi de fi de
by braking against the ta ta dum ta
sides. went up and come ta dum ta dum ta
down on her belly went fi de fi de
under the ladder fi fi de fi de
swung up her feet climbing ta dum ta dum
inside the ladder right dum ta ta dum
in my boy's face him struggling fi de fi
his own way up the outside. fi fi fi
her first name fiona age ta dum de
8 honey blond and discreet. fi de de

1956

Today an Ophelia

She sits braiding
her hair at
the sea's
edge—and
the tide
is coming
in! and
she sits in the
fringe of the
waves, braiding
her
hair, and
the tide—and
dark hair—and in
the greenblue water coming
in, seaweed

afloat—greenblue and
for once, wet dark
with the water
her dress is not
purple, but
no color at
all—her
hands, braiding
her
hair

1956

The Bath

he will insist on
reading things into her simplest act.
her bath, which she takes
because he wills it so. her bath
she takes to cleanse herself.
ritual. ritual always
in his life. she takes her bath
to ready herself.
and himself more often than not decides
she wants him unbathed. manlike.
what he is most pleased about is
her continuing bathing.
in his tub. in his water. wife.

1960

A Heart Full Of

a heart full of
garbage. that was
the novel she wanted
to write, rich and
beguiling in its angers.
i wonder how she
does it, forces her
way thru into something
comprehensible, makes of her
children presentable items
on her own agenda, supplies
her husband with affection
even in the middle of a
night when he has failed her,
refuses to remember as if
to deny it happened.
yet on his head spins that
light touch, and his chin
which her hand caressed
sprouts beardedly with
love. this is not a novel
but a way and light.

1962

A Prayer

for a wedding, 29 november 1963

because everyone knows exactly what's good for another
because very few see
because a man and a woman may just possibly look at each other
because in the insanity of human relationships there still may come a time we say:
  yes, yes

because a man or a woman can do anything he or she pleases
because you can reach any point in your life saying: now, i want this
because eventually it occurs we want each other, we want to know each other, even stupidly, even uglily
because there is at best a simple need in two people to try and reach some simple ground
because that simple ground is not so simple
because we are human beings gathered together whether we like it or not
because we are human beings reaching out to touch
because sometimes we grow
    we ask a blessing on this marriage
    we ask that some simplicity be allowed
    we ask their happiness
    we ask that this couple be known for what it is, and that the light shine upon it
    we ask a blessing for their marriage

1963

Sioux Song

for vdl

it is raining

it is raining

we sit together

we sit together

the weather is inside us

the weather is inside us

1978

BASIL KING | 1935–

Born in London, Basil King immigrated with his family to the United States in 1947 and settled in Detroit, Michigan. One of several students—including Ray Johnson and John Urbain—who came to BMC from Detroit's Cass Technical High School, King enrolled at the college from 1951 to 1956. King is a multidisciplinary artist who studied writing with Charles Olson, Robert Creeley, and Robert Duncan, music with Stefan Wolpe, and painting with Joseph Fiore and Esteban Vincente. In 1959, King and his wife, former BMC student Martha King, moved to New York City. There, he began his career as a professional painter while also illustrating small-press book and magazine covers, including LeRoi Jones/Amiri Baraka's *Preface to a Twenty-Volume Suicide Note* and the journal *Yūgen*. In 1985, King returned to writing and has since published a number of books, including *Mirage: A Poem in Twenty-Two Sections* (2003), *Learning to Draw / A History* (2011), *77 Beasts* (2007), and *There Are No Ghosts, There Are Portraits* (2023).

Josef Albers

Homage to the Square: Ascending, 1953

I am witness—
I saw the color
kick in—in—in
it thrust against
the wall, was not
relieved when it
awoke—it was faced
with a messenger
who with ignorance
had delivered a
message only
the rarefied would
be able to stomach.

2007

Pablo Picasso

Portrait of D.M., Paris, October 9, 1942

I am the manchild whose muse
        is stronger than the love
I have for this woman's mother
      dies, wanting her daughter's body
to suffer chest pains. The daughter rises
  as a man with a hard erection—
she fucks her mother,   to paint
       from the abstract
         to the figure, from the figure
to the abstract makes an edge
  of exquisite distance and distance
gives us our sensations

                    —until this war is over
                    craft defeats corruption

*

The muse is so strong
it will help me paint
My mother is dying
and wants to take me for herself

I don't want a hard erection—
I will not fuck my mother

I will call on the muse to be forgiven

We women have waited so long to paint

from the abstract
to the figure—from the figure
to the abstract makes an edge
of exquisite distance and distance
gives us our sensations—

—until this war is over
craft defeats corruption

*

This woman's dying mother
wants her daughter's body
to suffer chest pains. The daughter rises
as a man with a hard erection.
She fucks her mother. To paint
from the abstract
to the figure, from the figure
to the abstract makes an edge
of exquisite distance and distance
gives us our sensations.

until this war is over
—craft defeats corruption

*

I'm
so sorry
you're dying
inside me
there is
a space
for you
a desperate
space that
wanted you
to mother
me

until this war is over
craft defeats corruption

2007

Paul Gauguin

The Yellow Christ, 1889

This Jew's name is Jesus.
His father is a carpenter.
He came amongst us and told us a tale
that we thought was pornographic
and would get us in a lot of trouble.
So we listened and did nothing.
I guess we were wrong.
Powerful men thought him bad trouble
and framed it so he would be crucified.
We're sorry. You know, we've
begun to realize what he tried to do
and we love him.

2007

MARIE TAVROGES STILKIND | 1930–

Originally from Montréal, Québec, Marie Tavroges Stilkind attended BMC irregularly between 1951 and 1954. She heard about the college through fellow Montréaler and artist Dorothea Rockburne, who first attended in 1950. After BMC, Stilkind moved to New York City, where she worked as an editorial assistant for the *Juilliard Review* and became part of the avant-garde scene, socializing with figures such as Albert Fine, Philip Glass, and LeRoi Jones/Amiri Baraka. Playing a pivotal role in the mail art movement of the early 1960s, Stilkind was a close friend of BMC student and mail art practitioner Ray Johnson, who referred to her as "the secretary of the New York Correspondence School."[12]

To Fee Dawson

who never saw this poem

So nice to
visit with you again
on the pages
of Combustion.
When I think of you,
Fee Dawson,
I remember BMC
and the Smoky Mountains
in the spring.
Yellow green
on the tulip tree.
And you
teaching Tim, shy Tim,
to catch
a fast ball.
And Jorge and Joel
getting crew cuts
and soon there was
a baseball team
and everything
was All-American
and no one wanted
to make black night tea
for poetry readings
with Olson at two A.M.
Poetry that spring
was the crack of the ball
on wood,
the smell of cut grass
and exuberance,
Fee Dawson.
So nice to hear
your joyful cries
again.

composed ca. 1965; published in 2009

JONATHAN WILLIAMS | 1929–2008

One of Donald Allen's Black Mountain poets, Jonathan Williams was also a well-known and accomplished publisher, essayist, and photographer. In San Francisco, in 1951, with the help of artist and printer David Ruff, Williams founded the Jargon Society, one of the most important small presses in twentieth-century American literature. Based in both Highlands, North Carolina, and Yorkshire Dales, England, the Jargon Society published works by authors associated with BMC, including Charles Olson's *The Maximus Poems / 1–10* (1953), Robert Creeley's *The Immoral Proposition* (1953), Irving Layton's *The Improved Binoculars* (1956), Robert Duncan's *Letters: Poems, 1953–1956* (1958), Denise Levertov's *Overland to the Islands* (1958), and Larry Eigner's *On My Eyes* (1960). The press also published books by Buckminster Fuller, Mina Loy, Paul Metcalf, Lorine Niedecker, Kenneth Patchen, and Louis Zukofsky, among many others. Williams's own poetry draws heavily on the vernacular and natural surroundings of his native Appalachia. Of Williams's poetry, Guy Davenport writes that "[it] is the nucleus of his being, the radiant center. He has never written or spoken a dull sentence."[13] Born in Asheville, North Carolina, Williams studied at Princeton University and the Chicago Institute of Design. He first attended BMC in 1951 to study photography with Aaron Siskind and Harry Callahan. He worked closely with Olson in the summer of 1951 and, upon his return to the college in 1954 after completing military service in Germany (Williams was in the army medical corps), he studied writing with Creeley. His second book, *Amen/Huzza/Selah* (1960), is a collection of poems "local to life during The Last Days of Black Mountain College," and it includes "Three Tavern Songs in the Late Southern T'ang Manner."[14] After Williams's death and with the blessing of his longtime partner, Thomas Meyer, the Jonathan Williams Estate bequeathed the Jargon Society to the Black Mountain College Museum + Arts Center.

Three Tavern Songs in the Late Southern T'ang Manner

1. TRUNKENE IM FRÜHLING (MY VERSION)

or—who else go into the shrubbery
muttering

or shine the silver flashlight
at the female dormitory,
longingly?

questions, questions . . . always
constrictions—

ah, to sit
in the catbird seat!

2. AGAIN THE NIGHT!

so the moon, as she rose
red,
swung clean, from the hill,

but her face through the window had '*Heart of Kentucky*' on it, an
obfuscation (always a mystery), a
sour mash,

like this typewriter
crashing across the swampgrass,
as if brushing it
aside . . .

and trees, goddamn everywhere,
and figures of speech!

3. THE DESPERADO

so,
a bottle of bourbon on the top shelf, why
not?

or,
who are you, you
yankee, to ask *anything*?

you've been seeing too many drive-in movies;
that is,
nobody does,
in fact,
here,
drink—

only icewater, or
syllabub, sometimes,

in the gloaming,
tra-la

1960

The Distances to the Friend

Thoreau,
            grabbing on, hard,

a red, raw
            muskrat . . .

thought to eat it,
                      stifling all repulsion

so sat by the quagmire,
cranky, no cannibal, too
uninvolved
               to get to man

so simply

we, the
heirs, hear other rustlings:

the grass stirs like an
androgyne,
the man
in our hearts stands
his fear
on its head,
savagely—

              inversed, nervelessly,
we sweat past each other,
unrelieved:

bitter landscapes,
                    unlovely

Based on an incident at Walden Pond, Massachusetts.

1962

Silers Bald

(from "A Week from the Big Pigeon to the Little Tennessee River")

just in front of the
round iron john
in the beech grove

the fresh bear droppings
give you
something
to think about

1962

Some Southpaw Pitching

a riff for Charles Olson via Charles Ives

"let the song lie in the thing!" there's
music in anything! anything?

o there's poetry
in Mississippi; *exempli gratia*, the Iuka Drive-In:

I PASSED FOR WHITE plus
SNOW WHITE AND THE SEVEN SHADES

agreed?

Ives pitched for Hopkins Prep and beat
the Yale Freshmen and maybe pitched for Yale and beat
Dartmouth

once he stood in Dartmouth Common by the bon-fire
and heard the Glee-Club sing
"*Where O Where Are the Pea-Green Freshmen?*"

Ives, who knew how to take a lot off his knuckler,
took a lot off the tune, turning it
into the "Allegro" of the *Symphony #2*—
and Dvořák can't beat it

so, let the song lie in the ear, if it
hears it

where o where are the pea-green freshmen
d'antan?

even Helen Trent has gone to hell
in a boat,

where we all float—

or don't

The Shade of Ezra Pound once appeared to Charles Olson and uttered the poem's vatic first line. No one has quite understand what he meant, but it sounds like Heraclitus.

1962

Aunt Creasy, On Work:

shucks
I make the livin

uncle
just makes the livin
worthwile

1971

The Deracination

definition: *root*,
"a growing point,
an organ of absorption, an aereating organ,
a good reservoir, or
means of support"

Vernonia glauca, order *Compositae*,
"these tall perennials with
corymbose cymes of bright-purple heads of
tubular flowers
with conspicuous stigmas"

I do not know the Ironweed's root,
but I know it rules September

and where the flowers tower
in the wind there is a burr of
sound—empyrean . . . the mind
glows and the wind drifts . . .

epiphanies pull up
from roots—

epiphytic, making it up

out of the air

1971

The Hermit Cackleberry Brown, on Human Vanity:

caint call your name
but your face is easy

come sit

now some folks figure theyre
bettern
cowflop they
aint

not a bit

just good to hold the world together
liked hooved up ground

thats what

1971

Night Landscape in Nelson County, Kentucky

ah, Moon, shine
thou as amber in thy
charred-keg, hickory sky . . .

still as a still, steep
as a horse's face

1971

"Four-Way Gay"

Dave and Jack;
Rick and Jim;

Dave and Rick;
Jim and Jack;

Jim and Dave;
Jack and Rick—

plus fours!

1972

Funerary Ode for Charles Olson

like Apollinaire I was not in Camden when
Walt whispered to Horace,
Lift me up, Horace, I need to shit—
and then left us

like Apollinaire I was not in Gloucester
in January, 1970

I was in a stone cottage in Yorkshire,
writing, editing, and looking in the fire
for signs of the New Dark Ages

since the tongues and needles of the
"Terrible Knitters of Dentdale"
stopped clacking in the 19th century,
news travels slow up the River Dee:

card from Paul Metcalf:
"the Big O has climbed into his box
and put out to sea"

note from Ron Johnson:
"heart attack,
that abused, absurd bear-like body—
'and the mind go forth to the end of the world'"

. . . .

the nicest part of any of it
is that Bill Williams now has somebody to talk to
in the Asphodels
while waiting for Ezra

. . . so, dig Charles, first day out,
stumbling through the asphodels, figuring they are figwort,
shambling up to Doc Williams:
"Ah si, hombre, I am an archaeologist of morning!"

"Shit, Charlie, you're just a big Swede
in a turquoise skull-cap.
We were going to found a new universe together—
remember?"

. . . .

One day Mahler wept and said:
"Ich habe Papier geliebt!"
(Life's been nothing but paperwork!)

. . . .

so what about that word *amorvor*, Charles,
or the way you used to write *am O?*—
I love; or, *I am Olson?*

"we swarmeth in vile Canniball words," says Nashe—
foul & fair game for our anthropophagous friends & foes

to be called a Stuffed Cyclops who'd crawled
out of Ezra Pound's cave—that amused you;

or, to be called The Oldest Writer for Little Magazines
in the World . . .

to be called a cold man pretending to be hot,
to be called a man with no hearth—
that was something else,

like a man who made water-verse

. . . .

the song is heat! the song is
something to eat:
a mask made of fat appetite:
that baked fish for four he ate in whatever
Chinese restaurant in whatever city it happened to be;
the tiny reflection of the succulent Donner Party
in thick glasses;
the body of Herman Melville on a spit
at a Democratic Party barbecue in 1938 in Washington—
poetry, a form of *power*,

something you wielded like the poker hand
in the club-car with Roosevelt
headed for Cleveland . . .

he who controls rhythm
controls

the polls, the polis, the illiterate, the unwobbling pivot,
plus a few voles if you like

. . . .

cold, cold, on the bold
shore

let's just throw it out, what
may have been the ultimate, very large, size-16 achilles heel,
Charles . . .

it would not be the first time, New England;

nor the last,
since one of our erstwhile friends
has come to write the same letter to everything on earth,
each one signed "all love"

for love is not easy, now
that Pejorocracy is here—
for sure

. . . .

so, Charles, let us (and *you* as well as us)
take you at your word:
amorvor

let lust drag it off the word-list
down into the Bed Incarnate—

where heads have tongues up assholes,
and come's all over chests and fingers,
when your eyes finally tell you the poem is no place
for polite usage only

it is only when the beloved's come, shit, and heated juices
receive the same sanctification as one's own substance
that a state of *love* may be said to exist—
what poets call *sacramental* relationships, what Freudians
call excremental visions

we feed on each other in Elysian fires

the dead, who lived cold, are made to eat
asphodels instead

. . . .

Charles,
in my copy of *Call Me Ishmael*,
(which I sold 18 years later, in anger,
to some Jesuit on Long Island)
you wrote:

o, jonathan, to be furious
is to be frighted out of fear . .

like *Lear*
I believe it,

it surely is a queer time, the literati nastier than either
peasants or piranhas

. . . .

the severed head of Charles John Orpheus, Jr.
floats off Massachusetts

amorvor, voracious, and bereft,
I want to make a last supper of it—

like in the Marsden Hartley painting,
in Paradise

1972

"Actually, I Didn't Come Out of the Closet until 1971"

8-foot
buck-toothed
southern

gurl

1973

MICHAEL RUMAKER | 1932–2019

Born in Philadelphia and raised in National Park, New Jersey, Michael Rumaker started his undergraduate studies at Rider College in Trenton, New Jersey, before eventually enrolling at BMC in 1952. He graduated with honors in 1955, with Robert Duncan serving as his external examiner. Primarily known as a prose writer, Rumaker published his earliest fiction—a short story titled "The Truck"—in *BMR*. At BMC, he studied prose fiction with Robert Creeley, poetry with Charles Olson, and theater with Wesley Huss. Rumaker developed an especially close relationship with Olson and expressed how this relationship was both inspiring and taxing in *Black Mountain Days* (2003), his memoir chronicling the final years of the college. In 1970, Rumaker earned an MFA from Columbia University. His writings often consider the subjects of homosexuality and gay identity. Noteworthy works of prose include *The Butterfly* (1962), *Gringos and Other Stories* (1967), *A Day and Night at the Baths* (1979), and *Pagan Days* (1991). A volume of his selected poetry, *Pizza*, was published in 2005.

For Charles Olson

Yes, there are the anecdotes:
How you abhorred drafts
so your students almost passed out
in the smoke-filled classrooms
of Black Mountain;
how you sat in class
with a ragged gray
cashmere sweater
on your head
"to keep my brains warm";
the driver's seat of your old Ford
crushed back out of shape
from the bulk and weight
of your body;
who on first hearing "mother-fucker"
out of first baseman
    Fee Dawson's mouth
on the softball field,
your eyes bugged wide
you expelled a thin, high breath
of shock and delight.

A big man,
touch wasn't easy for you
but your arm around a shoulder,
a tentative touching of hands
(careful what you touched and how)
gave us a ground.

Shy of you,
you shocked me into life
being brutal to be kind
to teach me the shock of cruelty,
to be caring.

And once you wrote:
I will go down
bellowing like a hog,
a Celtic hog to the end.

Dream-king,
you taught us the meaning
and use of dreams;
moon-turbaned wiseman,
at the edge of
night and morning,
a further ground to investigate
to plow and make known.

Whose breath
was the rhythmical measure
of the man
and his content,
who taught us to be
archeologists of the self.

Archeologist of morning,
rooting
among the dead,
seizing their quickness
and delivering it whole, hot,
struggling and alive;
searching once-fleshed bones
to bring back across
the yawn of ages
alive
dead remnants
of a living past
to feed us.

Magician,
what was dead
you made alive,

what was dead in us
or sleeping
you touched with your dream heat
and brought to life.

Your tansy be all
that meadows your mind
in going

Your red-throated gentian
burst bright in your eyes
in goodbye.

2005

To a Motorcyclist Killed on Route 9W

From the second seat I see
the black Plymouth veer towards the bus,
light shower of sparks
as your motorcycle smashes into its fender.
Your long body flies slowly,
gracefully through the air
in the wide windshield
(light levis brilliant in the headlights)
and with a sickening rumble
the bus wheels
roll over your body.
I go out with the other men and see you,
face down,
you lie so final
on the tire-worn, exhaust-blackened concrete:
one arm flung out, the other
twisted by your side—
levis half way down your hips
revealing jockey shorts, label inside out,
brown suede boots with runover heels,

worn soles,
one crumpled boot lying close by,
droopy sock on your foot.
In the light of the fire
from your blazing motorcycle
your thick reddish hair glistens,
the bright spurts of blood on the cement
from your crushed chest.
Billow of flame bubbles high
up among the trees
as the gas tank of your cycle explodes.
The bus driver
runs with an extinguisher
he got from the bus.
Spitting, hissing, a thick
curtain of white, rubber-acrid smoke
rolls over the highway,
over your body,
hiding, shielding it.
"It's funny, we're still alive,"
the thin blond next to me says,
and over her shoulder,
reaching out to the hysterical woman
behind her,
"Say an Our Father, honey."
The police cars arrive,
whisking red lights
and squawking radios.
They light the scene with pink flares.
They discover you're from
    Rhode Island, 18.
It's not you.
It's ourselves we see
sprawled on the road.
We move closer together, helpless,
talk quietly in the early fall night,
stare, fascinated.
Ourselves we see

final and flung out on the cold road,
the public body now
exposed to the eyes of strangers,
ourselves exposed
for a moment in your death
final
the unlived thing you have become
stretched negligently
as in sleep
on the highway.

2005

MARTHA DAVIS KING | 1937–

Martha Davis King spent only three months at BMC in the summer of 1955 but that radical experience liberated her. She first learned about BMC when she saw issue 4 of *BMR*—with its reproductions of Franz Kline's abstract expressionist paintings—at the Bull's Head Bookshop in Chapel Hill, where she was then a student at the University of North Carolina. At BMC, King felt "a gust of profound expressively female freedom."[15] During that fabled summer, she studied theater with Wesley Huss and weaving with Tony Landreau. She immersed herself in the poetry of Charles Olson and Robert Creeley and in the abstract expressionism of Kline; she was also exposed, for the first time, to the music of Duke Ellington, Miles Davis, and Charlie Parker. She married painter, poet, and fellow BMC student Basil King in 1958; in 1959, the couple moved to New York City, where Martha Davis King continues to live, write, and publish. Her collections of poetry include *Women and Children First* (1975), *Weather* (1978), and *Imperfect Fit: Selected Poems* (2004).

Black Mountain Landscape

Swannanoa river
                    in a groove through the rocks
  where barefeet feel the smooth
  the light green river
                         sucks itself
                         water hair
                         milk hair
                                  pulse and curl

Above the flood plain
rows of corn
in sour clay
hardly mulch enough to raise a decent weed
since the skin-thin sheath of leaf mould
                                          leached away
only where loggers couldn't get 'em
cling the oak & beech, thicker by higher
huge shields of twigging
miles of celluloid where sap is moving
  vegetable abundance
  out of dirt
  as acid as an acorn

The valley rises and thins out
its up end curving like the handle of a spoon
Pancake clouds splotch across the valley floor
and rivers of light
spill past the sign for Stuckey's Pee cans
following the bent road
where farm boys park
gulp beer
and dream of beating city women

1978

65 and Raining

rising in Kyoto
a mist crosses Asia
up there
          where it's tomorrow

the children
gone for the day
rain beads on grass blades, and they
bend with the weight

65, says the radio, light
rain in Melbourne
in San Francisco
it is dark, 66 and clouds

64 in Kuala Lumpur
the mills of war
          stop

a cool swath across the world
the house
is quiet

in her dream she
stops
the red devourer feeding on terror
          is not goaded

drizzle in Bedlam noon
pause in Belfast

65 and raining
          in North Spain

the miners will rest
out of plastique, out,

almost, of rage
the millers of war
are quiet

    scars ache vaguely—
    New Delhi gutter dogs
    lift their snouts—
    raining and 65

clouds in London
rain is expected
65 in Bucharest
and we
in bed together
hear the radio announce
65 and raining
on the earth

2004

Subjects for poetry in the 20th century

List is mania
collections of images
the personal isn't
why I don't care about your grandmother in the sunset
why I do
the connections between things: yellow flags over and beyond
    national politics, warnings at sea, marsh flowers
conversions between things or from one thing to another thing
    lightning selects only the tent pole
    the pulse changes
seduction and numbness
the essential necessity of confusion
    out of dirt, temporary organization
    her fire gave me goosebumps

But it was more
subjects and poetry
            subjected
                        subjective
will it be clearer if you look under the table?

Will you be quiet?
            can quiet
                        quiet

Quiet and feel the squares on which we walk, drive;
the circles from which we drink, eat;
the oblongs we handle, raise, read, look out of, open, shut;
the rareness of triangles.

2004

JOHN WIENERS | 1934–2002

Born and raised in Milton, Massachusetts, John Wieners earned his undergraduate degree from Boston College in 1954. Inspired by hearing Charles Olson perform his poetry at the Charles Street Meeting House in 1954, Wieners (then employed as a librarian at Harvard University) enrolled at BMC, studying with Olson as well as Robert Creeley and Robert Duncan. Between 1957 and 1962, he edited and published three issues of the journal *Measure*, which he modeled after *BMR*. It featured the work of many BMC poets, including Olson, Creeley, and Duncan, as well as Ed Dorn, Larry Eigner, Edward Marshall, Michael Rumaker, and Jonathan Williams. With *The Hotel Wentley Poems* (1958) and Donald Allen's *NAP*, Wieners arrived on the new American scene, a startlingly original voice, writing poems that address homosexual desire, drug use, and mental health. In books such as *Behind the State Capitol, or Cincinnati Pike* (1975) and *The Journal of John Wieners Is to Be Called 707 Scott Street for Billie Holiday, 1959* (1996), Wieners—like Paul Blackburn—composed in a journal form, combining lyric poetry and diaristic prose. While he lived, for brief periods, in San Francisco in the late 1950s and New York City and Buffalo in the 1960s, he spent the bulk of his adult life in Boston's Beacon Hill neighborhood. Creeley once said of Wieners that he is "the greatest poet of emotion."[16]

A poem for cock suckers

Well we can go
in the queer bars w/
our long hair reaching
down to the ground and
we can sing our songs
of love like the black mama
on the juke box after all
what have we got left.

On our right the fairies
giggle in their lacquered
voices & blow
smoke in your eyes let them
it's a nigger's world
and we retain strength.
The gifts do not desert us,
fountains do not dry,
these are mountains
swelling for spring to cascade.

It is all here between
the powdered legs & painted
eyes of the fairy
Friends who do not fail us
Mary in our hour of
despair. Take not
away from me the small fires
I burn in the memory of love.

1958

A poem for painters

Our age bereft of nobility
How can our faces show it?
I look for love.
My lips stand out
dry and cracked with want
of it.
Oh it is well.

Again we go driven by forces
we have no control over. Only
in the poem
comes an image—that we rule
the line by the pen
in the painter's hand one foot
away from me.

Drawing the face
and its torture.
That is why no one dares tackle it.
Held as they are in the hands
of forces
they cannot understand.
That despair
is on my face and shall show
in the fine lines of any man.

I held love once in the palm of my hand.
See the lines there.
How we played
its game, are playing now
in the bounds of white and heartless fields.
Fall down on my head,
love, drench my flesh in the streams
of fine sprays. Like
French perfume
so that I light up as

morning glorys and
I am showered by the scent
of the finished line.

No circles
but that two parallels do cross
And carry our souls and
bodies together as the planets
Showing light on the surface
of our skin, knowing
that so much flows through
the veins underneath.
The cheeks puffed with it.
Our pockets full.

2

Pushed on by the incompletion
of what goes before me
I hesitate before this paper
scratching for the right words.
Paul Klee scratched for seven years
on smoked glass to develop
his line, LaVigne says: Look
at his face!   he who has spent
all night drawing mine.

The sun
also rises on the rooftops
beginning with violet.
I begin in blue knowing what's cool.

3

My middle name is Joseph and I
walk beside an ass on the way to
what Bethlehem, where a new babe is born.
Not the second hand of Yeats but
first prints on a cloudy windowpane.

4

America, you boil over

The cauldron scalds.
Flesh is scarred.
Eyes shot.

The street aswarm with
vipers and heavy armed bandits.
There are bandages on the wounds
but blood flows unabated.
Oh stop
up the drains.
We are run over.

5

Let us stay with what we know.
That love is my strength, that
I am overpowered by it:
Desire
that too
is on the face: gone stale.
When green was the bed my love
and I laid down upon.
Such it is, heart's complaint,
You hear upon a day in June.
And I see no end in view
when summer goes, as it will,
upon the roads, like singing
companions across the land.

South of Mission, Seattle,
over the Sierra Mountains,
the Middle West and Michigan,
moving east again, easy
coming into Chicago and

the cattle country, calling
to each other over canyons,
careful not to be caught
at night, they are still out,
the destroyers, and down
into the South, familiar land,
lush places, blue mountains
of Carolina, into Black Mountain
and you can sleep out, or
straight across into states

I cannot think of their names
this nation is so large, like
our hands, our love it lives
with no lover, looking only
for the beloved, back home
into the heart, New York,
New England, Vermont, green
mountains, and Massachusetts
my city, Boston and the sea
again to smell what this calm
ocean cannot tell us. The seasons.
Only the heart remembers
and records in the words

6

At last. I come to the last defense.

My poems contain no
wilde beestes, no
lady of the lake, music
of the spheres, or organ chants.

Only the score of a man's
struggle to stay with
what is his own, what
lies within him to do.

Without which is nothing.
And I come to this,
knowing the waste,
leaving the rest up to love
and its twisted faces,
my hands claw out at
only to draw back from the
blood already running there.

1958

The Magic of This Summer

June 23, 1963

The nights belong to us. They lie dreaming outside our windows, curled in the sun, there on the firescape. The nights lie dreaming outside us.

One does surely belong to Art. There do lie within us frontiers of art, assuming shape. Form does belong to some content. There is madness on my mind, assuming shape.

Form to be given, declared at any moment by
what lies outside, and within us. Some how or other, the
moment declares, us outside form to be given, declared
by shape, assuming us, our shape, forms remain
entirely given.

Let the truth of this moment last as long as my life
remains to be continually given, remains every moment,
to be given. The form declares
shape, given, of any, this moment, everything
declares itself in the moment, hidden itself in the declaration
of life, this moment, remains entirely given.

I sent a Post Card from Kansas City, Missouri
asking for money when I got to Washington D.C.
to Freude Mittleman, San Francisco,
Signed my grandfather's name
John Laffan
No Address Given

Is there anything in fragments of life, unrealized moments, that come on us, riding along Blue Hill Parkway, beyond the sunset, the moment of our life, come on, given over completely to the past, given over our life, entirely given, at any moment. This moment to be realized, shortly.

This means, you are to be given, at any moment, the fragments of past life.

A knock sounds on the door, it destroys the sense of well being, entirely, in the house. If there is well being entirely in the house. I am sensed with the sound of being familiar, over this content, the house to be inhabited by strangers.

It seems there is nothing, entirely given over to any moment, the bird does go along, on the firescape, the whole process, birds descend in sunlight.

Wings ascend the air. Nature displays a lovely shape, in the twittering trees one tries to escape.

The hand of the maker carves everything to be, come everything, to thy own shape.

For its own being, will come our shape. Form declares itself.

In the given moment

In every living being.

What is there to declare at any given moment,
of the form of our lives, what is there to be declared any more,
that the sun shines, there is nothing o no more lost, everything
given over in a moment, o lost and surrendered, my
castle in the sand, on the beach, o the castles surrendered,
in my air.

What is there to impose on
My life is not over. There is more to be given.
How may I say this? There is no sense of any danger;
still my life, by
back life given many more days.

God bless them, give over to them, entirely,
the sense of new consciousness you now certainly
possess.

Roll out many more days, impose on us, the sense of
being, our life more important than many beings may
possess, forgive us our punctuation; and spheres many
now possess may be invoked, to possess our senses.

Our new orders are; cannot be any more than there
are no more many new lives to be possessed.
A sense preserved of the past moment, a new life

The sense of continuity entirely destroyed by many
new senses, continually destroyed by many new
shapes o continually destroyed, o many new spheres,
many life entirely destroyed, continued by
many spheres, entirely lost, o continually destroyed
many lost by more o continually new generation.

There is no message more shapely than this
Who am I but a mouthpiece. There is no more
shapely kingdom than this to come. O my lost again
continually, o my spheres.

You possess entirely, o destroyer of my senses,
many strange and new things O possessor of

II.

How is the sentence to be ended?

As I write now, questions of form asked
how is mind-time taken? to be asked many questions
given the mind time enough to spare

time earned enough
to learn
There is time enough to ask many questions.

Not enough time. Any new life entirely lost, o my generation
to come O new generation, to come and be asked: Why?
Art is a question.

You cannot be lost, or entirely destroyed—there is
no generation to come, asked as you who are left are
continually asked; o how do you come by? And
why? There are no further any more to be asked,
entirely one question; what is there to make; what
more is there to ask?

What more is there to come many more asked; the question to come?
What more is there to come? is there any more, questions to
be asking? o come; there are many new questions to
ask; there? o how are the stars?

Is there life on any planet? O many
new stars continually fall and entirely destroyed, are
there any to come

Submit to many questions: Ask and it shall be asked of them also. You are entirely alone and lost, new and alone, lost. Shape then too takes place. Are there any new forms.

I hear the sound of rushing waters.

I see planets drifting in great blobs, through immense spaces

I don't want to see any more of this world. I close my eyes;   blue light!

These are associations, mental images, that do not ever exist. The mind composes itself entirely of images, that completely study the mind's way, even tho words written out picture only the mind's flashes

The mind, entirely composed of images creates a form, to be flowed through blood by many particles, entirely composed and transmitted this by many ways, to their life.

The mind, entirely composed of images, creates a poem. There are no different than we are.

There are no different spheres than yours

I heard a cat cry in my arm, assuming the shape of blood Cry aloud, in my arms.

o God help me o remind my spheres to protect me,
remind me of my own spheres,

as song spins out a melody
that the mood earns

spare there moments of my own past life;
to come, o be remembered

4:10

Now back to our continual reality, expressed in the afternoon
window. O reality, expressed in the past life, revive these
dying senses, o wonder at again! other window curtains
          blow in the sun.

          Now it can be done. The sun shines again in the window.
The heat radiates a light often heavenly; light more
in the window than any where else again.   The heat
often radiates a more long life. Dying heat. More.

                                        O let me be: rise,
                                                  shining again
off rooftops again. o let me be, rise off again
swimmers on the rooftops.
                              The heat often radiates
a lovely long life.
          O let me be, rise shining again
off the rooftops, swimmers in the after noon glow
of trees dry in the sun.
                              O let me be, rise again
o roofs hover in the trees; the lovers lie themselves
in the sun: o rise again;   o heat radiate; o left life
long and lovely, themselves, rise shining the afternoon
light.

1972

C H I L DREN OF THE WORKING CLASS

to Somes

from incarceration, Taunton State Hospital, 1972

gaunt, ugly deformed

broken from the womb, and horribly shriven
at the labor of their forefathers, if you check back

scout around grey before actual time
their sordid brains don't work right,
pinched men emaciated, piling up railroad ties and highway
ditches
blanched women, swollen and crudely numb
ered before the dark of dawn

scuttling by candlelight, one not to touch, that is, a signal panic
thick peasants after *the* attitude

at that time of their century, bleak and centrifugal
they carry about them, tough disciplines of copper Indianheads.

there are worse, whom you may never see, non-crucial around
the
spoke, these you do, seldom
locked in the Taunton State Hospital and other peon work farms
drudge from morning until night, abandoned within destitute
crevices odd clothes
intent on performing some particular task long has been far
removed
there is no hope, they locked-in key's; housed of course

and there fed, poorly
off sooted, plastic dishes, soiled grimy silver knives and forks,
stamped Department of Mental Health spoons
but the unshrinkable duties of any society
produces its ill-kempt, ignorant and sore idiosyncrasies.

There has never been a man yet, whom no matter how wise
can explain how a god, so beautiful he can create
the graces of formal gardens, the exquisite twilight sunsets
in splendor of elegant toolsmiths, still can yield the horror of

dwarfs, who cannot stand up straight with crushed skulls,
diseases on their legs and feet unshaven faces and women,
worn humped backs, deformed necks, hare lips, obese arms
distended rumps, there is not a flame shoots out could ex-
tinguish the torch of any liberty's state infection.

1907, My Mother was born, I am witness t-
o the exasperation of gallant human beings at g-
od, priestly fathers and Her Highness, Holy Mother the Church
persons who felt they were never given a chance, had n-
o luck and were flayed at suffering.

They produced children with phobias, manias and depression,
they cared little for their own metier, and kept watch upon
others, some change to get ahead

Yes life was hard for them, much more hard than for any blo
ated millionaire, who still lives on
their hard-earned monies. I feel I shall
have to be punished for writing this,
that the omniscient god is the rich one,
cared little for looks, less for Art,
still kept weekly films close for the
free dishes and scandal hot. Some how
though got cheated in health and upon
hearth. I am one of them. I am witness
not to Whitman's vision, but instead the
poorhouses, the mad city asylums and re-
lief worklines. Yes, I am witness not to
God's goodness, but his better or less scorn.

The First of May, The Commonwealth of State Massachusetts,
1972.

1975

(from *The Journal of John Wieners Is to Be Called 707 Scott Street for Billie Holiday, 1959*)
July 17

A poem does not have to be a major thing. Or a statement?
I am allowed to ask many things because it has been given
me the means to plunge into the depths and come up with
answers? No. Poems, which are
my salvation alone. The reader can do with them what he likes.
I feel right now even the reading of poems to an unknown
large? public is a shallow *act*, unless the reading be given for the
fact of clarity. The different *techne*
a man uses to make his salvation. That is why poetry
even tho it does deal with langue is no more *holy* act
than, say shitting.
Dis-
charge. Manifesting the
process of
is it life? Or the action between this and
non-action? *Lethargy vs.*
Violence.
For to take up arms against the void is attack, and the price of war
is high. Millions of syllables
shed over the falls of our saliva, millions of teardrops
roll out of our eyes. Giant screams echo through the halls of
our houses at night. We do not wish it. It is so. By the action
we are engaged in. Hundreds of days, months have to go by before
the spirits descend and the right word rolls out sharp and full of
fire air earth and water
off the tips of our
tongue. And one cannot avoid the days. They have
to parade by in all their carnage. The events of them like
images on a shield, we carry thru the streets of
the town
later on our way to the poetry reading. Drunk or
doped before that wild horde who presses in
to get a pick at the bloody hero. And is he?
You bet.

1996

(from *The Journal of John Wieners Is to Be Called 707 Scott Street for Billie Holiday, 1959*)
July 26

On the road again. America does not change. Nor do we, Olson says. We only reveal more of ourselves. Riding in the car with all the windows open. How can I rise to the events of our lives. I am a shrew and nagging bitch as my mother was. I am filled with doubt and too passive. I go where I am told. Anywhere. Take pleasure in doing what I am told. There is no comfort in Nature or God except for the weak. It is my fellow men that deliver me my life. Otherwise I wrap up in myself like an evening primrose in the sun. Nature is good for analogy. We think we learn lessons from her but she deserts us at the moment of action. That is why we remain savages. Underneath. And our civilization remains a jungle. Live it at night and see.

But traveling on the road to Sausalito, San Francisco then Big Sur, I see how much the earth still surrounds us. Willow Road juts out in my memory. Mission San Rafael Archangel. Redwood Highway. Where man is going now, who knows. The earth no longer need be his home. Maybe this means the end of the old world. And man, on the minutest of planets may and can range thru all of space. To the very frontiers, limits, barriers of outer worlds. Lucky Drive. End construction project. With what frightening speed we move ahead. This must be necessary: Paradise Drive. The children are quieting down now. The witch drives her old Chevrolet, her long black hair blowing out the window.

1996

The Black Mountain Blues

I want to go back to old black mountain this morning,
I want to sing old songs with Dorn and Charlie O,
I want to take my bleeding heart,
I wanta break my bleeding heart
all over this city's asphalt floor,
I want to swish a mountain shadow,
hear tree frogs say good morning, mister,
and the red clay roads will deep my feet in mud,
I want to sleep in the same pants every night
I want to eat spaghetti every night

with the ladies who play gay guitars
and the boys who lie down
in rain to see the stars,
I want the copperheads, the roses and the streams,
I want the mountains, and Lake Eden in my dreams
I want to go back to Black Mountain in the morning
and play ping pong in the cellar,
hear Billie Holliday through the woods
drink half a dollar wine till I'm drunk for good,
I want to leave the neon and the cement towers,
I want to spend my life in loneliness,
without a cheap lover to wash my face,
a lover who will fill my place when I turn my back,
I want to go back so fast
I want to be lonely,
I want only the shadow of those black mountains,
and kiss the rain, that's my roman fountains,
I want to catch lunar moths,
and pee on the chairs.
I want to walk down mornings,
and pick up the mail,
I want to see the men in grey come from the
county jails to clean our fields,
to wash our faces,
I want to go back to those empty rooms,
and taste the dirty delight of lonely nights,
I want to cry in bed again,
and sleep under windows that have no glass,
drink my beer with ten outcasts that make up
the people, make up for lovers
I leave behind me when I take for cover
under the warm and black hills of black mountain.
I want to roll my cigarettes again, and play piano,
with one finger, I want to walk down pathways and linger
by roses and japanese vines,
I want to hear Miles Davis sing again,
and old Bessie do swing again,
I want to hear the husbands and wives throw ink again

on each other's sink again,
those old tree frogs are calling me, the mountains,
are growing tall for me,
oh take me back, carry me back,
on the morning train, the tuesday train,
I shall go by the lumber yards,
and wait in the stations, the colored pardners,
I left behind, at Peek's, at all the
old familiar roads I bicycled,
I will ride again by the rapids,
and see the dogs catch lizards in the dawn,
oh those old grey mountains are calling,
those pink mountains are calling,
so it takes my lover away from me,
it brings me to a lonely country,
I go there, I run there, to see Charlie O,
and Connie O, with the dogs and babies who swear and wear no clothes,
I will give up my heart I will go in the dark to go back
to them someday, and take the beautiful bends, the road
that shows me my end, alone, alone, is the road I see,
but still I'll go there and I'll kiss the hornets and bees,
I'll hear foxes under my window,
I'll be afraid to go out in the dark, and I'll
whisper into my pillow, your light's gone out,
your light is up in the city, in bed with somebody else,
but it doesn't matter, in the mountains,
it doesn't matter in the hills, cuz there I'll be,
and there I'll wander from room to room,
from fellow to fonder, I'll take my
chances in the hills again,
I'll go and take my chances in the hills, again,
so mister man, buy a one-way ticket, I'm going back
dad I'm leaving this circuit, I'm cutting my space, I'm leaving
this time, I'm going on mountain, eastern mountain saving time,
so take your ticket for me, I'll kiss you goodbye,
I'll have nobody now, to kiss me and cry,
I'll have no lips to keep mine dry,
I'll be alone, there,

I'll be alone with nobody to care
for me,
but still I'm taking that trip,
and it's the end of the road,
but the end shall be high up
and I'll die with gold
clothes on,
in the black mountains of northern carolina,
I'll die and my face will have a silver-lining.

2002

PART IV | AFFILIATES

who visited Black Mountain College or published in the *Black Mountain Review* by year

PAUL METCALF | 1917–1999

The great-grandson of Herman Melville, Paul Metcalf was born in East Milton, Massachusetts. In 1946, he moved to the small community of Skyland, North Carolina, southwest of Black Mountain. Although he never enrolled at BMC, Metcalf and his wife often visited the nearby college, unofficially sitting in on classes and taking in student and faculty musical and theatrical performances. Composing genre-defying books that mix fiction, poetry, journalism, historical documents, and photography, Metcalf earned the admiration of Robert Creeley, Guy Davenport, and Jonathan Williams. He employed a collage method derived from his reading of Ezra Pound (*The Cantos*), William Carlos Williams (*Paterson*), and Charles Olson (*The Maximus Poems*). Metcalf's major works include *Genoa* (1965), *Patagonia* (1971), *The Middle Passage* (1976), and *I-57* (1988). Like Olson, Metcalf was especially concerned with the relationship of language to myth, history, and place.

Author's Note

I am a lifelong baseball fan, brought up with, and still pledging allegiance to, the Boston Red Sox. I therefore need no lessons in suffering. Despite being relentlessly partisan, though, I believe that I recognize Quality, wherever it appears. It was not difficult for me to be attracted, early on, to Mr. Willie Howard Mays. The attention and affection I have directed toward him, over the years, was perhaps eased by the fact that he played in the "other league." (Had he been a dreaded Yankee, this poem no doubt would not have been written.)

In my casual baseball reading, I stumbled on a paperback called *My Greatest Day in Baseball*, in which several well-known players chose a particular day or play to celebrate—and for Willie, it was this unearthly throw. What caught my eye, in the description, was this phrase: "So that he threw like a discus thrower."

Baseball is drama. It is also comedy (grown men playing a kid's game, for high pay)—but it is comic in the highest sense of that term. It occurred to me that good comedy is produced when the artist takes an absurd idea and pursues it literally and seriously, to its conclusion. Why not take Willie's throw and treat it as Willie's throw *back*—back to the infield, the catcher—and back in history, to the Greek Olympiad—Willie as the young Greek, hurling the discus?

From there on, it was just a question of mining the sources, and letting the pieces fall together: Willie the young Greek, hurling the discus in the Polo Grounds, August 25, 1951.

The throw went *back*. May it, with this small celebration, hurtle forward, from Greece, to New York, to wherever the games may be played. Cheers!

—Paul Metcalf

Willie's Throw

I REMEMBER
what I think nobody else remembers . . .
the way the clouds were against the sky . . .
they were no longer white
but ribbed with gray too,
and you had the feeling that
if you could reach high enough
you could
get the gray out of there.

Still, for the greatest day ever for Willie Howard Mays, you have to go all the way back to his rookie season in 1951. That was the year the Giants made their miraculous comeback in the last six weeks of the season to tie the Dodgers, who had led by 13½ games in mid-August . . .

And the one play that may have turned around the whole year for both teams came on August 15. The Giants' streak had just about started—four in a row—and they were playing Brooklyn at the Polo Grounds. It was a 1–1 ball game, eighth inning, one out, Billy Cox on third, Ralph Branca on first and Carl Furillo up. In the stands there were 21,007 fidgety fans.

I lived with my Aunt Sarah and her family. I was born, May 6, 1931, not in Fairfield but in a nearby place with almost the same name—Westfield—but the marriage of my father and mother didn't last much more than a year after that, and then I went to live at Aunt Sarah's house in Fairfield.

They were kids themselves, my mother and father—no more than 18, either one of them, when I was born. But he was a baseball player, and my mother was a wonderful athlete herself—a star runner who held a couple of women's track records in that part of the country . . .

Furillo hit a fly ball into right center field. Mays, playing over in left-center for the notorious pull-hitting Furillo, had to come a long distance to make the catch. Make it he did, on the dead run, gloved hand extended and that was the second out. But Cox on third had tagged up and was heading home with the lead run. And Cox could run like a deer. When Mays caught the fly ball, running full speed toward the right field foul line, he was moving away from the play. If he stopped dead and threw, he couldn't possibly get any zip on the ball . . .

. . . STRAIGHTWAY HE DREW ALL EYES UPON HIMSELF, WHEN THEY BEHELD HIS FRAME, SUCH PROMISE OF GREAT DEEDS WAS THERE.

. . . So he improvised. He caught the ball, planted his left foot and pivoted away from the plate . . .

What I did, though, was catch the ball and kind of let
its force in my glove help spin me completely around.

. . . so that he threw like a discus thrower . . .

The art of throwing from a circle 8 ft. 2½ in. in diameter to the greatest distance, and so that it falls within a 90° sector marked on the ground, an implement weighing 8 lb. 6.4 oz. known as a discus. The sport was common in the days of Homer, who mentions it repeatedly. It formed part of the pentathlon, or quintuple games, in the ancient Olympic games . . .

Fans in the bleachers must have wondered what in the world their boy was doing.

. . . The discus must be slung out and not really thrown at all; the athlete's difficulty lies in controlling an implement which can be retained under and against the hand and wrist only by centrifugal force and such slight pressure as the tips of the fingers are able to exert.

AT ONCE, THEN, CONFIDENT IN HIS POWERS HE MEASURES, NOT THE ROUGH ACRES OF THE PLAIN, BUT THE SKY'S EXPANSE WITH HIS RIGHT ARM, AND WITH EITHER KNEE BENT EARTHWARD HE GATHERS UP HIS STRENGTH AND WHIRLS THE DISK ABOVE HIM AND HIDES IT IN THE CLOUDS.

One time, outside of a flower store, I saw an emblem
of this guy with wings that said you could send flowers
by wire. And when the wind blew on the overhead
utility lines and made the wires sing, I'd always think to
myself that must be flowers going through the
wires, somebody sending them to somebody else . . .

. . . WHAT POWER HAS MAN AGAINST THE GODS?

Preparatory to making a throw the athlete holds the discus in the right (best) hand so that the edge rests against the joints of the fingers nearest to the tips. He takes up his position in the rear half of an 8 ft. 2½ in. circle with the feet about 18 in. apart and his left side turned in the direction in which the throw is to be made. The discus is swung up above the head, where it is met and supported by the fingers of the left hand. The right arm next swings back until it reaches a point behind and higher than the right shoulder. From this position, after two or three preliminary swings have been made and the right hand is at its highest point, the athlete commences a 1¼ turn in a kind of dancing time with the right arm hanging loosely down. The first pivotal movement is upon the left foot; when a half turn has been made the weight is transferred to the right foot, upon which the turning movement continues. As the left foot again takes the ground, at the front edge of the circle, the right leg begins to push the body forward and there is a violent turn of the right shoulder, but the arm is still kept trailing behind and the actual throwing movement does not commence until the right arm is well off the right shoulder. The left leg forms a point of resistance as the throw is made and the discus departs through the air mounting upwards . . .

But Willie, making a complete whirling pivot on the dead run, cut loose with a tremendous peg . . .

> . . . AND HOLDING IT ALOFT SUMMONS UP THE STRENGTH OF HIS UNYIELDING SIDE AND VIGOROUS ARMS, AND FLINGS IT WITH A MIGHTY WHIRL, SPRINGING FORWARD AFTER IT HIMSELF. WITH A TERRIFIC BOUND THE QUOIT FLIES THROUGH THE EMPTY AIR, AND EVEN IN ITS FLIGHT REMEMBERS THE HAND THAT FLUNG IT AND KEEPS IT TO ITS DUE PATH, NOR ATTAINS A DOUBTFUL OR A NEIGHBORING GOAL . . .

The throw came to the plate as a bullet and Whitey Lockman, the cut-off man . . .

(. . . the good Lord willin' and the creeks don't rise . . .)

. . . let it go through and Wes Westrum, the catcher, caught it belt high and slapped a tag on a desperately sliding Cox. For a long time . . . the stands were silent, not quite certain they had seen right. Then they exploded when they realized Mays had turned a certain run into a miracle inning-ending double play.

. . . AND MAKES TREMBLE THE GREEN BUTTRESSES AND SHADY HEIGHTS OF THE THEATER . . .

EDDIE BRANNICK: *The finest play I ever saw.*
CHARLIE DRESSEN: *He'll have to do it again before I'll believe it.*
CARL FURILLO: *The play is impossible. And that's that.*

THE BOX SCORE

BROOKLYN

	A.B	R.	H.	P.	A.
Furillo rf	4	0	1	5	0
Reese ss	4	1	1	1	2
Snider cf	4	0	0	2	0
Pafko lf	4	0	0	1	0
Campan'la c ..	3	0	1	5	0
Hodges 1b	3	0	0	8	0
Cox 3b	3	0	2	1	1
Ter'l'ger 2b ...	2	0	0	1	3
Robinson 2b ..	1	0	0	0	0
Branca p	3	0	1	0	2
TOTALS ...	31	1	6	24	8

NEW YORK

	A.B	R.	H.	P.	A.
Stanky 2b	3	0	1	1	3
Dark ss	4	1	1	1	1
Mueller rf	3	0	0	2	0
Irvin lf	3	0	1	2	0
Lockman 1b ..	3	0	0	10	0
Mays cf	3	1	1	3	1
Westrum c ..	3	1	1	7	1
Hearn p	3	0	0	0	2
TOTALS ...	28	3	5	27	11

BROOKLYN	**000**	**000**	**100**	**—1**
NEW YORK	**100**	**000**	**02x**	**—3**

RBI–Irvin, Campanella, Westrum 2. 2b–Dark. HR–Westrum. DB–Branca, Rees & Hodges; Mays & Westrum. LOB–Brooklyn 3, New York 2. BB–Off Branca 1. SO—Branca 5, Hearn 5. WP–Hearn. Balk–Hearn. Hearn–(W, 11-7). Branca–(L, 10-4). Umpires–Warneke, Goetz, Jorda, & Dascoli.T–2:10.A–21,007.

DR. UHLEY: *According to the textbooks every human being has a kind of layer of fat on his back . . .*
WILLIE: *So?*
DR. UHLEY: *So?*
WILLIE: *I mean, what's the problem?*
DR. UHLEY: *The problem is you don't have any fat.*

WILLIE: *I thought you said everybody does.*

DR. UHLEY: *I didn't say everybody does. The book says everybody does. Up till now, the book's been right.*

WILLIE: *Well, if I don't have the fat, what do I have?*

DR. UHLEY: *Willie, all you've got for a back is one continuous muscle.*

Bibliography

Carmichael, John P., editor. *My Greatest Day in Baseball.* New York, 1968. *Encyclopedia Britannica.* Chicago, 1943 edition.

Mays, Willie & Charles Einstein. *Willie Mays: My Life in and out of Baseball.* New York, 1966.

New York Times. August 16, 1951.

Statius, Publis Papinus. *Thebaid.* J. H. Mozeley, trans. 2 Vol., London & Cambridge, 1961.

1979

PAUL BLACKBURN | 1926–1971

One of Donald Allen's Black Mountain poets, Paul Blackburn was born in St. Albans, Vermont. Like Paul Carroll, Larry Eigner, and Denise Levertov, Blackburn never visited the BMC campus. In the late 1940s, at the encouragement of his mentor, Ezra Pound, Blackburn began corresponding with Robert Creeley, who later invited Blackburn to be a contributing editor of *BMR*. Through Creeley, Blackburn forged fruitful relationships with Cid Corman, the publisher of *Origin*, and BMC poets such as Levertov, Charles Olson, Joel Oppenheimer, and Jonathan Williams. Serving as the New York distributor of *BMR*, Blackburn ensured the magazine's circulation in Greenwich Village's 1950s bohemian scene. He infused his "open form" poetics—derived from Pound and Williams and later developed alongside Olson, Creeley, and Robert Duncan—with the diction, imagery, and tempo of New York City. For example, he popularized the poetry subgenre of the "subway poem" and, later, like John Wieners, composed in journal form. Unfortunately, his poetic inventiveness and keen social observations are sometimes accompanied by the sexual objectification of women. A key organizer of poetry readings in the early 1960s at Café Le Metro and St. Mark's Church in-the-Bowery, Blackburn was also an admired translator of Provençal troubadour verse; the Spanish medieval epic *El cantar de mio Cid* (*The Poem of the Cid*); poetry by Federico García Lorca, Octavio Paz, and Pablo Picasso; and short stories by Julio Cortázar.

The Continuity

The bricklayer tells the busdriver
and I have nothing to do but listen:

Th' holdup at the liquor-store, d'ja hear?
            a detective
watch't   'm for ten minutes
            He took it anyway
            Got away down Broadway   Yeah?
                                                Yeah.

                        And me:

                the one on the Circle?
                                                Yeah.
Yeah?   I was in there early tonight.

                The continuity.
            A dollar forty-
two that I spent on a bottle of wine
is now in a man's pocket going down Broadway.

Thus far the transmission is oral.

Then a cornerboy borrows my pencil
to keep track of his sale of newspapers.

1954

The Yawn

The black-haired girl

with the big

brown

eyes

on the Queens train coming

in to work, so

opens her mouth so beautifully

wide

in a ya-aawn, that

two stops after she has left the train

I have only to think of her   and I

o-oh-aaaww-hm

wow !

1958

Clickety-Clack

(for Lawrence Ferlinghetti)

I took
a coney island of the mind
to the coney
island of the flesh
the brighton local
riding
past church avenue, beverly, cortelyou, past
avenues h & j
king's highway, neck road, sheepshead bay,
brighton, all the way to stillwell
avenue
that hotbed of assignation
clickety-clack

I had started reading when I got on
and somewhere down past newkirk reached
number 29 and read aloud
The crowd
in the train
looked startled at first but settled down
to enjoy the bit
even if they did think I
was insane or something
and when I reached the line : " the cock
of flesh at last cries out and has his glory
moment God "
some girl sitting opposite me with golden hair
fresh from the bottle began to stare dis-
approvingly and wiggle as tho she had ants
somewhere where it counted
And sorry to say
5 lines later the poem finished and I
started to laugh like hell Aware
of the dirty look I was getting I

stared back at her thighs imagining
what she had inside those toreador pants besides
                    her bathing suit and, well
                    we both got off at stillwell
Watching her high backside sway and swish down that
street of tattoo artists, franks 12 inches long, past
                    the wax museum and a soft-drink
                    stand with its white inside,
I stepped beside her and said: " Let's
fling that old garment of repentance, baby ! "
              smitten, I
hadn't noticed her 2 brothers were behind me

                    clickety-clack

                    Horseman, pass by

1960

Two Songs for the Opp

1. Stay drunk!

   that's my motto .

   Then you'll never have to know

   if the girl love you or no

                    (hee hee hee

                    nor will she

2. Play gui-

   tar, go to the bar

hope there's one hand will caress

and undress

But pints to go

before you sleep

(har,   har,

nobody care

1963

The 1965 Season

Bottom of the 7th, the
first time Berra has caught all season :
he leads off & singles, that
makes it 2 for 3 .
But those Mets

Bases loaded and no outs; one run in. The
Phils change pitchers &
Ed Roebuck of Brooklyn Dodgers fame comes in
& strikes out his first batter.
Then the Phils make a double play.
Well,
one run is better than nothing,
        that makes 2 .

Top of the 8th, the Mets
amazing—a double play—
It takes a couple of more men, but
Al Jackson strikes out his 10th man in the game.

That ties the club record.

Roebuck strikes out his 1st batter this inning, too.
Then Kranepool lines to left &
          Christopher flies out short center,
                    ends that half.

"Number 9, Jim Hickman into left for Christopher.
Number 3, Billy Cowan, into center for Swoboda."
Defensive moves, o Casey.
But Thomas rips a single past Klaus at third.
Tony Taylor also singles between third and short.
Gus Triandos with 2 strikes, and Jackson
sends thru a wild pitch, the batters move up,
here we go, &
                    well, Jackson strikes him out
                    —a new Mets' record with 11 .
okay, there's one out.
Ruben Amaro, sacrifice fly, drives Thomas in.
John Wesley Convington on deck : 6 homeruns
11 RBI's (o, he had his at Milwaukee in
          57–58, those great years)   .   He
goes to 3 & 2, takes the payoff, it
goes to Hunt, to Kranepool
          (Cookie Rojas on deck)
                                        in time .
                                        it's all over

METS   2
PHILLIES   1

          Well, it's a game, no?

1966

16 Sloppy Haiku

for Bob Reardon

I say what I mean

Nothing else is

given to do, say,

even poems

*

First large

table on the left

as you enter

His chair is turned up

*

Two years ago

Jim died

doing battle with a truck

on Third Avenue

from a motorbike seat

shaking and

cold sober

*

Love is not enuf

Friendship is not enuf

Not even art

is / Life is too much

*

It has been

seasonably cold

messy weather, the

length of his

illness

*

Bad weather over-

head, slush underfoot

Who'd want to get

out of the hospital

anyway?

*

God's blood drained

donations are required

One pint per man, no

deposit, no return

*

His three sisters,

Crapsey, Topsey, and Morgan le Faye,

want to plant him in Arlington Cemetery

Eat him slowly

*

Apostates are usually interested

in poetic values and relationships

not dogma

*

Briar-rose, primrose,

and periwinkle, all

three of you bitches can

kiss my French-Irish ass

*

Cinquefoil and bat's blood

got at the wake of the new moon,

(add poplar leaves and soot)

will protect witches against cramps

while flying

*

Nothing not accepted,

nothing not exchanged,

that sense of it .

The possibility, not

farewell

*

We try

hard as we can

to be only what we are, fulcrum

for the work .

*

Isn't . is

it not terrible, Eunice,

that there's a love

doesn't need an object?

*

A sound you'll never

hear again:

pissing in the toilet

about 3 A.M.

*

He had a tendency to finish

what he did

cleanly,

minus something

Find it .

1966

Journal 5.XI.67

(from *The Journals*)

How is it I keep remembering
after all those / these facts,
this flack
keeps . coming?
It all drives back upon the brain .
After yesterday, two things were
plain-ly set against the mindfall
The sandspit in Arkansas
after a motorcycle ride in the November day
was warmed 3 cigarettes & talk
Or how explain the marks of branches in the
sand, with no mantrack near . Complexities
of the very simple—what?
Standing at the
edge of I had to pee
into the Mississippi . And
later, cottonheaded from whiskey,
did not spend, tho she did from my
tongue . this young wife
of someone else, too up tight from
cars & bikes pulling into the driveway
where was her car? It had run
out of gas . o yes.
The anxiety (plus too much whiskey) kept me down .
Here was a quim I wanted to do wonderful things in
taste was sweet and sour
The rest had left : Bobby & Lee on bike
it must have been damnably cold
that hour of morning
Bobby's nose falling off . the wind
up Lee's sleeves . And all for
a spider hanging inconclusively
swinging, flowers in the vermouth

bottle, yellow, chrysanthemums, cost 75 ¢ a bunch
          at the market as opposed .

Two cups of coffee and the magazine in
the bathroom . would be .
CYCLE WORLD 1966 . The Road Test
Annual . which only Sara
wins . An-other
terrible Sunday morning in the world,
everybody juiced and coffeed
Memphis is on the river, cold
Sunday paper on the porch & torch
the flowers stand
     there
the motor warming up
          turning over
The arm stretches out again
to
  no / one /there .

1975

WILLIAM BRONK | 1918–1999

Aside from the time he studied at Dartmouth College and Harvard University, William Bronk spent most of his life in Hudson Falls, New York, where, after serving in the Second World War and briefly teaching at Union College, he ran the family coal and lumber business until he retired in the late 1970s. In the 1950s, Bronk's poetry was published in "little" magazines such as *BMR* and *Origin* and in more mainstream publications such as the *New Yorker* and *Poetry*. Often compared to Wallace Stevens, Bronk uses poetic language to explore philosophical ideas (e.g., metaphysics and ethics) and interrogate fixed notions of time and space. He imagines poetry as the ideal expressive mode for the individual living in an uncertain age—a way of making and accessing "a world beyond our world which holds our world."[1] Although he did not follow projective verse principles, Bronk earned the admiration of both Charles Olson and Robert Creeley, and he was, according to David W. Clippinger, the final poet cut from Donald Allen's *NAP* manuscript.[2] In 1982, he received the National Book Award for Poetry for *Life Supports: New and Collected Poems* (1981).

At Tikal

Mountains they knew, and jungle, the sun, the stars—
these seemed to be there. But even after they slashed
the jungle and burned it and planted the comforting corn,
they were discontent. They wanted the shape of things.
They imagined a world and it was as if it were there
—a world with stars in their places and rain that came
when they called. It closed them in. Stone by stone,
as they built this city, these temples, they built this world.
They believed it. This was the world, and they,
of course, were the people. Now trees make up
assemblies and crowd in the wide plazas. Trees
climb the stupendous steps and rubble them.
In the jungle, the temples are little mountains again.

It is always hard like this, not having a world,
to imagine one, to go to the far edge
apart and imagine, to wall whether in
or out, to build a kind of cage for the sake
of feeling the bars around us, to give shape to a world.
And oh, it is always a world and not the world.

1956

Blue Spruces in Pairs, a Bird Bath Between

Seen by starlight from the window, fat
blue spruces patch the lawn with darker dark.

Arranged in pairs. People no longer plant
these trees in pairs, with bird baths set between.

Fashions in ornamental planting change.
Houses and yards lose style in twenty years.

Seen by starlight. The universal stars.
Something here is certainly laughably wrong.

Ideas are always wrong. Their separateness
causes a threat to neuter each other out

and leave us without a world as it does here:
heavens and styles collide meaninglessly.

The unsubmissive mind has freedom to be
nothing, worldless—not to exist at all.

Because the various world we sense is not
ever apprehended as one, or formed as one,

ideas are always wrong, always unfixed,
and often their power to make the world real is lost.

Huge factors stand ready to leap in
to alter or destroy a world we defend alone.

1964

For an Early Italian Musician

Listening now to his music, how
one wishes to have been the musician, and so
to be beautiful forever as his music is,
and he in it, who is now
only his music, which is his world.

How one always wishes for an end
—to be complete.

And there is also this:
that one wishes to last, that one needs to make
a world for survival, which cannot be done
simply, or soon, but by a slow

crystal on crystal accretion of a made
world, a world made to last.

One is nothing with no world.

1964

The Real World

The real world is no world though without
our knowing it may well be. We can't
say anything about it: how it is
or why, what way it may, but it is there.

They studied the animals, how they react,
earth sciences, measured the interplay
of energies, money matters, how man
treats man, or has in time,—his history.

Nothing we say makes sense, finally.
All right; we believe certain things.
There are things we can say within that belief unless
they negate it. None of them deals with a real world.

There is a real world which does make sense.
It is beyond our knowing or speaking but it is there.

1972

PAUL CARROLL | 1927–1996

Born in Chicago, Carroll served in the US Navy, then attended Illinois Wesleyan University before transferring to the University of Chicago, where he graduated with an MA in English literature in 1952. Like Paul Blackburn, Larry Eigner, and Denise Levertov, Carroll did not study at or visit BMC. However, his Beat-influenced poetry circulated in magazines of the postwar period, including *BMR* and *Origin*. Though a formidable poet, Carroll is often remembered as an editor who championed provocative literature. From 1957 to 1958, Carroll—a graduate student at the time—worked as an editor, alongside Irving Rosenthal, at the *Chicago Review*, which published excerpts from William Burroughs's *Naked Lunch* (1959) in the Spring 1958 and Fall 1958 issues. He resigned from that post when the University of Chicago's administration pressured the magazine's editors to redact passages from the soon-to-be-published winter issue that included further selections from Burroughs's novel. Those Burroughs excerpts were ultimately published in a new magazine Carroll cofounded with Rosenthal called *Big Table*. Carroll edited issues 2–5 of *Big Table*, showcasing new American poets, including John Ashbery, LeRoi Jones/Amiri Baraka, Paul Blackburn, Robert Creeley, Robert Duncan, Allen Ginsberg, and Denise Levertov. Carroll taught for many years at the University of Illinois at Chicago, where he started the Program for Writers. He also founded the Poetry Center of Chicago and won the Chicago Poet's Award in 1985. After retiring from teaching in 1992, Carroll died in 1996 near Vilas, North Carolina, about an hour north of Asheville and Black Mountain. He published several volumes of poetry, including *Odes* (1969), *The Luke Poems* (1971), *New and Selected Poems* (1978), and *The Garden of Earthly Delights* (1986). Along with Charles Olson's "The Kingfishers" and Robert Duncan's "A Poem Beginning with a Line by Pindar," Carroll's "Father" helped establish the reputation of BMC writers.

Father

How sick I get
of your ghost. And
of looking at this tintype on my desk
of you as a cocky kid—
Kilkenney's coast, rocks & suncracked turf
giving the resilience to your countenance
as you try to seem so nonchalant, posing
in a rented Sunday morning-suit
spats & bowler hat:
a greenhorn off the boat. Yet something in

that twist of fist, knuckles taut
around the cane-knob, shows
how you already seem to know you will transform
that old cow-pasture of Hyde Park
into your own oyster.

The way you did.

And that other picture—
stuck somewhere in the dresser drawer
among the Christmas handkerchiefs,
the rubbers, poems & busted rosary beads.
Posed beneath 3 palms
on Tampa Beach's boardwalk,
a stocky man who made his millions by himself.
And can quarrel with congressmen from Washington
about the New Deal bank acts.
Or call Mayor Kelly crooked to his face.

Hair, bone,
brains & cock & skin
rotten in the earth these 16 years.
Remember, father, how Monsignor Keelty
(whose mouth you always said
looked exactly like a turkey's ass)
boomed out Latin above your coffin at Mount Olivet?

But as the raw October rain
rasped against our limousine
guiding the creeping cars back into Chicago,
Jack, your first born,
picked his nose:
and for an instant flicked a look
to ask if I too knew
you were dead for good—
St. Patrick's paradise a club
for priests & politicians
you wouldn't get caught dead in.
You used to like to call me "Bill." And kiss me.
Or take me to the Brookfield Zoo. Or stuff
english toffee in my mouth—but always
only after you had cursed
& with a bedroom slipper whacked
the tar out of Jack. This morning,

broke as usual,
no woman in my bed,
I threw 6 bucks away
for a shave & haircut at the Drake.
And looked again for you. On Oak St. beach

gazing beyond the bathers & the boats
I suddenly searched the horizon, father,
for that old snapshot of Picasso
& his woman Dora Maar.
Picasso bald & 60. But both
in exaltation, emerging
with incredible sexual dignity
from the waters of the Golfe Juan.

The sun tattooed light on the lake.
A red bone of a fish.
The semen of the ghost.

I left the lake. But tripped
in the quick dark
of the Division St. underpass. Then picked a way past
newspaper scraps, puddles
& a puckered beachball.
I looked for dirty drawings on the wall.
Traffic crunches overhead.
This underpass is endless.

1960

Plotinus Refuses to Sit for a Portrait

If watching
pigeons flittering
in and out of the Arch of Titus, catching
that exact angle
at which belly blackens, leaving
only pimply skin of wings
to usher in the early Roman dusk,

has any value,
then so have these:
to recognize apricots are not precisely globular;
or catch desire twitch
in a widow's eye
like hunch of leaves of ailanthus tree
preparing for winter;

or see sun, rising,
leek in crevices
of cobbles along the Via Appia. Prizing
such things,
his fingers most famous
in Rome, Carterius justly boasts
with oil or charcoal sketch

he guarantees
a kind of immortality.
Asked to pose, Plotinus shrugs and laughs.
That god
he's got inside
twists, restless. Art a fake. It's life. And life?
Hay for the animals.

1969

Song in the Studio of Paul Klee

The moon of the Moors is not outside tonight.
It is in the heart of an old angora cat
and beats as she sleeps
in my lap. Tomorrow afternoon
the final leaf
will fall. It will be blue.
And if by chance it condescends to float
on this blue windowsill
we will hear, as it hits, the tinkle of a flute
or wood cuckoos popping from six cuckoo clocks.
These slovenly clouds that pass
between the cubes of muscle in my brain
are those I counted once
on a cold and polished marble table top
at uncle's restaurant;
or flat on my back from the bottom of a boat
I shall one day see
while feeling the rolls of the boat as the pilot plunges the pole
and sails to where there is no moon at all.

1969

Song After Making Love

Sometimes I want to be a cloud
Drifting like a barnacle goose or a galleon
Into the winter home of God

The green of these trees
The grass green as oxygen
The green of my excited heart

Shadows of bird between the bones
Blood feels sweet as if moving in maple trees
A part of me is grass

I close my eyes
I'm empty
At the same time full
Like a galaxy in daylight

2008

LARRY EIGNER | 1927–1996

Born with cerebral palsy because of a poorly executed forceps delivery, Larry Eigner lived for much of his life with his parents, Bessie and Israel, in Swampscott, Massachusetts. He completed high school through homeschooling (local teachers came to the family home) and college-level coursework by correspondence through the University of Chicago. After a chance encounter with Cid Corman's radio show, *This Is Poetry*, in 1949, Eigner struck up a friendship with Corman, who, in turn, introduced him to Robert Creeley; he soon became friends with poets such as Robert Duncan, Denise Levertov, Charles Olson, and Jonathan Williams. Eigner—who typed his poems on a 1940 Royal manual typewriter with only his right index finger and thumb—was especially impressed by, and drawn to, Olson's projective use of the typewriter and reimagining of the page's spatial possibilities. On the "glassed-in front porch" from which he typed his poems and correspondence in Swampscott, Eigner attentively observed, contemplated, and documented the daily passing phenomena.[3] Creeley's Divers Press published Eigner's first book, *From the Sustaining Air*, in 1953; Williams's Jargon Society published Eigner's first major volume, *On My Eyes*, in 1960, with Olson and Levertov helping select poems for inclusion; and that same year Donald Allen categorized him as one of the Black Mountain poets in *NAP*. In 1978, he moved to Berkeley, California, and entered a group home (Cornerstone House), and in 1979 he settled, finally, into a house purchased by his brother and conservator, Richard. Poets Robert Grenier and Kathleen Frumkin shared the home with Eigner and served as his legal caretakers for a decade. During this late period, Eigner became a popular and influential figure in the Bay Area poetry scene. In 2010, Stanford University Press issued the four-volume *Collected Poems of Larry Eigner* (edited by Curtis Faville and Robert Grenier). The University of Alabama Press published *Letters to Jargon: The Correspondence between Larry Eigner and Jonathan Williams* (edited by Andrew Rippeon) in 2019 and *Sustaining Air: The Life of Larry Eigner* by Jennifer Bartlett (with contributions by George Hart) in 2023.[4]

F e s t e

The children were frightened by crescendoes
cars coming fowards in the movies

That is,before they found out love,
that is, Comedy

          the cheeks blew
  music rises and continues

and the sea does

and there were no accidents today
the bombs showered us in the air

composed in 1951

V o i c e , F r e e

 come to stand through
 intimate dark
               a
 sympathetic surface

slide threshold of words
 by sincere, easy
   breath registered
                    a

   sober
   synonymous story

composed ca. 1951–53

from the sustaining air

fresh air

There is the clarity of shore
And shadow, mostly, brilliance

summer
        the billows of August

When, wandering, I look from my page

I say nothing

   when asked

I am, finally, an incompetent, after all

composed in 1953

IT SOUNDED

 and tangled dry—

          like fire
      at the start of the day
         the engines
               control
but the wind in the twigs
or thistles, stalk

      the birds are violent
      the spring

 they function by shouting

 suddenly

all day

the houses stand some paint in
glass the dusty sun

with the fresh air

and the man who fixes the roof

top and

the transformer below

nothing except the wires
and the trees

    and the boys climbing
                 the shed
          (to leap
          and break

composed in 1955

Keep me still, for I do not want to dream

I live in this house, walls being plastered
all my life. the apple tree still standing
my life built, the minutes keeping on
the walls cross, standing around
                        a distinct company
    projection, the clothes wave
          briefly, touch beyond eyes

weed the garden
the light burns away the street
the peaceful corn salt in the empty night,

among chickens, sparrows and dogs,
the pigeons limping easily on the roof,
the cat sticking his limbs through the sewer
his claws agape, naked
pondering

  he goes to sleep and wakes up
   he plays dead, hanging ..
              rain melts
   and hail fans on the wind

     the thistles, when they get old

  nearly everything gets in
  and then we close up

          the flowers are hidden lately

composed in 1956

the knowledge of death, and now
 knowledge of the stars

    there is one end
                and the endless

   Room at the center

     passage /in no time

    a rail   thickets hills   grass

composed in 1960

so the words go up
into thin air

parlor   the speaking
room

birds pass the window
a plane lengthens through fog
or cloud bends away
the curves together

the phone the hallway
all my life

composed in 1965

IRVING LAYTON | 1912–2006

The Romanian-born Irving Layton was raised and educated in Montréal, Québec. He earned a BS in agriculture from MacDonald College and an MA in political science from McGill University. A leading proponent of modernism in Canada, Layton began corresponding with Robert Creeley and Charles Olson in 1953, initiating the cross-cultural exchanges between American and Canadian poets represented in the pages of Canadian magazines like *Contact* and *CIV/n*. That same year, in September, Olson invited Layton, over the phone, to join the faculty at BMC, though he never made it down to the campus; according to Ekbert Faas and Sabrina Reed, "Due to his past political activities as 'a hot left-winger,' Layton himself was not allowed to cross the US border."[5] Donald Allen considered including Layton in *NAP* but ultimately decided against it because of his citizenship—though no author's poetry appeared more frequently in *BMR*. Layton also served on the editorial board of *BMR*. Creeley's Divers Press and Jonathan Williams's Jargon Society published two of Layton's early collections of poetry: *In the Midst of My Fever* (1954) and *The Improved Binoculars* (1956), respectively.

Westmount Doll

For saying this
curse me to see seven Canadian winters
        but your emptied stare
is the death of all poets. You, depthless,
and your face a school, a discipline,
    magic away the martyrdoms, dissipate
the tragic pneumas in my brain-box
to as little meaning as
            disturbed flox on wet sand.

Or hex me to see
the great black-bearded Agamemnon
        slain by a danceband leader
:bonged on the head on the polished floor:
yet wreathing your brittle fingers you make
    a sweatless funnel through which fall,
insubstantial, love, and mysterious
as the contempt for the harmless
            the desire to strike and dishonour.

Certainly, what fazes me
    even more than the satisfaction
you take in your throat and white shoulders
is that all dark verse,
            Hebrew or Sophoclean,
in your cascading neighbourhood seems
aberrant, out-of-keeping,
a lout or playboy
                        if you know what I mean
discussing the schizoid features
of the Absolute.

1956

A Tall Man Executes a Jig

I

So the man spread his blanket on the field
And watched the shafts of light between the tufts
And felt the sun push the grass towards him;
The noise he heard was that of whizzing flies,
The whistlings of some small imprudent birds,
And the ambiguous rumbles of cars
That made him look up at the sky, aware
Of the gnats that tilted against the wind
And in the sunlight turned to jigging motes.
Fruitflies he'd call them except there was no fruit
About, spoiling to hatch these glitterings,
These nervous dots for which the mind supplied
The closing sentences from Thucydides,
Or from Euclid having a savage nightmare.

II

Jig jig, jig jig. Like miniscule black links
Of a chain played with by some playful
Unapparent hand or the palpitant
Summer haze bored with the hour's stillness.
He felt the sting and tingle afterwards
Of those leaving their orthodox unrest,
Leaving their undulant excitation
To drop upon his sleeveless arm. The grass,
Even the wildflowers become black hairs
And himself a maddened speck among them.
Still the assaults of the small flies made him
Glad at last, until he saw purest joy
In their frantic jiggings under a hair,
So changed from those in the unrestraining air.

III

He stood up and felt himself enormous.
Felt as might Donatello over stone,
Or Plato, or as a man who has held
A loved and lovely woman in his arms
And feels his forehead touch the emptied sky
Where all antinomies flood into light.
Yet jig jig jig, the haloing black jots
Meshed with the wheeling fire of the sun:
Motion without meaning, disquietude
Without sense or purpose, ephemerides
That mottled the resting summer air till
Gusts swept them from his sight like wisps of smoke.
Yet they returned, bring a bee who, seeing
But a tall man, left him for a marigold.

IV

He doffed his aureole of gnats and moved
Out of the field as the sun sank down,
A dying god upon the blood-red hills.
Ambition, pride, the ecstasy of sex,
And all circumstances of delight and grief,
That blood upon the mountain's side, that flood
Washed into a clear incredible pool
Below the ruddied peaks that pierced the sun.
He stood still and waited. If ever
The hour of revelation was come
It was now, here on the transfigured steep.
The sky darkened. Some birds chirped. Nothing else.
He thought the dying god had gone to sleep:
An Indian fakir on his mat of nails.

V

And on the summit of the asphalt road
Which stretched towards the fiery town, the man
Saw one hill raised like a hairy arm, dark

With pines and cedars against the stricken sun
—The arm of Moses or of Joshua.
He dropped his head and let fall the halo
Of mountains, purpling and silent as time,
To see temptation coiled before his feet:
A violated grass snake that lugged
Its intestine like a small red valise.
A cold-eyed skinflint it now was, and not
The manifest of that joyful wisdom,
The mirth and arrogant green flame of life;
Or earth's vivid tongue that flicked in praise of earth.

VI

And the man wept because pity was useless.
"Your jig's up; the flies come like kites," he said
And watched the grass snake crawl towards the hedge,
Convulsing and dragging into the dark
The satchel filled with curses for the earth,
For the odours of warm sedge, and the sun,
A blood-red organ in the dying sky.
Backwards it fell into a grassy ditch
Exposing its underside, white as milk,
And mocked by wisps of hay between its jaws;
And then it stiffened to its final length.
But though it opened its thin mouth to scream
A last silent scream that shook the black sky,
Adamant and fierce, the tall man did not curse.

VII

Beside the rigid snake the man stretched out
In fellowship of death; he lay silent
And still in the heavy grass with eyes shut,
Inhaling the moist odours of the night
Through which his mind tunnelled with flicking tongue
Backwards to caves, mounds, and sunken ledges
And desolate cliffs where come only kites,

And where of perished badgers and racoons
The claws alone remain, gripping the earth.
Meanwhile the green snake crept upon the sky,
Huge, his mailed coat glittering with stars that made
The night bright, and blowing thin wreaths of cloud
Athwart the moon; and as the weary man
Stood up, coiled above his head, transforming all.

1963

DENISE LEVERTOV | 1923–1997

Denise Levertov was the only woman anthologized as a Black Mountain poet in Donald Allen's *NAP*. Like Paul Blackburn, Paul Carroll, and Larry Eigner, she did not study at the college, but she did publish her poetry in *BMR* and *Origin*. Levertov was born in Ilford, Essex, England, to a Russian father and Welsh mother. As a child in Ilford and, later, as a teen in London, she took lessons in painting and especially ballet, while also demonstrating a keen interest in poetry. During the Second World War, however, much of her time and energy was devoted to service in the Civil Nursing Reserve. Upon immigrating to the United States in 1948, Levertov established ties to BMC primarily through Robert Creeley and Robert Duncan. She was introduced to Creeley through her husband, Mitchell Goodman, formerly a schoolmate of Creeley's at Harvard; with Duncan, Levertov participated in a voluminous correspondence that began in 1952. Living in the United States and immersing herself in the poetry and poetics of William Carlos Williams and Charles Olson, Levertov soon discovered an American idiom of her own—"new rhythms in which to write, in accordance with new rhythms of life and speech."[6] This shift in her writing is especially present in *Overland to the Islands* (1958) and *With Eyes at the Back of Our Heads* (1960). Like Olson's "Projective Verse," Levertov's "Some Notes on Organic Form" is one of the touchstones of the new American poetics.

Everything that Acts is Actual

From the tawny light
from the rainy nights
from the imagination finding
itself and more than itself
alone and more than alone
at the bottom of the well where the moon lives,
can you pull me

into December? a lowland
of space, perception of space
towering of shadows of clouds blown upon
clouds over
                    new ground, new made
under heavy December footsteps? *the only*
way to live?

The flawed moon
acts on the truth, and makes
an autumn of tentative
silences.
You lived, but somewhere else,
your presence touched others, ring upon ring,
and changed. Did you think
I would not change?

                                    The black moon
turns away, its work done. A tenderness,
unspoken autumn.
We are faithful
only to the imagination. *What the*
imagination
                seizes
as beauty must be truth. What holds you
to what you see of me is
that grasp alone.

1957

Merritt Parkway

        As if it were
forever that they move, that we
        keep moving—

                Under a wan sky where
                as the lights went on a star
                        pierced the haze & now
                follows steadily
                                a constant
                above our six lanes
                the dreamlike continuum . . .

And the people—ourselves!
      the humans from inside the
      cars, apparent
      only at gasoline stops
                            unsure,
        eyeing each other
                        drink coffee hastily at the
                slot machines & hurry
        back to the cars
                vanish
                into them forever, to
                keep moving—

Houses now & then beyond the
sealed road, the trees / trees, bushes
passing by, passing
        the cars that
                keep moving ahead of
        us, past us, pressing behind us
                                        and

over left, those that come
toward us shining too brightly
moving relentlessly

in six lanes, gliding
north & south, speeding with
a slurred sound—

1958

The Artist

(From the Spanish translation of Toltec Códice de la Real Academia, fol. 315, v.
With the help of Elvira Abascal, who understood the original Toltec.)

The artist: disciple, abundant, multiple, restless.
The true artist: capable, practicing, skillful;
maintains a dialogue with his heart, meets things with his mind.

The true artist: draws out all from his heart,
works with delight, makes things with calm, with sagacity,
works like a true Toltec, composes his objects, works dexterously, invents;
arranges materials, adorns them, makes them adjust.

The carrion artist: works at random, sneers at the people,
makes things opaque, brushes across the surface of the face of things,
works without care, defrauds people, is a thief.

1960

Pleasures

I like to find
what's not found
at once, but lies

within something of another nature,
in repose, distinct.
Gull feathers of glass, hidden

in white pulp: the bones of squid
which I pull out and lay
blade by blade on the draining board—

    tapered as if for swiftness, to pierce
    the heart, but fragile, substance
    belying design.   Or a fruit, *mamey*,

cased in rough brown peel, the flesh
rose-amber, and the seed:
the seed a stone of wood, carved and

polished, walnut-colored, formed
like a brazilnut, but large,
large enough to fill
the hungry palm of a hand.

I like the juicy stem of grass that grows
within the coarser leaf folded round,
and the butteryellow glow
in the narrow flute from which the morning-glory
opens blue and cool on a hot morning.

1960

Life at War

The disasters numb within us
caught in the chest, rolling
in the brain like pebbles. The feeling
resembles lumps of raw dough

weighing down a child's stomach on baking day.
Or Rilke said it, 'My heart . . .
Could I say of it, it overflows
with bitterness . . . but no, as though

its contents were simply balled into
formless lumps, thus
do I carry it about.'
The same war

continues.
We have breathed the grits of it in, all our lives,
our lungs are pocked with it,
the mucous membrane of our dreams
coated with it, the imagination
filmed over with the gray filth of it:

the knowledge that humankind,
delicate Man, whose flesh
responds to a caress, whose eyes
are flowers that perceive the stars,

whose music excels the music of birds,
whose laughter matches the laughter of dogs,
whose understanding manifests designs
fairer than the spider's most intricate web,

still turns without surprise, with mere regret
to the scheduled breaking open of breasts whose milk
runs out over the entrails of still-alive babies,

transformation of witnessing eyes to pulp-fragments,
implosion of skinned penises into carcass-gulleys.

We are the humans, men who can make;
whose language imagines *mercy*,
lovingkindness we have believed one another
mirrored forms of a God we felt as good—

who do these acts, who convince ourselves
it is necessary; these acts are done
to our own flesh; burned human flesh
is smelling in Vietnam as I write.

Yes, this is the knowledge that jostles for space
in our bodies along with all we
go on knowing of joy, of love;

our nerve filaments twitch with its presence
day and night,
nothing we say has not the husky phlegm of it in the saying,
nothing we do has the quickness, the sureness,
the deep intelligence living at peace would have.

1971

Prayer for Revolutionary Love

That a woman not ask a man to leave meaningful work to follow her.
That a man not ask a woman to leave meaningful work to follow him.

That no one try to put Eros in bondage.
But that no one put a cudgel in the hands of Eros.

That our loyalty to one another and our loyalty to our work
not be set in false conflict.

That our love for each other give us love for each other's work.
That our love for each other's work give us love for one another.

That our love for each other's work give us love for one another.
That our love for each other give us love for each other's work.

That our love for each other, if need be,
give way to absence. And the unknown.

That we endure absence, if need be,
without losing love for each other.
Without closing our doors to the unknown.

1971

GAEL TURNBULL | 1928–2004

Born in Edinburgh, Scotland, Gael Turnbull studied, worked, and published in Canada, the United States, and England for many years. After earning his bachelor's degree at Cambridge University in 1948 and his medical degree from the University of Pennsylvania in 1951, Turnbull practiced medicine in Northern Ontario, Canada, and in Santa Barbara, California, before returning to England in 1963. A transnational figure, Turnbull published his early poetry in post–Second World War avant-garde magazines, including *BMR* and *Origin* in the United States and *Contact* and *CIV/n* in Canada. He helped introduce BMC poets such as Robert Creeley, Ed Dorn, and Charles Olson to an English audience through his magazine *Migrant* and Migrant Press, which he cofounded with Michael Shayer. His collected poetry, *There Are Words*, was published in 2006.

Bjarni Spike-Helgi's Son

The man who bred me,
breeds me yet.

That father whom I scarcely knew
but as an overbearing ox
who begrudged even the sky
above his neighbor's head,
who stirred mean quarrels,
killed and then was killed—

while I went in peace,
well loved by all who knew me,

wishing no part
with what I was already part.

*

We all went to the court, and I name Geitir as my father's slayer, and Geitir named himself and asked for atonement, not ashamed, but as a just man who wished a just outcome.

And the atonement was paid, one hundred of silver according to the law, and another thirty for the ambush.

And we swore oaths together, in the sight of all men, to keep our trust.

*

It was my mother brought them—

she
who bleeds in secret

and gives birth in blood,
gave me my blood,
binds us
by blood—

in a shut room,
snow over the windows,
the hearth stoked, incandescent—

reproach
thrust upon me,
a bundle of torn clothes,
twisted together concealing
something like charred pitch
caked in the weave,
something dark,
his,
my father's . . .

*

O Geitir, I have kept my trust.
Although you fell beneath my axe,
I did not strike,
and not at you.

Your head upon my knee.
Your question
(I will always hear,
though you never spoke),
"Who killed me?"

Whom you killed,
killed you,
killed me.

*

That night I walked alone.

No man saw the face I hid.

In night I walk.

No man sees the man I hide.

1956

An Irish Monk on Lindisfarne, about 650 AD

A hesitation of the tide
betrays this island, daily.

On Iona, at dusk
(ago, how long ago?)
often (did it happen?)
I saw the Lord walking
in the surf amidst the gulls,
calling, 'Come. Have joy in Me.'

Yes, with these eyes.

Now, on strange rocks
(faintly through the wall)
echoing, the same sea roars.

Detail is my toil.
In chapel, verse by verse—

in the kitchen, loaf by loaf—
with my pen, word by word—

by imitation,
illumination.

The patience of the bricklayer
is assumed in the dream of the architect.

*

On the road coming, five days' travel, a Pict woman (big mouth and small bones) gave me shelter, and laughed (part scorn, part pity) at my journey. 'What do you hope for, even if you get there, that you couldn't have had twice over in Ireland?'

Then I told her of the darkness amongst the barbarians and the great light in the monasteries at home, and she replied, 'Will they thank you for that, you so young and naive, and why should you go, you out of so many?'

I said that I heard a voice calling, and she said, 'So men dream, are unsatisfied, wear their legs out with walking, and you scarcely a boy out of school.'

So she laughed, and I leaned my head on my hands, feeling the thickness of dust in each palm.

Then she told me there was not another of her race left in that valley, not one, nothing left. 'And all in three generations. Once even Rome feared us. Now my children are mongrels. And my husband has left me. No matter. Or great matter. I am still a Pict.'

Then she fed me, put herbs on my feet, wished me well, and I blessed her but she said, 'Save that for yourself;

you will need it, when your heart turns rancid, and your
joints begin to stiffen on the foreign roads. Remember
me, when you come, returning.'

So she mocked; and sometimes, even now, ten years later,
I hear it as I waken (receding in a dream), that laughter,
broad, without malice.

*

Returning,
in the mind, still there,
home:
– devout green hills
– intimate peat smoke
– a cow-bell beseeching
– warm fleece in my bed
– fresh water, fresh, a brook

Here:
– rain clouds like beggars' rags
– stench of burned weed
– fret of the chain-mail sea
– hard knees on cold stone
– dry saliva, salt fish

The gulls cry:
– believe
– achieve

The bells reply:
– some
– some

At the lowest ebb
you can leave dryshod
this fitful island.

1956

EBBE BORREGAARD (GERARD BOAR) | 1933–

Originally from Long Island, New York, Ebbe Borregaard is traditionally associated with poets of the San Francisco Renaissance, including Helen Adam, Robin Blaser, Robert Duncan, Madeline Gleason, and Jack Spicer. Borregaard was accepted at BMC for the fall 1956 semester; however, when he arrived on campus, classes never started. Instead, Charles Olson announced that the Lake Eden campus was closing, so Borregaard left for San Francisco. He is included as an affiliate because of the campus visit and his long association with the BMC community that subsequently gathered in San Francisco. In 1960, Borregaard helped plan for Blaser and Spicer's White Rabbit College, a San Francisco–based reinvention of BMC that—with the exception of a single course by Duncan on the history of poetry—never fully materialized, and he briefly ran the Oannes Press, which published Helen and Pat Adam's ballad opera *San Francisco's Burning* (1963) and copublished James Alexander's *Eturnature: A Wavering Light thru Eternity* (1965) with Open Space. Borregaard's publications include *The Wapitis* (1958), *Leanto* (1960), and *Sketches for 13 Sonnets* (1969), a series of free-verse sonnets written under the anagrammatic pseudonym Gerard Boar. These poems riff on the traditional theme of unrequited love.

Does music ramify love—I sing so sweet
of all that is in & beneath the sea, it makes me weak
My love goes off everywhere from me,
princeps she is a trembling palacial fire
who warms me evenly,
orchids & faggots tend her ascending
with false ire & mirth bending every hearth
with wine & punches entertain & then expire.
•
Resting tho a kiss can blow a flame
bywith a smokey post
who warns her of torrents which careen from lame mtns,
and all the salt and coasting foam never
put this fire out.

1969

For what do I race these corridors of courtesy
from here on tell me love in poetry
Aye, and you, I am fickle too,
so rest in me now dumb fool
claspt in such inhospitable devotion—
POOOT, this is for them behind
near on to me.
Love is lost as it is to me,
she fell away like fruit blown down with wind,
POOOT that I am, headlong I carry
my fawnsey quills dug in my sides
in which contemporary diseases ride.
On either hand groves of grievous tyranny
in which to hang yr golden tapestry.

1969

From my draining heart a shadow stalks
sometimes unique but more often drawn
hopeless to love
therefor tangent in bleeding nights two spirits vent
love's delight
& transgress abstract intensity—does such joy
display a leavey peck of goods all ghosts employ,
what with inviting love to dip well in,
bunk fortuning bestial agony—now does my
spectre mistris union take
Now does my base heart cease to ake
•
Like the meager, counterfeit made intense
I delineate my awful wretchedness.

1969

To a lover one word, to a loser the world
what dominion have you for me chose, in god's name,
have I been abandond somewhere lovelame,
or been with yr signature on the firestars of feebler domains
In the world our worlds spin
in yr world I whirl within
for love not vers you me curse
& thrown up into yr firmament there I old thefts reimburse
while my life does yaw & vaude
in devertissements caw,
a gem, a gem for a loser's purse
a word to contemplate the univers.

1969

AFTERWORD | Joseph Bathanti

In 1972, Arthur Craft, one of my writing teachers (the most personally influential writing teacher I would ever encounter) at the University of Pittsburgh, where I was then matriculating and secretly burning to be a writer, opened the hatch of his silver Chevy Vega to reveal a haphazard trove of books he was discarding.

I scooped up a number of them, and I'm sure I still own them. But the only one I remember among them, that I indeed cherish, lo, these unfathomably impossible-to-believe fifty-two years later, is *The New American Poetry: 1945–1960* (*NAP*), edited by Donald Allen, an Evergreen Original from Grove Press, with a 1960 copyright and a price tag of $2.95. A plain stolid paperback of 454 pages, in its fifteenth printing, its title, editor, and forty-four contributors queue unceremoniously down the front of it.

Skirmished horizontally across the cover is what can only be the furling red and white stripes of the American flag—no stars, just five red stripes, disembodied from the greater field. I've pored over the acknowledgments in attempt to discover the origin of the cover art but to no avail. The cover design, however, is de rigueur, completely appropriate, it seems, for a volume called *NAP*—a riff on poetry, a riff on the flag, a riff on America, and more than anything, a riff on *new*.

By 1960, the year Allen's book appeared, Black Mountain College's (BMC) fabled doors had only been closed a mere three years. I was seven years old. John Kennedy, our newly elected president, invited the great poet Robert Frost to ring in his presidency by reading a poem at the 1961 inauguration—an elegant flourish no other American president had insisted upon before and, sadly, only three others have since. How prescient of JFK to herald the New Frontier with a poem. Out of his presidency, a new America and a new American poetry would indeed spring. Frost was charming and inimitably irascible, the era's iconic stand-in for Walt Whitman, as he recited, in a gale, bareheaded, "The Gift Outright," which begins with the iambic near admonition "The land was ours before we were the land's."[1]

The 1960s had, if nothing else, nominally signed into office as well, though the decade's official parturition had begun much earlier—certainly in part at BMC, from 1933 to 1957, in its obscure mountain valley in Buncombe County, North Carolina.

The autumn afternoon in 1972 that I peered into Craft's Vega, the 1960s still theoretically roiling—and, in all ignorance and good intention, plucked from it a book that I would carry all my life, that would indeed, like so many books, change my life—I had never heard of BMC. It was also that very same year, 1972, that Martin Duberman's *Black Mountain: An Exploration in Community* auspiciously, and also unbeknownst to me, had been published—another book, like Allen's, handed to me by someone who has profoundly influenced me, that changed my life and launched me deeply, pathologically, into the fascinating never-ending allure of BMC.

In 1972, I cast my first presidential ballot as an American citizen. The incumbent, Richard Nixon, defeated my candidate, George McGovern, in a landslide, nullifying McGovern's promise to end the Vietnam War. While American troop strength in Vietnam was at an all-time low, the Paris Peace Talks nevertheless remained stalled. "Watergate" had entered the national lexicon. My draft status was 1-A.

I suppose I was drawn to Allen's anthology because I was fooling around with writing poems and had begun, in my classes at Pitt, to seriously read poetry. The book was already beat up the day I grabbed it. The cover was near torn off; the spine cracked; pages foxed, yellowing, and watermarked. Today it's worse for the wear, and every so often I Scotch-tape it in strategic places to keep it from literally falling apart.

In 1972, the writers I would have recognized from the table of contents were Lawrence Ferlinghetti, Allen Ginsberg, Jack Kerouac, and perhaps Gary Snyder. I had somehow latched on to the Beats but in the most osmotic fashion imaginable. I am certain I had never read anything by them, but I was aware that I needed to. Interestingly enough, I was reading in one of my literature classes William Carlos Williams and Ezra Pound, the prophets of the Beats and Black Mountaineers, though at the time the conduit tithing them all together was, for me, ocean-wide and way beyond my ken.

Then, in 1985, I met and became fast friends with Ronald H. Bayes (1932–2021), then and now a giant of North Carolina poetry and longtime writer in residence at St. Andrews University in Laurinburg, North Carolina, where I had just accepted a teaching job. It was Ron who laid in my hands Duberman's spectacular history of BMC. In short, BMC sunk a syringe into me and I was instantly hooked. "Enchanted" is a better word—as if a spell had been wrought. And I was a little embarrassed. How in the world had I, a college professor, a well-educated fellow, who had just published his first chapbook of poems, escaped knowing about the most astonishing, fire-breathing experiment in the annals of American education?

Ron and St. Andrews were repositories of Black Mountain scholarship and lore, specifically the literary arts that prospered under Charles Olson's leadership from 1951 to 1957. What's more, Ron certainly qualifies for honorary membership among the ranks of the Black Mountain writers. His disposition and aesthetic as a writer closely parallel theirs.

Intimate with Charles Olson, Ed Dorn, Jonathan Williams, Joel Oppenheimer, and Fielding Dawson and a very close friend of Robert Creeley's (a frequent visitor to St. Andrews) until Creeley's death, Ron hosted a number of them over the years at St. Andrews. In 1974, he inspired a Black Mountain Festival on campus that featured all of the writers above minus Olson and Dawson, along with John Cage, Merce Cunningham, Buckminster Fuller, and Duberman. In 1975, Dawson and M. C. Richards showed up on campus, and Oppenheimer returned for the entire month of January 1977.

Duberman's history of Black Mountain returned me to my bookshelves. I whipped out my tattered *NAP* and finally got around to really reading not only Donald Allen's crucial preface but also the poets and poems in question that I hadn't looked over with any practiced industry for the better part of fifteen years.

Allen's preface boldly and somewhat narrowly laid down the strictures for what constituted the School of Black Mountain Poetry—at least back in 1960. Again, it's important to note that BMC had closed but three years earlier and a legitimate accounting of its reach and importance was clearly impossible back then. It remains today a fairly well-kept secret; in 1960 it was a thorough anomaly. Allen, though dogmatic, deserves his due for instigating the discussion and, in truth, dubbing the Black Mountain poets, according them the status of a realized literary movement. What's more, he situates them in the hierarchy of what he calls "these new younger poets" in four other schools or movements: the San Francisco Poets, the Beat Generation, the New York Poets, and an uncategorized amorphous collective comprising poets who defy category and float among the other schools.[2]

The ten poets canonized by Allen as Black Mountain poets in *NAP*—in the order in which he lists them—are Charles Olson, Robert Duncan, Denise Levertov, Paul Blackburn, Robert Creeley, Paul Carroll, Larry Eigner, Edward Dorn, Jonathan Williams, and Joel Oppenheimer. Four of these poets—Levertov, Blackburn, Carroll, and Eigner—never actually set foot on the BMC campus but were associated with the college for having published in affiliated magazines, *Origin* and the *Black Mountain Review*.

It struck me then, though never more so than now, that the rubric for determining who is a Black Mountain poet would require radical expansion to accommodate M. C. Richards, Fielding Dawson, Russell Edson, Paul Goodman, Jane Mayhall, Paul Metcalf, Hilda Morley, John Wieners, and Michael Rumaker, all of whom were keenly associated with the college.

But thankfully all that's been remedied by *The Anthology of Black Mountain College Poetry*, in which a goodly number of other worthy poets, now represented in this new and hopefully exhaustive anthology, rightfully take their places and complete this pantheon.

I also discovered through Allen's anthology and Duberman's history Charles Olson, who remains for me the most fascinating, the most maddening, of the lavish cast of Black Mountaineers. During Olson's tenure as BMC's last rector, from 1953 to 1957, the literary arts, notably poetry, exploded, took center stage, and launched, of course, the Black Mountain group of poets.

After a part-time stint at BMC in the late 1940s, Olson showed up at BMC for good in the summer of 1951, fresh from several months in the Yucatán, where he had been studying Mayan glyphs. Foremost a poet, Olson was also a mystic, theologian, historian, and philosopher. At 6'7" and 250 pounds (assessments of his dimensions vary but always lean toward hyperbole), his mere presence was astonishing. A dervish of boundless energy and verbal pyrotechnics, it tended to be Olson, the man, the mountainous charismatic, who impacted people, who in truth swept them off their feet for better or worse—and not his writing, though the relationship between the man and his work is seamless albeit megalomaniacal.

One of Olson's chief contributions to the world of poetry remains his famous essay "Projective Verse"—which I found myself seduced and flummoxed by when I first encountered it in Allen's anthology. "Projective Verse" promulgates a break with canonical American and English poets. At the time of its initial publication, in 1950 in *Poetry New York*, the essay was exclusively aligned with the still-forming counterculture and underground movements in fringe poetic communities. While Olson's "Projective Verse" is a terrifically influential essay—one that mid- and late twentieth-century poets, regardless of their affiliation with particular schools, would have been aware of—I can't help but wonder how widely it is still read.

Olson makes clear in "Projective Verse" that "the line comes (I swear it) from the breath, from the breathing of the man who writes, at the moment that he writes, and thus is, it is here that, the daily work, the WORK, gets in, for only he, the man who writes, can declare, at every moment, the line its metric and its ending—where its breathing, shall come to, termination."[3] Using the breath to calibrate lines can certainly be traced clear back to Whitman, then to William Carlos Williams, who, along with Ezra Pound, was, again, the darling of the Black Mountain poets as well as of the Beats. Allen Ginsberg, of course, also believed the breath to be the measure of the poetic line. Olson reveled in the sacrosanctity of the instant in which one composes, the ordained yet still-to-be-discovered organic epiphany—whenness as Muse—something the Beats would capitalize upon, most notably Jack Kerouac.

"Projective Verse" is digressive, frenetic, holographic, and most of all, imbued with Olson's wild makeshift presence. It owes its inspiration to physics, biology, epistemology, and ontology. But perhaps the most fascinating point the essay makes is that poetry is a conflation and synthesis of so many seemingly disparate elements that it remains at best a psychical process that ineluctably springs from a person's specific history and biochemistry—in addition to their unconscious—as well as the all-important mystery of a particular place and time in which the composition occurs and from which it takes its cues.

The poet is a force field that draws in energy from particulars and then transmits this energy, without altering its essence, to the reader. If a poem is composed in a moment in time and is thus influenced rhythmically by whatever forces are abroad at that moment, then the poem, again, becomes an organism and takes on a life of its own. By the same token, the reader approaches the poem in a moment in time, yet obviously at a remove from the instant of the poem's conception and composition. Nevertheless, there occurs, theoretically, enlightenment of an incomparable sort (as I imagine it), a kind of synergistic epiphany between poet and reader.

We don't abide in stasis but flux—and one of Olson's salient points is the protean constitution of verse. He unabashedly invokes the Muse. The same Muse that, for a shimmering ephemeral interstice in time, resided palpably at BMC, in this case specifically at its Lake Eden campus for the better part of the 1950s (though given the list of luminaries who graced BMC, it remains abundantly and mind-blowingly apparent that the Muse worked overtime at both college campuses during its twenty-four-year existence).

It is gratifying, but also a tad jarring, to see the municipality of Black Mountain listed in Allen's preface along with Berkeley, San Francisco, Boston, and New York City as hot spots for the emerging avant-garde of the period—especially when one conceptualizes Black Mountain in the 1950s, not to mention in 1933 when the first pioneering students and faculty of the newly founded BMC arrived by train in the tiny village. But in truth, what did provincial, very rural Black Mountain—the place, the locus, its geography, its ether and ethos, immured gloriously yet invisibly in the heart of Appalachia—have in common with its obviously more sophisticated cosmopolitan counterparts in Berkley, San Francisco, Boston, and New York?

Gauging place as inspiration, as shaping oeuvre, as the Muse incarnate, requires what in fiction we call "the willing suspension of disbelief." But nothing less than a kind of willed predestined magic, true intuitive mysticism, the Muse in spades, was at play at Black Mountain during those Olson years that produced a cadre of writers, unapologetically experimental, derivative of no one except perhaps one another, that would profoundly influence not only its own generation but generations to come. *The Anthology of Black Mountain College Poetry* champions, restores, rediscovers, uncovers, and introduces an exponentially more diverse roster than Donald Allen, clairvoyant though he was, dished up in 1960. Including more names and titles than Allen did sixty-four years ago, this anthology expresses the ongoing, fertile yield and influence of BMC in these ensuing years.

ACKNOWLEDGMENTS

Blake Hobby extends his thanks to the following: Alex Alesi, Joseph Bathanti, John Becker, the Black Mountain College Museum + Arts Center, Connie Bostic, Rand Brandes, Brian Butler, Grace Campbell, John Cheek, Julia Connor, Erin Dickey, Oguz Erdur, Gary Ettari, Thomas Frank, Kilian Giannini, Mary Emma Harris, Cori Heich, June Zinn Hobby, Basil King, Martha King, Steve Lansford, Jolene Mechanic, Alice Michahelles, Alessandro Porco, Jacob Riley, Alice Sebrell, David Silver, Heather South, Michael von Uchtrup, UNC Asheville students, faculty, and staff, the Western Regional Archives of North Carolina (Oteen), William S. Wilson, and Mary Zogzas.

Alessandro Porco extends his thanks to the following: Ammiel Alcalay, Charmaine Cadeau, Stephen Cain, Jason Camlot, Cara Cilano, Jean-Christophe Cloutier, Julia Connor, Robbie Dewhurst, Steve Evans, Melissa Floyd (Wilmington lifesaver), Seth Forrest, Ben Friedlander, Jason Frye, Lauren Frye, Kaplan Harris, Josh Hoeynck, Stacy Hubbard, Justin Katko, Vincent Katz, Damien Keane, Brittney Knotts, Ben Lee, Jerry Lieblich, Kate Maddalena, Derek Mosley, the Piner family, the Porco family (especially Lynda and Giovanni), Andrew Rippeon, Karis Shearer, Dale Smith, Chelsea Spengemann, Scott Stevens, Michael Seth Stewart, Tracy Ware, Kyle Waugh, and Erin Wunker; special thanks to Liz and Moez Surani, along with Zara and Laiq; colleagues at UNC Wilmington, especially Michelle Britt, Don Bushman, Amanda Coyne, Nicholas Crawford, Sarah Hallenbeck, Allison Harris, Juan Carlos Kase, Jennifer Lozano, Dan Noland, Lee Schweninger, Meghan Sweeney, and Andy Tolhurst; undergraduate and graduate students in my courses on Black Mountain College and American poetry; organizers, participants, and attendees at the annual ReVIEWING Black Mountain College International Conference; James Maynard, curator of the Poetry Collection at the University at Buffalo; Heather South, lead archivist at the Western Regional Archives of North Carolina (Oteen); Jeff Arnal and Alice Sebrell at the Black Mountain College Museum + Arts Center; the anonymous peer reviewers, who provided comments and suggestions that strengthened the manuscript; the editorial team at UNC Press, especially Valerie Burton, Lucas Church, and Iza Wojciechowska; and, finally, Blake Hobby and Joseph Bathanti.

Joseph Bathanti extends his thanks to the following: Alex Albright, Appalachian State University Center for Appalachian Studies and the Appalachian Studies Academic Program, Appalachian State University Department of English, Appalachian State University Department of Interdisciplinary Studies, Appalachian State University Watauga Residential College, Jeff Arnal, Sandra Ballard, Joan Bathanti, Melissa Watterworth Batt, the Black Mountain College Museum + Arts Center, Greta Browning, Valerie Burton, Maryrose Carroll, Katherine Chaddock, Lucas Church, Jeff Davis, Fielding Dawson, Mary Emma Harris, Fred Hay, Blake Hobby, Whitney Jones, Vincent Katz, Basil King, Martha King, Irwin Kremen, Susan Maldovan, James Maynard, Pamela Myers, Alessandro Porco, Mary Anne Redding, Alice Sebrell, Heather South, Anne Waldman, the Western Regional Archives of North Carolina (Oteen), Russell Williams, Iza Wojciechowska, and the W. L. Eury Appalachian Collection.

APPENDIX

The editors, the University of North Carolina Press, and the Black Mountain College Museum + Arts Center have made efforts, over many years, to secure rights to reprint the poems included in the present anthology. Unfortunately, we have not been able to secure permissions for the work of three poets: George Zabriskie, Max Finstein, and Edward Marshall. However, we are providing below a header note and a list of selected works for each poet, thus acknowledging their significant contributions to the history of Black Mountain College poetry.

GEORGE ZABRISKIE | 1918–1989

Faculty

Born in Caldwell, New Jersey, George Zabriskie moved to Durham, North Carolina, to attend Duke University in 1937. He graduated in 1941. In that same year, Zabriskie published a volume of poems, *The Mind's Geography*. In 1942, he received a John Simon Guggenheim Memorial Foundation Fellowship. During the 1944–45 academic year at BMC, Zabriskie taught three courses: the Psychodynamics of Creativity, Modern Poetry, and Verse Writing. He introduced students to the poetry of Hart Crane, E. E. Cummings, T. S. Eliot, Wallace Stevens, and William Carlos Williams. In 1945, he published *Like the Root*, a book-length poem with illustrations by his wife, Elizabeth Hewlett Capehart Zabriskie. According to Martin Duberman, Zabriskie "lived in the community as something of a recluse," liking the school and its academic freedom but missing city life.[1] In a short memoir, Zabriskie describes BMC as seemingly "the worst possible place to live" but "certainly the best possible place to teach."[2] Even though he did not stay long at BMC, Zabriskie met painter Lyonel Feininger there, and the two men shared a lifelong friendship. Zabriskie also taught at the University of Louisville and Marietta College before relocating to Washington, DC, around 1950. He worked a variety of jobs before landing at the *Washington Post*, where he was a member of the paper's classifieds department from 1969 to 1989.

Selected Works

Zabriskie, George. *Like the Root*. New York: Coward-McCann, 1945.
———. *The Mind's Geography*. New York: Knopf, 1941.

MAX FINSTEIN | 1924–1982

Affiliate

First visiting BMC in the early 1950s but never formally enrolling, Max Finstein later socialized with former BMC students and faculty members, namely Robert Creeley, Fielding Dawson, and Joel Oppenheimer, in New York City and New Mexico. In the late 1960s, Finstein helped establish two communes in New Mexico: the New Buffalo Commune and the Reality Construction Company. Finstein's books include *Savonarola's Tune* (1959), *The Disappearance of Mountains* (1966), and *There's Always a Moon in America* (1968). His poetry combines the hipster feel of the Beats, the prosodic technique of Creeley, and the man-about-town imagery of Paul Blackburn. As Gilbert Sorrentino writes in his foreword to *Savonarola's Tune*, "If the poem is a machine then Finstein's is perhaps a punch press, the die cast truly, the product exact to calibration, dross on the floor—for the porter."[3]

Selected Works

Finstein, Max. *The Disappearance of Mountains*. San Francisco: Wild Dog, 1966.
———. *Savonarola's Tune*. New York: Laurence Hellenberg/Totem, 1959.
———. *Selected Poems*. Santa Fe, NM: Desert Review, 1980.
———. *There's Always a Moon in America*. San Francisco: Cranium, 1968.

EDWARD MARSHALL | 1932–2005

Affiliate

Born in Chichester, New Hampshire, Edward Marshall studied at the University of New Hampshire, New England College, and Columbia University. Marshall's "Leave the Word Alone" is an iconic new American poem. It circulated around the BMC campus in 1955 and 1956 and was a favorite of Charles Olson's. He believed the poem to be a significant achievement in projective verse. In a letter to Marshall about "Leave the Word Alone," Olson writes, "That's a fine thing you've done here, Marshall—very *true*, and *quick*, very *thick*. It *speaks* very much. It is *very* personal and formal at once. And *form-wise* it is very true—the peopling, the protests, the end [italics in original]."[4] According to Robert Duncan, Marshall's poem was "in 1956 the exciting poem for everybody at Black Mountain."[5] And Allen Ginsberg has acknowledged Marshall's poem's influence on his own "Kaddish": "I copied [Marshall's] freedom of form, and wildness of line, and homeliness of personal reference."[6] In 1957, "Leave the Word Alone" appeared in the final issue of the *Black Mountain Review*. Later, at the urging of Olson, it was included in Donald Allen's *The New American Poetry: 1945–1960*.

Selected Works

Marshall, Edward. *Hellan, Hellan*. San Francisco: Auerhahn, 1960.
———. *Leave the Word Alone*. New York: Pequod, 1979.
———. *Transit Glory*. New York: Carp and Whitefish, 1967.

NOTES

Preface

1. Plato, *Symposium*, 205b–205d.
2. Allen, preface, xi.
3. Harris, *Arts at Black Mountain*, 7.

Introduction

1. In an unpublished letter from 19 October 1933, Theodore Dreier—one of the school's founders—indicates that BMC's student body had increased from nineteen to twenty-two. See Dreier, excerpt from letter, 19 October 1933, folder 13, PC.1956.30, in Dreier, BMC Collection. According to the Western Regional Archives' lead archivist, Heather South, the slight increase was likely the result of day students enrolling at the college. In late November, Josef and Anni Albers arrived on campus from Germany; thus the total faculty by year's end was twelve.
2. Adamic, "Education on a Mountain," 519; Duberman, *Black Mountain*, 24–25; Erickson, "Progressive Education," 77–80; Harris, *Arts at Black Mountain*, 8. See also Rice, *I Came Out of the Eighteenth Century*; and Reynolds, *Visions and Vanities*.
3. Duberman, *Black Mountain*, 11–24; Harris, *Arts at Black Mountain*, 2–7; Molesworth, "Imaginary Landscape," 30; Reynolds, "Socrates and Serendipity," 34–36.
4. Duberman, *Black Mountain*, 2, 6–7; Harris, *Arts at Black Mountain*, 2; Reynolds, "Socrates and Serendipity," 37.
5. Adamic, "Education on a Mountain," 519; Duberman, *Black Mountain*, 24–28; Erickson, "Progressive Education," 77–79; Harris, *Arts at Black Mountain*, 15–16; Reynolds, "Socrates and Serendipity," 36–38.
6. Rice, "Fundamentalism and the Higher Learning," 595.
7. Duberman, *Black Mountain*, 1–10; Harris, *Arts at Black Mountain*, 2.
8. Duberman, *Black Mountain*, 38–39; Harris, *Arts at Black Mountain*, 7, 16.
9. Rice, "Black Mountain College Memoirs," 12.
10. Duberman, *Black Mountain*, 26, 37.
11. Duberman, *Black Mountain*, 25; Harris, *Arts at Black Mountain*, 7, 47; Silver, "Building Autonomy," 121.
12. Duberman, *Black Mountain*, 18–20; Harris, *Arts at Black Mountain*, 6.
13. Duberman, *Black Mountain*, 21; Harris, *Arts at Black Mountain*, 6.
14. Duberman, *Black Mountain*, 14–15; Harris, *Arts at Black Mountain*, 47.
15. Harris, *Arts at Black Mountain*, 52.

16. Duberman, *Black Mountain*, 25, 153–71. See also Bellard, "Design-Build Program," 133, 135; Erickson, "A. Lawrence Kocher," 142; Harris, *Arts at Black Mountain*, 56–66.
17. Duberman, *Black Mountain*, 41–63; Harris, *Arts at Black Mountain*, 16–24; Molesworth, "Imaginary Landscape," 47. See also Horowitz and Danilowitz, *Josef Albers*.
18. Molesworth, "Imaginary Landscape," 47–51.
19. Duberman, *Black Mountain*, 290–92; Harris, *Arts at Black Mountain*, 76, 93–96; Hiam, "Arnold Schoenberg and Musical Interpretation," 115, 117; Molesworth, "Imaginary Landscape," 42, 45.
20. Harris, *Arts at Black Mountain*, 93.
21. Harris, *Arts at Black Mountain*, 140–46.
22. Cage, "Defense of Satie"; Díaz, "Summer Session 1948"; Duberman, *Black Mountain*, 282–304; Harris, *Arts at Black Mountain*, 146–56; Harris, "John Cage at Black Mountain."
23. Duberman, *Black Mountain*, 38; Harris, *Arts at Black Mountain*, 46. See also Burns, "'Creative Writing.'"
24. For an example of Robert Wunsch's poetry, see Wunsch, "Lilies of the Valley."
25. Harris, *Arts at Black Mountain*, 38–40.
26. Harris, *Arts at Black Mountain*, 46; Peters, *May Sarton*, 133–34; Sarton to Polly Thayer Starr, 27 October 1940, in Sarton, *Selected Letters*, 171.
27. Zabriskie, "Black Mountain College," 25.
28. "Creative Writing Group."
29. Duberman, *Black Mountain*, 354–56; Evans, "Charles Olson," 317; Harris, *Arts at Black Mountain*, 172–77. For a larger overview of Olson's life at BMC, see Clark, *Charles Olson*.
30. Creeley, "*Black Mountain Review*"; Duberman, *Black Mountain*, 417–21, 434–35; Duncan, "Black Mountain College"; Harris, *Arts at Black Mountain*, 212–13.
31. Duberman, *Black Mountain*, 422–39; Harris, *Arts at Black Mountain*, 240.
32. Dawson, *Black Mountain Book*, 132. See also Lane, *Black Mountain College*; and Rumaker, *Black Mountain Days*.
33. Morley, "Few Mixed Recollections," 317.
34. Rumaker, *Black Mountain Days*, 532.
35. Duberman, *Black Mountain*, 426.
36. Duberman, *Black Mountain*, 426.
37. Duberman, *Black Mountain*, 426–27; Harris, *Arts at Black Mountain*, 177.
38. Harris, *Arts at Black Mountain*, 175.
39. Harris, *Arts at Black Mountain*, 177.
40. Harris, *Arts at Black Mountain*, 240.
41. Metcalf, "Where Do You Put the Horse?," 24.
42. Woods, "Black Mountain and Associates," 974.
43. Creeley, "*Black Mountain Review*"; Duberman, *Black Mountain*, 411–17; Evans, "*Black Mountain Review*"; Power, "In, Around, and About *The Black Mountain Review*"; Woods, "Black Mountain and Associates."
44. Olson to Corman, 14 December 1953, in Olson and Corman, *Complete Correspondence*, 2:103.

45. Creeley, "*Black Mountain Review*," 507, 512.
46. Creeley, "*Black Mountain Review*," 508.
47. Creeley, "*Black Mountain Review*," 509.
48. Duberman, *Black Mountain*, 413.
49. Full bibliographic entries for the first magazine appearances of these poems are available in the works cited: see Creeley, "Old Song"; Duncan, "Letters for Denise Levertov"; Levertov, "Everything that Acts is Actual"; Olson, "On First Looking"; Bronk, "For an Early Italian Musician"; Carroll, "Plotinus Refuses To Sit"; Eigner, "A Fete"; Layton, "Lacquered Westmount Doll"; Morley, "'Seldom is a Gothic head'"; Oppenheimer, "Today an Ophelia"; and Turnbull, "Bjarni." Note: in some instances, poem titles and texts have been edited and revised between the first magazine appearance in *BMR* and the final, authoritative book publication, with the present anthology privileging the latter. For example, Layton's "Lacquered Westmount Doll" is reprinted here as "Westmount Doll."
50. Molesworth, "Imaginary Landscape," 48.
51. Harris, *Arts at Black Mountain*, 91–104.
52. Harris, *Arts at Black Mountain*, 158, 231; Molesworth, "Imaginary Landscape," 48.
53. Black Mountain College brochure, folder 3, box 1, in Richards, Papers; also quoted in Molesworth, "Imaginary Landscape," 47.
54. Olson, "Human Universe," 155.
55. See Barron, *Exiles and Emigrés*; Joseph Horowitz, *Artists in Exile*; and Cohen, *Stefan Wolpe*.
56. See Glass, *Counterculture Colophon*; and Glass, *Rebel Publisher*.
57. Bob Perelman, "On Don Allen, *The New American Poetry*," *Jacket2*, 29 April 2011, https://jacket2.org/article/don-allen-new-american-poetry.
58. See, e.g., Creeley to Olson, 21 July 1951, 13 April, 20 June 1952, in Creeley and Olson, *Complete Correspondence*, 6:175–77, 9:244–51, 10:164–69; and 8 April 1953, in Creeley, *Selected Letters*, 109–14. See also Creeley, "Form."
59. Evans, "Charles Olson," 318. See also Rosenberg, "American Action Painters."
60. Allen, preface, xi.
61. Allen, preface, xi.
62. Jones, *New American Poetry Circuit*.
63. Olson, "Projective Verse," 387.
64. Olson, "Projective Verse," 387.
65. Olson, "Projective Verse," 388.
66. Olson, "Projective Verse," 394.
67. Duncan, *Collected Later Poems*, 3.
68. O'Hara, *Collected Poems*, 231.
69. Ginsberg, "Howl, Parts I and II," 182.
70. Allen, preface, xiii.
71. Allen, preface, xii.
72. Olson reading at Beloit College, 26 March 1968, quoted in Robert Creeley to Ammiel Alcalay, 1 December 2003, in Creeley, *Selected Letters*, 416.
73. Wieners, "Biographical Note," 445.

74. Alcalay, preface, x.
75. Golding, "*New American Poetry* Revisited."
76. Allen, afterword, 447–48.
77. Olson to Allen, 17 June 1958, 12 September 1959, in Allen and Olson, *Poet to Publisher*, 42, 60.
78. Clippinger, *Mind's Landscape*, 167; Golding, "*New American Poetry* Revisited," 184.
79. Clippinger, *Mind's Landscape*, 164.
80. Clippinger, *Mind's Landscape*, 164.
81. Allen to Olson, 9 September 1959, in Allen and Olson, *Poet to Publisher*, 59.
82. Dawson, *Black Mountain Book*, 7.
83. Dawson, *Black Mountain Book*, 7.
84. Stilkind, "To Fee Dawson," 41.
85. Wieners, "Black Mountain Blues," 311.
86. Goodman, "Advance-Guard Writing," 375.
87. Martha King, *Weather*, 44.
88. Dawson, *Black Mountain Book*, 17.
89. Richards, "Excerpts from 'Black Mountain College,'" 171–74; Richards, *Opening Our Moral Eye*, 69–70.
90. Richards, *Centering*, 68–69, 70 (quote).
91. Richards, *Centering*, 70.
92. Richards, *Centering*, 64.
93. Olson to Richards, 7 June 1950, folder 6, box 1, in Richards, Papers.
94. Duberman, *Black Mountain*, 507–8; Harris, *Arts at Black Mountain*, 197; Nin, *Diary*, 22–23; Richards, "Excerpts from 'Black Mountain College,'" 172.
95. Duberman, *Black Mountain*, 261; Lane, "Black Mountain Book," 216; Tite, "Black Mountain Press," 197.
96. Tite, "Black Mountain Press," 197.
97. Harris, *Arts at Black Mountain*, 197.
98. Morley, *Turning*, xiii.
99. Mayhall, *Givers and Takers 2*, 66.
100. Selden Rodman, review of *A Way of Happening*, by Ruth Herschberger, *New York Times*, 9 May 1948, BR14; Ashbery to Herschberger, 30 December 2000, box 8, in Herschberger, Papers; Ashbery, *Other Traditions*, 5.
101. Herschberger, *Way of Happening*, 3.
102. Barcena, "Texture of the South"; Duberman, *Black Mountain*, 176–86; Wilkins, "Social Justice at BMC."
103. Barcena, "Texture of the South," 210; Duberman, *Black Mountain*, 180; Wilkins, "Social Justice at BMC."
104. Green, "Note on the Mush War," 199–200.
105. Nielsen, *Integral Music*, 127–28.
106. See Mackey, *Discrepant Engagement*; Pizza, *Dissonant Voices*; Thomas, *Don't Deny My Name*; and Turco, "Amiri Baraka's Black Mountain."
107. Weber, introduction, n.p.
108. Albers, *Poems and Drawings*, n.p.

109. Quasha, "From 'DiaLogos,'" 471; Alpert, "Postmodern Oral Poetry."
110. Alpert, "Postmodern Oral Poetry," 668.
111. Urbain, "1930," 98.
112. Harrison, *Joys and Perplexities*, 72.
113. Goodman, *Collected Poems*, 196.
114. Cage, *X*, 109.
115. Stein, *Susan Weil*, 3–5.
116. Basil King, *77 Beasts*, 40.
117. Levy and Negro, *Poems by Gerard Legro*, 70.
118. Olson to Ferry, 7 August 1951, in Olson, *Selected Letters*, 141.
119. Olson to Ferry, 7 August 1951, in Olson, *Selected Letters*, 141. See also Voyce, "Alternative Degrees," 86.
120. Richards, *Opening Our Moral Eye*, 61.

Part I

1. Weber, introduction, n.p.
2. Weber, introduction, n.p.
3. Dawson, *Black Mountain Book*, 16–17.
4. Creeley, preface; Kunitz, preface.
5. Olson, "Projective Verse," 387.
6. Olson, "Projective Verse," 387.
7. Creeley's "Old Song" was published under the pen name Thomas White. The poem appeared in issue 4 of *BMR*. For more information on Creeley's "Thomas White," see Faas and Trombacco, *Robert Creeley*, 148; and Creeley to Irving Layton, 8 January 1954, in Layton and Creeley, *Complete Correspondence*, 88–92.
8. Duncan, "Black Mountain College."

Part II

1. Sarton to Koteliansky, 1 November 1940, quoted in Peters, *May Sarton*, 134. See also Sarton to Polly Thayer Starr, 27 October 1940, in Sarton, *Selected Letters*, 170–72.
2. Russell Davenport, "Bucky Fuller's Notebook," vii.
3. Goodman, "Advance-Guard Writing," 376.
4. Levertov, *Poet in the World*, 234.

Part III

1. Mayhall to Lois Redmond, 9 April 1995, quoted in Bostic and Sebrell, *Shape of Imagination*, 34.
2. Herschberger quoted in Love, *Feminists Who Changed America*, 211.
3. Peggy Bennett Cole, unpublished manuscript, quoted in Duberman, *Black Mountain*, 222.
4. Johnson, interview.
5. Jungermann, *Primary Perceptions*, 53.
6. Lane, "Black Mountain Book," 218.

7. Roberts, "'Carolina Moon,'" 206–7.
8. Kinnell, *Poems of François Villon*, acknowledgments.
9. Gerd Stern, "From Beat Scene Poet to Psychedelic Multimedia Artist in San Francisco and Beyond, 1948–1978," interview by Victoria Morris Byerly, 1996, Regional Oral History Office, University of California, Berkeley, http://content.cdlib.org/view?docId=kt409nb28g&doc.view=entire_text.
10. Stein, *Susan Weil*, 2.
11. VanDerBeek, "Culture," 16.
12. Marie Tavroges Stilkind, "The Mail-Interview," interview by Ruud Janssen, 28 July 1997, International Union of Mail-Artists, www.iuoma.org/stilkind.html.
13. Guy Davenport, introduction, 11.
14. Williams, *Ear in Bartram's Tree*, n.p.
15. Martha King, "Three Months in 1955."
16. Creeley quoted in Wieners, *Supplication*, biographical note.

Part IV

1. Bronk, *Life Supports*, 33.
2. Clippinger, *Mind's Landscape*, 164.
3. Robert Grenier, "Larry Eigner Biography," Electronic Poetry Center, 2010, http://writing.upenn.edu/epc/authors/eigner/bio_grenier.html.
4. Eigner's poems are organized here chronologically according to composition dates rather than publication dates. This decision follows from the model established by Stanford University Press's *Collected Poems of Larry Eigner* and University of Alabama Press's *Calligraphy Typewriters: The Selected Poems of Larry Eigner*, both edited by Curtis Faville and Robert Grenier. The textual history of Eigner's magazine and book publications is complicated by a variety of presumptive editorial interventions (e.g., the use of first lines as titles) related, in part, to Eigner's disability. As Faville explains, "Nearly all Larry's books were edited during his lifetime: by other hands. Apparently it was thought—and I'm not clear about exactly why this was deemed to be necessary—that Larry was unable to do it himself, and needed this 'help' to do it. It may have been as a result of his modesty, or his sense of mental 'confusion' which was an effect of his prose writing—people tended to think he was scattered, or unfocused, or perhaps they thought his disability made him 'disorganized.'" Curtis Faville, "Commentary on Larry Eigner's 'On My Eyes': A Response to Charles Bernstein's 1960 Symposium Presentation," *Jacket2*, 3 May 2011, https://jacket2.org/article/commentary-larry-eigners-my-eyes. In contrast, Faville and Grenier have produced "authoritative, 'established texts'" based on Eigner's typescripts; see "A Note on the Text," in Eigner, *Collected Poems*, 1:xiv–xvii. We have relied on Faville and Grenier's textual scholarship in our editorial practice, reprinting those authoritative texts. For example, in "F e s t e," we have preserved Eigner's spelling ("fowards" rather than "forward") and punctuation ("is,before" rather than "is, before"). In addition, like the Stanford and Alabama editions, we have used the Courier computer typeface to reproduce the look and feel of Eigner's Royal manual typewriter's typeface.
5. Faas and Reed, introduction, xi.
6. Levertov, "Biographical Note," 410.

Afterword

1. Frost, *Poetry of Robert Frost*, 348.
2. Allen, preface, xi.
3. Olson, "Projective Verse," 389–90.

Appendix

1. Duberman, *Black Mountain*, 226.
2. Zabriskie, "Black Mountain College," 25.
3. Sorrentino, foreword.
4. Olson to Marshall, October 1955, quoted in Maud, *Charles Olson's Reading*, 114.
5. Robert Duncan, interview by Ann Charters, in Wagstaff, *Poet's Mind*, 249.
6. Ginsberg, introduction; also quoted in Varner, *Historical Dictionary*, 174.

WORKS CITED

Adamic, Louis. "Education on a Mountain: The Story of Black Mountain College." *Harper's Magazine*, April 1936, 516–30.

Albers, Josef. *Poems and Drawings*. New Haven, CT: Yale University Press, 2006. First published 1958 by Readymade (New Haven).

Alcalay, Ammiel. Preface to Wieners, *Stars Seen in Person*, vii–xiv.

Allen, Donald. Afterword to *New American Poetry*, 447–50.

———, ed. *The New American Poetry: 1945–1960*. Berkeley: University of California Press, 1999. First published 1960 by Grove (New York).

———. Preface to *New American Poetry*, xi–xiv.

Allen, Donald, and George F. Butterick, eds. *The Postmoderns: The New American Poetry Revised*. New York: Grove, 1982.

Allen, Donald, and Charles Olson. *Poet to Publisher: Charles Olson's Correspondence with Donald Allen*. Edited by Ralph Maud. Vancouver, BC: Talonbooks, 2003.

Alpert, Barry. "Postmodern Oral Poetry: Buckminster Fuller, John Cage, and David Antin." *boundary 2* 3, no. 3 (Spring 1975): 665–82.

Ashbery, John. *Other Traditions*. Cambridge, MA: Harvard University Press, 2000.

Barcena, Brian. "Texture of the South: Roland Hayes and Integration at Black Mountain College." In Molesworth and Erickson, *Leap Before You Look*, 208–11.

Barron, Stephanie, ed. *Exiles and Emigrés: The Flight of European Artists from Hitler*. Los Angeles: Los Angeles County Museum of Art, 1997.

Bellard, Lauren. "The Design-Build Program at Lake Eden." In Molesworth and Erickson, *Leap Before You Look*, 132–41.

Bostic, Connie, and Alice Sebrell, eds. *The Shape of Imagination: Women of Black Mountain College*. Asheville, NC: Black Mountain College Museum + Arts Center, 2008.

Bronk, William. "For an Early Italian Musician." *Black Mountain Review*, no. 5 (Summer 1955): 166.

———. *Life Supports: New and Collected Poems*. San Francisco: North Point, 1981.

Burns, Lucy. "'Creative Writing [. . .] has a place in the curriculum': Robert Wunsch at Black Mountain College, 1933–43." *Journal of Black Mountain College Studies*, no. 11 (2020). www.blackmountaincollege.org/robert-wunsch-at-black-mountain-college.

Cage, John. "Defense of Satie." In *John Cage: An Anthology*, edited by Richard Kostelanetz, 77–83. New York: Da Capo, 1991.

———. *X: Writings '79–'82*. Middletown, CT: Wesleyan University Press, 1983.

Carroll, Paul. "Plotinus Refuses To Sit For A Portrait." *Black Mountain Review* 1, no. 4 (Winter 1954): 16.

Clark, Tom. *Charles Olson: The Allegory of a Poet's Life*. New York: W. W. Norton, 1991.

Clippinger, David. *The Mind's Landscape: William Bronk and Twentieth-Century American Poetry*. Newark: University of Delaware Press, 2006.

Cohen, Brigid. *Stefan Wolpe and the Avant-Garde Diaspora*. New York: Cambridge University Press, 2012.

"Creative Writing Group." *Black Mountain College Community Bulletin*, November 1946, n.p. Black Mountain College Records, 1933–56. Western Regional Archives, State Archives of North Carolina, Asheville.

Creeley, Robert. "*The Black Mountain Review*." In *Collected Essays of Robert Creeley*, 505–15.

———. *The Collected Essays of Robert Creeley*. Berkeley: University of California Press, 1989.

———. "Form." In *Collected Essays of Robert Creeley*, 590–92.

——— [Thomas White, pseud.]. "Old Song." *Black Mountain Review* 1, no. 4 (Winter 1954): 17.

———. Preface to Morley, *Blessing Outside Us*, n.p.

———. *Selected Letters*. Edited by Rod Smith, Kaplan Harris, and Peter Baker. Berkeley: University of California Press, 2014.

Creeley, Robert, and Charles Olson. *The Complete Correspondence*. Edited by George F. Butterick. 10 vols. Santa Barbara, CA: Black Sparrow, 1980–96.

Davenport, Guy. Introduction to Williams, *Palpable Elysium*, 9–11.

Davenport, Russell. "Bucky Fuller's Notebook." In Fuller, *Untitled Epic Poems on the History of Industrialization*, v–xii.

Dawson, Fielding. *The Black Mountain Book: A New Edition*. Rocky Mount: North Carolina Wesleyan College Press, 1991. First published 1970 by Croton (New York).

Díaz, Eva. "Summer Session 1948." In Molesworth and Erickson, *Leap Before You Look*, 218–21.

Dreier, Theodore, and Barbara Loines Dreier. Black Mountain College Collection. Western Regional Archives, State Archives of North Carolina, Asheville.

Duberman, Martin. *Black Mountain: An Exploration in Community*. Evanston, IL: Northwestern University Press, 2009. First published 1972 by Dutton (New York).

Duncan, Robert. "Black Mountain College." In "Ten Prose Pieces, 1945 to 1978," transcribed and edited by Robert J. Bertholf and James Maynard. *Jacket*, no. 28 (October 2005). http://jacketmagazine.com/28/dunc-bert-10prose.html#x7.

———. *The Collected Later Poems and Plays*. Edited by Peter Quartermain. Berkeley: University of California Press, 2014.

———. "Letters for Denise Levertov: An A Muse Meant." *Black Mountain Review* 1, no. 3 (Fall 1954): 19–22.

Eigner, Larry. *Calligraphy Typewriters: The Selected Poems of Larry Eigner*. Edited by Curtis Faville and Robert Grenier. Tuscaloosa: University of Alabama Press, 2016.

———. *The Collected Poems of Larry Eigner*. Edited by Curtis Faville and Robert Grenier. 4 vols. Stanford, CA: Stanford University Press, 2010.

———. "A Fete." *Black Mountain Review* 1, no. 1 (Spring 1954): 33.

Erickson, Ruth. "A. Lawrence Kocher: Stool and Side Table." In Molesworth and Erickson, *Leap Before You Look*, 142–43.

———. "A Progressive Education." In Molesworth and Erickson, *Leap Before You Look*, 76–80.

Evans, Steve. "*Black Mountain Review*." In Molesworth and Erickson, *Leap Before You Look*, 346–49.

———. "Charles Olson." In Molesworth and Erickson, *Leap Before You Look*, 316–21.

Faas, Ekbert, and Sabrina Reed. Introduction to Layton and Creeley, *Complete Correspondence*, ix–xxix.

Faas, Ekbert, and Maria Trombacco. *Robert Creeley: A Biography*. Montréal, QC: McGill-Queen's University Press, 2001.

Frost, Robert. *The Poetry of Robert Frost: The Collected Poems*. Edited by Edward Connery Lathem. New York: Henry Holt, 1969.

Fuller, Buckminster. *Untitled Epic Poem on the History of Industrialization*. New York: Touchstone/Simon and Schuster, 1970. First published 1962 by Jargon Society (Highlands, NC).

Glass, Loren. *Counterculture Colophon: Grove Press, the Evergreen Review, and the Incorporation of the Avant-Garde*. Stanford, CA: Stanford University Press, 2013.

———. *Rebel Publisher: Grove Press and the Revolution of the Word*. New York: Seven Stories, 2018.

Ginsberg, Allen. "Howl, Parts I and II." In Allen, *New American Poetry*, 182–90.

———. Introduction to *Leave the Word Alone*, by Edward Marshall, n.p. New York: Pequod, 1979.

Golding, Alan. "*The New American Poetry* Revisited, Again." *Contemporary Literature* 32, no. 2 (1998): 180–211.

Goodman, Paul. "Advance-Guard Writing, 1900–1950." *Kenyon Review* 13, no. 3 (1951): 357–80.

———. *Collected Poems*. Edited by Taylor Stoehr. New York: Random House, 1973.

Green, Jesse. "A Note on the Mush War." In Lane, *Black Mountain College*, 199–201.

Harris, Mary Emma. *The Arts at Black Mountain College*. Cambridge, MA: MIT Press, 1987.

———. "John Cage at Black Mountain: A Preliminary Thinking." *Journal of Black Mountain College Studies*, no. 4 (2012). www.blackmountainstudiesjournal.org/volume4/mary-emma-harris-john-cage-at-black-mountain-a-preliminary-thinking.

Harrison, Lou. *Joys and Perplexities: Selected Poems of Lou Harrison*. Winston-Salem, NC: Jargon Society, 1992.

Herschberger, Ruth. Papers. Sophia Smith Collection, SSC-MS-00280. Smith College Special Collections, Northampton, MA.

———. *A Way of Happening*. New York: Pellegrini and Cudahy, 1948.

Hiam, Jonathan. "Arnold Schoenberg and Musical Interpretation at the Black Mountain College Summer Music Institute of 1944." In Molesworth and Erickson, *Leap Before You Look*, 114–19.

Horowitz, Frederick A., and Brenda Danilowitz. *Josef Albers: To Open Eyes*. New York: Phaidon, 2006.

Horowitz, Joseph. *Artists in Exile: How Refugees from the Twentieth Century War and Revolution Transformed the American Performing Arts*. New York: Harper Perennial, 2008.

Johnson, Ray. Interview by Diane Spodarek and Randy Delbeke. *Detroit Artists Monthly* 3, no. 2 (February 1978). www.jpallas.com/hh/rj/DAMintervw-RayJ.html.
———. *The Paper Snake*. New York: Something Else, 1965.
Jones, Jeanetta L. *The New American Poetry Circuit: First Season, 1970–71*. San Francisco: New American Poetry Circuit, 1970.
Jungermann, Eva Schlein. *Primary Perceptions: Poetry and Prose Snippets*. Phoenix, AZ: Bridgewood, 2000.
Katz, Vincent, ed. *Black Mountain College: Experiment in Art*. Cambridge, MA: MIT Press, 2013.
King, Basil. *77 Beasts: Basil King's Beastiary*. New York: Marsh Hawk, 2007.
King, Martha. "Three Months in 1955: A Memoir of Black Mountain College." *Jacket*, no. 40 (2010). http://jacketmagazine.com/40/king-martha-black-mountain.shtml.
———. *Weather*. New York: New Rivers, 1978.
Kinnell, Galway, trans. *The Poems of François Villon*. New York: New American Library, 1965.
Kunitz, Stanley. Preface to Morley, *To Hold in My Hand*, n.p.
Lane, Mervin Louis. "A Black Mountain Book." In Lane, *Black Mountain College*, 215–19.
———, ed. *Black Mountain College: Sprouted Seeds—an Anthology of Personal Accounts*. Knoxville: University of Tennessee Press, 1990.
Layton, Irving. "Lacquered Westmount Doll." *Black Mountain Review* 1, no. 1 (Spring 1954): 19.
Layton, Irving, and Robert Creeley. *The Complete Correspondence, 1953–1978*. Edited by Ekbert Faas and Sabrina Reed. Montréal: McGill-Queen's University Press, 1990.
Levertov, Denise "Biographical Note." In Allen and Butterick, *Postmoderns*, 409–11.
———. "Everything that Acts is Actual." *Black Mountain Review*, no. 7 (Fall 1957): 160–61.
———. *The Poet in the World*. New York: New Directions, 1973.
Levy, Jerrold, and Richard Negro. *Poems by Gerard Legro*. Edited by Alessandro Porco. Toronto, ON: Book*hug/Department of Reissue, 2016. First published privately 1949 at the Black Mountain College Print Shop (Black Mountain, NC).
Love, Barbara J., ed. *Feminists Who Changed America, 1963–1975*. Urbana: University of Illinois Press, 2006.
Mackey, Nathaniel. *Discrepant Engagement: Dissonance, Cross-Culturality, and Experimental Writing*. New York: Cambridge University Press, 1993.
Maud, Ralph. *Charles Olson's Reading: A Biography*. Carbondale: Southern Illinois University Press, 1996.
Mayhall, Jane. *Givers and Takers 2*. New York: Eakins, 1973.
Metcalf, Paul. *Collected Works*. 3 vols. Minneapolis: Coffee House, 1996–97.
———. "Where Do You Put the Horse?" In *Collected Works*, 3:1–100.
Molesworth, Helen A. "Imaginary Landscape." In Molesworth and Erickson, *Leap Before You Look*, 25–75.
Molesworth, Helen A., and Ruth Erickson, eds. *Leap Before You Look: Black Mountain College, 1933–1957*. Boston: Institute of Contemporary Art, 2015.
Morley, Hilda. *A Blessing Outside Us*. Woods Hole, MA: Pourboire, 1976.

———. "A Few Mixed Recollections." In Lane, *Black Mountain College*, 317–18.
———. "'Seldom is a Gothic head more beautiful than when broken.'" *Black Mountain Review*, no. 6 (Spring 1956): 40.
———. *To Hold in My Hand: Selected Poems, 1955–1983*. New York: Sheep Meadow, 1983.
———. *The Turning*. Wakefield, RI: Asphodel, 1998.
Nielsen, Aldon Lynn. *Integral Music: Languages of African American Innovation*. Tuscaloosa: University of Alabama Press, 2004.
Nin, Anaïs. *The Diary of Anaïs Nin, 1947–1955*. Edited by Gunther Stuhlmann. New York: Harcourt Brace Jovanovich, 1974.
O'Hara, Frank. *The Collected Poems of Frank O'Hara*. Edited by Donald Allen. Berkeley: University of California Press, 1995.
Olson, Charles. *Collected Prose*. Edited by Donald Allen and Benjamin Friedlander. Berkeley: University of California Press, 1997.
———. "Human Universe." In *Collected Prose*, 155–66.
———. "On First Looking Out Of La Cosa's Eyes." *Black Mountain Review* 1, no. 1 (Spring 1954): 3–7.
———. "Projective Verse." In Allen, *New American Poetry*, 386–97.
———. *Selected Letters*. Edited by Ralph Maud. Berkeley: University of California Press, 2000.
Olson, Charles, and Cid Corman. *The Complete Correspondence, 1950–1964*. Edited by George Evans. 2 vols. Orono: University of Maine Press, 1989.
Oppenheimer, Joel. "Today an Ophelia." *Black Mountain Review*, no. 6 (Spring 1956): 37.
Peters, Margot. *May Sarton: A Biography*. New York: Knopf, 1997.
Pizza, Joseph. *Dissonant Voices: Race: Jazz, and Innovative Poetics in Midcentury America*. Iowa City: University of Iowa Press, 2023.
Power, Kevin. "In, Around, and About *The Black Mountain Review*: Robert Creeley and Company." In Katz, *Black Mountain College*, 271–95.
Quasha, George. "From 'DiaLogos: Between the Written and the Oral in Contemporary Poetry.'" In *Symposium of the Whole: A Range of Discourse toward an Ethnopoetics*, edited by Jerome Rothenberg and Diane Rothenberg, 462–74. Berkeley: University of California Press, 1983.
Reynolds, Katherine Chaddock. "Socrates and Serendipity: Ungainly Beginnings of an Improbable College." *North Carolina Literary Review* 2, no. 2 (1995): 32–44.
———. *Visions and Vanities: John Andrew Rice of Black Mountain College*. Baton Rouge: Louisiana State University Press, 1998.
Rice, John Andrew. "Black Mountain College Memoirs." In Lane, *Black Mountain College*, 10–24.
———. "Fundamentalism and the Higher Learning." *Harper's Magazine*, May 1937, 587–97.
———. *I Came Out of the Eighteenth Century*. Columbia: University of South Carolina Press, 2014. First published 1942 by Harper and Brothers (New York).
Richards, Mary Caroline. *Centering in Pottery, Poetry, and the Person*. 2nd ed. Middletown, CT: Wesleyan University Press, 1973.
———. "Excerpts from 'Black Mountain College: A Golden Seed.'" In Lane, *Black Mountain College*, 170–75.

———. *Opening Our Moral Eye: Essays, Talks, and Poems Embracing Creativity and Community*. Edited by Deborah J. Haynes. Aurora, CO: Lindisfarne, 1996.
———. Papers. 1898–2007, bulk 1942–99. Getty Research Institute, Los Angeles.
Roberts, Richard [Dick]. "'Carolina Moon.'" In Lane, *Black Mountain College*, 206–7.
Rosenberg, Harold. "The American Action Painters." *ARTnews*, January 1952, 22–23, 48–50.
Rumaker, Michael. *Black Mountain Days: A Memoir*. Asheville, NC: Black Mountain, 2003.
Sarton, May. *Selected Letters, 1916–1954*. Edited by Susan Sherman. New York: W. W. Norton, 1997.
Silver, David. "Building Autonomy, Creating Community: The Farm and Work Program at Black Mountain College." In Molesworth and Erickson, *Leap Before You Look*, 120–23.
Sorrentino, Gilbert. Foreword to *Savonarola's Tune*, by Max Finstein, 3. New York: Laurence Hellenberg/Totem, 1959.
Stein, Donna. *Susan Weil: Full Circle*. Asheville, NC: Black Mountain College Museum + Arts Center, 1998.
Stilkind, Marie Tavroges. "To Fee Dawson." In Bostic and Sebrell, *Shape of Imagination*, 41.
Thomas, Lorenzo. *Don't Deny My Name: Words and Music and the Black Intellectual Tradition*. Edited by Aldon Lynn Nielsen. Ann Arbor: University of Michigan Press, 2008.
Tite, Jim. "The Black Mountain Press." In Lane, *Black Mountain College*, 196–97.
Turco, Lewis. "Amiri Baraka's Black Mountain." In *Twayne Companion to Contemporary Literature in English*, edited by R. H. W. Dillard and Amanda Cockrell, 77–85. New York: Thomson Gale, 2002.
Turnbull, Gael. "Bjarni." *Black Mountain Review* 1, no. 4 (Winter 1954): 18–20.
Urbain, John. "1930." *New York Quarterly*, no. 41 (1990): 98.
VanDerBeek, Stan. "Culture: Intercom and Expanded Cinema—a Proposal and Manifesto." *Film Culture*, no. 40 (Spring 1966): 15–18.
Varner, Paul. *Historical Dictionary of the Beat Movement*. Toronto, ON: Scarecrow, 2012.
Voyce, Stephen. "Alternative Degrees: 'Works in Open' at Black Mountain College." In *After the Program Era: The Past, Present, and Future of Creative Writing in the University*, edited by Loren Glass, 85–104. Iowa City: University of Iowa Press, 2016.
Wagstaff, Christopher, ed. *A Poet's Mind: Collected Interviews with Robert Duncan, 1960–1985*. Berkeley, CA: North Atlantic Books, 2012.
Weber, Nicholas Fox. Introduction to Albers, *Poems and Drawings*, n.p.
Weil, Susan. *Out of Bounds: Collage Poems*. N.p.: Self-published, 2012.
Wieners, John. "Biographical Note." In Allen, *New American Poetry*, 445.
———. "The Black Mountain Blues." In Katz, *Black Mountain College*, 311–13.
———. *Supplication: Selected Poems of John Wieners*. Edited by Joshua Beckman, C. A. Conrad, and Robert Dewhurst. Seattle: Wave Books, 2015.
Wilkins, Micah. "Social Justice at BMC before the Civil Rights Age: Desegregation, Racial Inclusion, and Racial Equality at BMC." *Journal of Black Mountain College*

Studies, no. 6 (Summer 2014). www.blackmountainstudiesjournal.org/volume6/6-17-micah-wilkins.
Williams, Jonathan. *An Ear in Bartram's Tree: Selected Poems, 1957–1967*. Chapel Hill: University of North Carolina Press, 1969.
———. *A Palpable Elysium: Portraits of Genius and Solitude*. Boston: David R. Godine, 2002.
Woods, Tim. "Black Mountain and Associates: *Origin* (1951–2007) and *The Black Mountain Review* (1954–7)." In *North America, 1894–1950*, edited by Peter Brooker and Andrew Thacker, 966–82. Vol. 2 of *The Oxford Cultural History of Modernist Magazines*. New York: Oxford University Press, 2012.
Wunsch, W. R. "Lilies of the Valley." *Carolina Review*, December 1936, 5.
Zabriskie, George. "Black Mountain College: A Personal Memoir, 1944–45." *Form*, no. 5 (1967): 24–27.

FURTHER READINGS

These sources are selected to help readers locate more BMC poetry and learn more about BMC's history and influence. While representative of a range of primary and secondary works, this list is not exhaustive.

Aji, Hélène. "The Common Pedagogy of the Uncommon: Building Aesthetic Community from the Ezuniversity to Black Mountain College and Beyond." In *Modernist Communities across Cultures and Media*, edited by Caroline Pollentier and Sarah Wilson, 68–86. Gainesville: University Press of Florida, 2019.

Albers, Anni. "Handweaving Today: Textile Work at Black Mountain College." *Weaver* 6, no. 1 (January–February 1941): 3–7.

———. *On Weaving*. Middletown, CT: Wesleyan University Press, 1965.

———. *Selected Writings on Design*. Edited by Brenda Danilowitz. Middletown, CT: Wesleyan University Press, 2001.

Albers, Josef. "Art as Experience." *Progressive Education*, no. 12 (October 1935): 391–93.

———. "Concerning Art Instruction." *Black Mountain College Bulletin*, no. 2 (June 1934): 2–7.

———. "The Educational Value of Manual Work and Handicraft in Relation to Architecture." In *New Architecture and City Planning*, edited by Paul Zucker, 688–94. New York: Philosophical Library, 1944.

———. *Interaction of Color*. 50th anniversary ed. New Haven, CT: Yale University Press, 2013.

———. "A Note on the Arts in Education." *American Magazine of Art* 29, no. 4 (April 1936): 233.

Albers, Josef, and Donald Judd. *Form and Color*. New York: Pace Wildenstein, 2007.

Albers, Josef, and Wassily Kandinsky. *Friends in Exile: A Decade of Correspondence, 1929–1940*. Edited by Nicholas Fox Weber. New York: Hudson Hills, 2010.

Albright, Alex, ed. "The Black Mountain College Issue." Special issue, *North Carolina Literary Review* 2, no. 2 (1995).

Alcalay, Ammiel. *A Little History*. New York: re:public/UpSet Press, 2013.

Aldan, Daisy, ed. *A New Folder—Americans: Poems and Drawings*. New York: Folder Editions, 1959.

Allen, Donald, and Warren Tallman, eds. *The Poetics of the New American Poetry*. New York: Grove, 1973.

Allen, Felicity, ed. *Education*. Cambridge, MA: MIT Press, 2011.

Altieri, Charles. *Enlarging the Temple: New Directions in American Poetry during the 1960s*. Lewisburg, PA: Bucknell University Press, 1979.

Alves, Bill, and Brett Campbell. *Lou Harrison: American Musical Maverick*. Bloomington: Indiana University Press, 2017.

Anderson, Elliott, and Mary Kinzie, eds. "The Little Magazine in America: A Modern Documentary History." Special issue, *Tri Quarterly*, no. 43 (Fall 1978).

Andrew, Jason, ed. *Jack Tworkov: Accident of Choice, the Artist at Black Mountain College 1952*. Asheville, NC: Black Mountain College Museum + Arts Center, 2011.

Artaud, Antonin. *The Theater and Its Double*. Translated by Mary Caroline Richards. New York: Grove, 1958.

Ashbery, John. *Other Traditions*. Cambridge, MA: Harvard University Press, 2000.

Ashby, Sylvia Girsch. *Anne of Green Gables*. Adapted from L. M. Montgomery's novel. Boston: Baker's Plays, 1992.

———. Collection. Western Regional Archives, State Archives of North Carolina, Asheville.

Baraka, Amiri. *The Autobiography of LeRoi Jones*. Chicago: Lawrence Hill Books, 1997.

———. *The LeRoi Jones/Amiri Baraka Reader*. Edited by William J. Harris. New York: Thunder's Mouth, 1991.

———. *S.O.S.: Poems 1961–2013*. New York: Grove, 2016.

Baraka, Amiri, and Edward Dorn. *The Collected Letters*. Edited by Claudia Moreno Pisano. Albuquerque: University of New Mexico Press, 2013.

Bartlett, Jennifer. "*Limits / are what any of us / are inside: The Life and Work of Larry Eigner*—from Chapter 14 Berkeley/Independent Living." *Wordgathering* 7, no. 1 (2013). www.wordgathering.com/past_issues/issue25/reviews/bartlett.html.

———. *Sustaining Air: The Life of Larry Eigner*. With contributions by George Hart. Tuscaloosa: University of Alabama Press, 2023.

Bartlett, Jennifer, and George Hart, eds. *Momentous Inclusions: The Life and Work of Larry Eigner*. Albuquerque: University of New Mexico Press, 2021.

Basinski, Michael, ed. *Jargon at Forty, 1951–1991: An Exhibition and Celebration*. Buffalo: Poetry and Rare Books Collection, State University of New York at Buffalo, 1991.

Basualdo, Carlos, and Erica Battle, eds. *Dancing around the Bride: Cage, Cunningham, Johns, Rauschenberg, and Duchamp*. New Haven, CT: Yale University Press, 2012.

Bathanti, Joseph, ed. "Black Mountain College." Special issue, *Appalachian Journal* 44–45, nos. 3–4/1–2 (2017/2018).

———. "The Mythic School of the Mountain: Black Mountain College." *Our State*, April 2014, 158–72.

Bauhaus-Archiv Berlin. *Bauhaus: A Conceptual Model*. Ostfildern, Germany: Hatje Cantz, 2009.

Bayer, Herbert, Ise Gropius, and Walter Gropius, eds. *Bauhaus 1919–1928*. New York: Museum of Modern Art, 1938.

Beach, Christopher. "The New American Poetry and the postmodern avant-garde." In *The Cambridge Introduction to Twentieth-Century American Poetry*, 189–209. New York: Cambridge University Press, 2003.

Belgrad, Daniel. *The Culture of Spontaneity: Improvisation and the Arts in Postwar America*. Chicago: University of Chicago Press, 1998.

Bell, Charles Greenleaf. *Delta Return*. Bloomington: Indiana University Press, 1956.

———. *Five Chambered Heart*. New York: Persea Books, 1986.
———. *Millennial Harvest: The Life and Collected Poems of Charles Greenleaf Bell*. Santa Fe, NM: Lumen Books, 2006.
———. *Songs for a New America*. Bloomington: Indiana University Press, 1953.
Benfey, Christopher. *Red Brick, Black Mountain, White Clay: Reflections on Art, Family, and Survival*. New York: Penguin, 2012.
Bennett, Peggy. *The Varmints*. New York: Knopf, 1947.
Bentley, Eric. "Report from the Academy: The Experimental College." *Partisan Review* 12, no. 3 (Summer 1945): 422–30.
Bergdoll, Barry, and Leah Dickerman, eds. *Bauhaus 1919–1933: Workshops for Modernity*. New York: Museum of Modern Art, 2009.
Bernstein, David W., and Christopher Hatch, eds. *Writings through John Cage's Music, Poetry, and Art*. Chicago: University of Chicago Press, 2001.
Bertolf, Robert J., and Dale Smith, eds. *Imagining Persons: Robert Duncan's Lectures on Charles Olson*. Albuquerque: University of New Mexico Press, 2017.
Bezner, Kevin. "From Black Mountain College to Nuyorican Poets Café: Lineage, Tradition, and Community in Postmodern Poetry." *Cincinnati Poetry Review*, no. 26 (1995): 77–85.
Blackburn, Paul. *The Collected Poems of Paul Blackburn*. Edited by Edith Jarolim. New York: Persea Books, 1985.
———. *The Journals*. Edited by Robert Kelly. Santa Barbara, CA: Black Sparrow, 1977.
———, trans. *Proensa: An Anthology of Troubadour Poetry*. Edited by George Economou. New York: New York Review of Books, 2017. First published 1978 by University of California Press (Berkeley).
Black Mountain College Bulletin, nos. 1–8, 1933–44.
Black Mountain College Bulletin/Bulletin-Newsletter, vols. 1–12, 1942–56.
Black Mountain College Community Bulletin, 1942–47.
Black Mountain College Newsletter, nos. 1–17, 1938–42.
Blocklyn, Philip. "'It's Right the Way It Is': Printing at Black Mountain College." *Journal of Black Mountain College Studies*, no. 12 (2021). www.blackmountaincollege.org/blocklyn-printing.
Boar, Gerard [Ebbe Borregaard]. *Sketches for 13 Sonnets*. Berkeley, CA: Oyez, 1969.
Borchardt-Hume, Achim, ed. *Albers and Moholy-Nagy: From the Bauhaus to the New World*. New Haven, CT: Yale University Press, 2006.
Borezo, Amy. *Raising the Supine Dome*. Orange, MA: Shelter Bookworks, 2010.
Borregaard, Ebbe. *Leanto*. San Francisco: privately published, 1960.
———. *The Wapitis*. San Francisco: White Rabbit, 1958.
Boyd, Jack, and Fielding Dawson. *2 & 4 Poems*. Black Mountain, NC: Black Mountain College Print Shop, 1950.
Boyer, Jean Pierre, and Emmanuel Ponsart, eds. *Dossier Charles Olson: Black Mountain College*. Marseille, France: Centre international de poésie, 2010.
Bradnock, Lucy. *No More Masterpieces: Modern Art after Artaud*. New Haven, CT: Yale University Press, 2021.
Brand, Juliane, and Christopher Hailey, eds. *Constructive Dissonance: Arnold Schoenberg*

and the Transformations of Twentieth-Century Culture. Berkeley: University of California Press, 1997.
Brandes, Rand, Lee Ann Brown, and Leslie Rindoks. *Far from the Centers of Ambition: A Celebration of Black Mountain College*. Davidson, NC: Lorimer, 2012.
Breedlove, Brian. *Loud Rebellions and Silent Revolutions: Black Mountain College's Legacy*. Saarbrücken, Germany: Scholars' Press, 2014.
Breslin, Paul. "Black Mountain: A Critique of the Curriculum." *Poetry*, no. 136 (July 1980): 219–39.
Bronk, William. *Bursts of Light: The Collected Later Poems*. Edited by David Clippinger. Greenfield, MA: Talisman House, 2012.
———. *Vectors and Smoothable Curves: The Collected Essays of William Bronk*. Greenfield, MA: Talisman House, 1996. First published 1983 by North Point (San Francisco).
Brown, Carolyn. *Chance and Circumstance: Twenty Years with Cage and Cunningham*. New York: Knopf, 2007.
Butler, Brian. *Dan Rice at Black Mountain College: Painter among the Poets*. Asheville, NC: Black Mountain College Museum + Arts Center, 2014.
———. *Emerson Woelffer: At the Center and at the Edge*. Asheville, NC: Black Mountain College Museum + Arts Center, 2008.
Butler, Brian, and Blake Hobby, eds. *Journal of Black Mountain College Studies*, vols. 1–8 (2005–15). www.blackmountainstudiesjournal.org.
Butor, Michel. *Gregory Masurovsky: A World in Black and White*. Asheville, NC: Black Mountain College Museum + Arts Center, 2004.
Byers, Mark. *Charles Olson and American Modernism: The Practice of the Self*. New York: Oxford University Press, 2018.
Cage, John. "An Autobiographical Statement." *Southwest Review* 76, no. 1 (Winter 1991): 59–76.
———. *Empty Words*. Middletown, CT: Wesleyan University Press, 1979.
———. *4′33″*. Frankfurt, Germany: C. F. Peters, 2012.
———. *Haiku*. Black Mountain, NC: Black Mountain College Music Press, 1952.
———. Interview by Michael Kirby and Richard Schechner. In Sandford, *Happenings and Other Acts*, 51–71.
———. *M: Writings*. Middletown, CT: Wesleyan University Press, 1973.
———. *Selected Letters*. Edited by Laura Kuhn. Middletown, CT: Wesleyan University Press, 2016.
———. *Silence*. Middletown, CT: Wesleyan University Press, 1961.
———. *Water Walk*. London: Edition Peters, 1959.
———. *A Year from Monday: New Lectures and Writings*. Middletown, CT: Wesleyan University Press, 1967.
Carroll, Paul. *The Beaver Dam Road Poems*. Boone, NC: Big Table Books, 1994.
———. "Father." In Allen, *New American Poetry*, 88–89.
———. *The Garden of Earthly Delights*. Chicago: Chicago Office of Fine Arts, 1986.
———. *The Luke Poems*. Chicago: Big Table, 1971.
———. *New and Selected Poems*. Chicago: Yellow, 1978.
———. *Odes*. Chicago: Big Table, 1969.

———. "Song After Making Love." *Cold Mountain Review* 36, no. 2 (Spring 2008): 30.
Carter, Jon Horne. "A Community Far Afield: Black Mountain College and the Southern Estrangement of the Avant-Garde." In *The Bohemian South: Creating Countercultures, from Poe to Punk*, edited by Shawn Chandler Bingham and Lindsey A. Freeman, 54–72. Chapel Hill: University of North Carolina Press, 2017.
Charters, Samuel. *Some Poems/Poets: Studies in American Underground Poetry since 1945*. Berkeley, CA: Oyez, 1971.
Chase, Marilyn. *Everything She Touched: The Life of Ruth Asawa*. San Francisco: Chronicle Books, 2020.
Chevlowe, Susan, ed. *Common Man, Mythic Vision: The Paintings of Ben Shahn*. Princeton, NJ: Princeton University Press, 1998.
Christensen, Paul. *Charles Olson: Call Him Ishmael*. Austin: University of Texas Press, 1979.
Chu, Hsiao-Yun, and Roberto G. Trujillo, eds. *New Views on R. Buckminster Fuller*. Stanford, CA: Stanford University Press, 2009.
Clark, Camille. "Black Mountain College: A Pioneer in Southern Racial Integration." *Journal of Blacks in Higher Education*, no. 51 (Spring 2006): 46–58.
Clark, Tom. *Edward Dorn: A World of Difference*. Berkeley, CA: North Atlantic Books, 2002.
———. *Robert Creeley and the Genius of the American Common Place*. New York: New Directions, 1993.
Clarkson, Austin, ed. *On the Music of Stefan Wolpe: Essays and Recollections*. Hillsdale, NY: Pendragon, 2003.
Cole, William, ed. *The Birds and the Beasts Were There*. Cleveland, OH: World, 1963.
———, ed. *Eight Lines and Under: An Anthology of Short, Short Poems*. New York: Macmillan, 1967.
Collier, Caroline, and Michael Harrison, eds. *Starting at Zero: Black Mountain College 1933–1957*. Bristol, UK: Arnolfini, 2005.
Cometti, Jean-Pierre, and Éric Giraud, eds. *Black Mountain College art, démocratie, utopie*. Marseille, France: Centre international de poésie, 2014.
Conniff, Brian. "Reconsidering Black Mountain: The Poetry of Hilda Morley." *American Literature* 65, no. 1 (1993): 117–30.
Cooper, Robert, ed. "Nine American Poets." Special issue, *Artisan*, no. 2 (Spring 1953).
Corkran, David H. "With Eyes on the Ground: Black Mountain Years." In Lane, *Black Mountain College*, 139–42.
Cornell, Daniell, ed. *The Sculpture of Ruth Asawa: Contours in the Air*. San Francisco: Fine Arts Museums of San Francisco, 2006.
Corso, Gregory. "For Black Mountain." *Yūgen*, no. 4 (1959): 28.
———. "For Black Mountain—2." *Yūgen*, no. 7 (1961): 30.
Creasy, Jonathan C., ed. *Black Mountain Poems: An Anthology*. New York: New Directions, 2019.
Creeley, Robert. *All That Is Lovely in Men*. With drawings by Dan Rice. Asheville, NC: Jargon Society, 1955.
———. *The Collected Poems of Robert Creeley, 1945–1975*. Berkeley: University of California Press, 2006.

———. *The Collected Poems of Robert Creeley, 1975–2005*. Berkeley: University of California Press, 2006.
———. *Collected Prose*. Chicago: Dalkey Archive, 2001.
———. *Contexts of Poetry: Interviews, 1961–1971*. Bolinas, CA: Four Seasons Foundation, 1973.
———. *The Immoral Proposition*. Karlsruhe-Durlach/Baden, Germany: Jargon Society, 1953.
———. "An Ode." In Katz, *Black Mountain College*, 309.
Cuddihy, Michael, ed. "Hilda Morley/Language Poets." Special double issue, *Ironwood*, no. 20 (1982).
Cunningham, Merce. "Space Time and Dance." 1952. In *Merce Cunningham: Dancing in Space and Time*, edited by Richard Kostelanetz, 37–39. New York: A Cappella Books, 1992.
Dahlberg, Edward. *Because I Was Flesh*. London: Methuen, 1963.
———. *Bottom Dogs*. New York: Simon and Schuster, 1930.
———. *Cipango's Hinder Door*. Austin: University of Texas Press, 1965.
Danilowitz, Brenda. *The Prints of Josef Albers: A Catalogue Raisonné, 1915–1976*. Manchester, VT: Hudson Hills, 2010.
Darwent, Charles. "From Bauhaus to Black Mountain." *Modern Painters* 14, no. 4 (Winter 2002): 48–49.
Davey, Frank. "Black Days on Black Mountain." *Tamarack Review*, no. 35 (1965): 62–71.
Davidson, Michael. *Guys Like Us: Citing Masculinity in Cold War Poetics*. Chicago: University of Chicago Press, 2004.
Dawson, Fielding. "At Black Mountain College Just after Charley Olson's Famous Essay was Published in *Poetry New York* (1950)." *Olson: The Journal of the Charles Olson Archives*, no. 2 (1974): 69.
———. *An Emotional Memoir of Franz Kline*. New York: Pantheon Books, 1967.
———. *Fielding Dawson on Duberman's Black Mountain, and B. H. Friedman's Biography of Jackson Pollock*. Toronto, ON: Coach House, 1973.
———. *A Simple Wish for a Sincere and Meaningful Christmas*. Black Mountain, NC: Black Mountain College Print Shop, 1949.
———. *6 Stories of the Love of Life*. Black Mountain, NC: Black Mountain College Print Shop, 1950.
de Kooning, Elaine. "Albers Paints a Picture." *Art News*, November 1950, 40–43, 57–58.
———. "De Kooning Memories: Starting Out in the 1940s." *Vogue*, December 1983, 352–53, 393–94.
de Kooning, Willem. *Collected Writings*. New York: Hanuman Books, 1988.
Delbos, Stephan. *The New American Poetry and Cold War Nationalism*. Cham, Switzerland: Palgrave Macmillan, 2021.
de Visscher, Eric. "'There's no such thing as silence . . .': John Cage's Poetics of Silence." In *Writings about John Cage*, edited by Richard Kostelanetz, 117–33. Ann Arbor: University of Michigan Press, 1993.
Dewey, Anne Day. *Beyond Maximus: The Construction of Public Voices in Black Mountain Poetry*. Stanford, CA: Stanford University Press, 2007.

Dewey, John. *Art as Experience*. New York: Perigee Books, 1934.
———. *Democracy and Education*. New York: Macmillan, 1916.
———. *Experience and Education*. 1938. Reprint, New York: Simon and Schuster, 1997.
Diamond, Monty, dir. *Black Mountain College: A Thumbnail Sketch*. Burlington, VT: Monty Diamond Films, 1989.
Díaz, Eva. *Black Mountain College, an Exhibition Series: Its Time and Place, Experiments in Material and Form, Collaborations and Interdisciplinary Dialogues*. Asheville, NC: Asheville Art Museum, 2006. Exhibition catalog.
———. "The Ethics of Perception: Josef Albers in the United States." *Art Bulletin* 90, no. 2 (June 2008): 260–85.
———. *The Experimenters: Chance and Design at Black Mountain College*. Chicago: University of Chicago Press, 2015.
Dorn, Edward. *Collected Poems*. Edited by Jennifer Dunbar Dorn with Justin Katko, Reitha Pattison, and Kyle Waugh. Manchester, UK: Carcanet, 2012.
———. *Ed Dorn Live: Lectures, Interviews, and Outtakes*. Edited by Joseph Richey. Ann Arbor: University of Michigan Press, 2007.
———. *Way More West: New and Selected Poems*. Edited by Michael Rothenberg. New York: Penguin, 2007.
———. *What I See in the Maximus Poems*. Ventura, CA: Migrant, 1960.
Duncan, Robert. *The Collected Early Poems and Plays*. Edited by Peter Quartermain. Berkeley: University of California Press, 2012.
———. *Collected Essays and Other Prose*. Edited by James Maynard. Berkeley: University of California Press, 2014.
———. *The H.D. Book*. Edited by Michael Boughn and Victor Coleman. Berkeley: University of California Press, 2011.
———. *Medea at Kolchis: The Maiden Head*. Berkeley, CA: Oyez, 1965.
———. *The Song of the Border-Guard*. Illustrated by Cy Twombly. Black Mountain, NC: Black Mountain College Graphics Workshop, 1952.
Duncan, Robert, and Denise Levertov. *The Letters of Robert Duncan and Denise Levertov*. Edited by Robert J. Bertholf and Albert Gelpi. Stanford, CA: Stanford University Press, 2003.
Duncan, Robert, and Charles Olson. *An Open Map: The Correspondence of Robert Duncan and Charles Olson*. Edited by Robert J. Bertholf and Dale M. Smith. Albuquerque: University of New Mexico Press, 2017.
Dunn, Carolyn, and Kevin Killian. *Eyewitness: From Black Mountain to White Rabbit*. New York: Granary Books, 2015.
DuPlessis, Rachel Blau. *Purple Passages: Pound, Eliot, Zukofsky, Olson, Creeley, and the Ends of Patriarchal Poetry*. Iowa City: University of Iowa Press, 2012.
Edelstein, J. M. *A Jargon Society Checklist, 1951–1979*. New York: Books and Company, 1979.
Edith C. Blum Art Institute. *The Black Mountain Poets: The Emergence of an American School of Poetics*. Annandale-on-Hudson, NY: Edith C. Blum Art Institute/Bard College, 1987.
Edson, Russell. *Ceremonies in Bachelor Space*. Black Mountain, NC: Grapnel, 1951.

———. *Little Mr. Prose Poem: The Selected Poems of Russell Edson*. Edited by Craig Morgan Teicher. Rochester, NY: BOA Editions, 2022.
———. *The Tunnel: Selected Poems*. Oberlin, OH: Oberlin College Press, 1994.
Eigner, Larry. *Area Lights Heights: Writings, 1954–1989*. Edited by Benjamin Friedlander. New York: Roof Books, 1989.
Eigner, Larry, and Jonathan Williams. *Letters to Jargon: The Correspondence between Larry Eigner and Jonathan Williams*. Edited by Andrew Rippeon. Tuscaloosa: University of Alabama Press, 2016.
Ellert, JoAnn C. "The Bauhaus and Black Mountain College." *Journal of General Education* 24, no. 3 (1972): 144–72.
Epstein, Andrew. "The Black Mountain Poets." In *The Cambridge Introduction to American Poetry since 1945*, 28–42. New York: Cambridge University Press, 2022.
Evans, Steve. "Robert Duncan: Song of the Borderguard." In Molesworth and Erickson, *Leap Before You Look*, 338–41.
Faas, Ekbert, ed. *Towards a New American Poetics: Essays and Interviews*. Santa Barbara, CA: Black Sparrow, 1978.
Fabio, Sarah Webster, and Mary Parks Washington. "A Downhome Recipe from a Black Soul Mother's Workshop." In *A Mirror, a Soul: A Two-Part Volume of Poems*, by Sarah Webster Fabio, 2. San Francisco: J. Richardson, 1969.
Ferrini, Henry, dir. *Polis Is This: Charles Olson and the Persistence of Place*. Gloucester, MA: Ferrini Productions, 2007.
Fetterman, William. *John Cage's Theatre Pieces: Notations and Performances*. New York: Routledge, 2010.
Field, Tom. *Tom Field: Paintings from Black Mountain College and the Beat Era*. San Francisco: 871 Fine Arts, 1996.
Forrest, Seth Johnson. "'Thus far the transmission is oral': Orality, Aurality, and the Poetry of the Black Mountain School." PhD diss., University of California, Davis, 2008.
Foster, Edward Halsey. *Understanding the Black Mountain Poets*. Columbia: University of South Carolina Press, 1995.
Foster, F. A. *Black Mountain College: 1933–1956*. Montreat, NC: self-published, 1987.
Foster, Hal, Rosalind Krauss, Yve-Alain Bois, Benjamin H. D. Buchloh, and David Joselit. *Art since 1900: Modernism, Antimodernism, Postmodernism*. 3rd ed. 2 vols. New York: Thames and Hudson, 2016.
Frank, Thomas E., and Julie J. Thomson, eds. *Journal of Black Mountain College Studies*, vols. 9–14 (2019–23). www.blackmountainstudiesjournal.org.
Fredman, Stephen, and Steve McCaffery, eds. *Form, Power, and Person in Robert Creeley's Life and Work*. Iowa City: University of Iowa Press, 2010.
Frisch, Walter, ed. *Schoenberg and His World*. Princeton, NJ: Princeton University Press, 1999.
Fuller, Buckminster. *Ideas and Integrities: A Spontaneous Autobiographical Disclosure*. New York: Collier Books, 1963.
———. *Intuition*. Garden City, NY: Doubleday, 1972.
———. *Operating Manual for Spaceship Earth*. New York: E. P. Dutton, 1978.

Gold, Bobby, Kelly Gold, and Alice Sebrell. *Breaking New Ground: The Studio Potter and Black Mountain College*. Asheville, NC: Black Mountain College Museum + Arts Center, 2007.

Golding, Alan. "The Black Mountain School." In *The Cambridge Companion to American Poets*, edited by Mark Richardson, 340–54. New York: Cambridge University Press, 2015.

———. *From Outlaw to Classic: Canons in American Poetry*. Madison: University of Wisconsin Press, 1995.

Golding, Alan, Steven Loevy, and Buzz Spector, eds. "Black Mountain and Since: Objectivist Writing in America." Special issue, *Chicago Review* 30, no. 3 (1979).

Goldstein, Carl. "Teaching Modernism: What Albers Learned in the Bauhaus and Taught to Rauschenberg, Noland, and Hesse." *Arts Magazine* 54, no. 4 (December 1979): 108–16.

Goodman, Paul. *Hawkweed*. New York: Random House, 1967.

———. *Homespun of Oatmeal Gray*. New York: Random House, 1970.

———. *The Lordly Hudson*. New York: Macmillan, 1962.

———. *North Percy*. Los Angeles: Black Sparrow, 1968.

Goodman, Paul, and Percival Goodman. *Communitas: Means of Livelihood and Ways of Life*. New York: Columbia University Press, 1947.

Green, Jesse. *Seven Poems*. Portland, OR: Reed College Graphic Arts Workshop, 1950.

———. "Williams' *Kora in Hell*: The Opening of the Poem as 'Field of Action.'" *Contemporary Literature* 13, no. 3 (1972): 295–314.

Haas, Karen E., ed. *Josef Albers: In Black and White*. Boston: Boston University Art Gallery, 2000.

Hair, Ross. *Avant-Folk: Small Press Poetry Networks from 1950 to the Present*. Liverpool, UK: Liverpool University Press, 2016.

Harris, Kaplan. "Black Mountain Poetry." In *The Cambridge Companion to Modern American Poetry*, edited by Walter Kalaidjian, 155–66. New York: Cambridge University Press, 2015.

Harris, Mary Emma. "On Discovering Black Mountain College." *North Carolina Literary Review* 2, no. 2 (1995): 93–94.

———. *Remembering Black Mountain College*. Asheville, NC: Black Mountain College Museum + Arts Center, 1996.

———. "Was It a Real College or Did We Just Make It Up Ourselves?" *Journal of Black Mountain College Studies*, no. 7 (2015). www.blackmountaincollege.org/volume7/was-it-a-real-college-mary-emma-harris.

Hayden, Robert C. *Singing for All People: Roland Hayes—a Biography*. Boston: Select, 1995.

Hays, K. Michael, and Dana Miller, eds. *Buckminster Fuller: Starting with the Universe*. New Haven, CT: Yale University Press, 2008.

Hellman, Robert. "Four Poems." In Lane, *Black Mountain College*, 323–25.

Hellman, Robert, and Richard F. O'Gorman, trans. *Fabliaux: Ribald Tales from the Old French for the First Time Done into English*. Illustrated by Ashley Bryan. London: Arthur Barker, 1965.

Herd, David, ed. *Contemporary Olson*. Manchester, UK: Manchester University Press, 2016.
Herschberger, Ruth. *Adam's Rib*. New York: Pellegrini and Cudahy, 1948.
———. *Nature and Love Poems*. New York: Eakins, 1969.
———. "The Structure of Metaphor." *Kenyon Review* 5, no. 3 (1943): 433–43.
Hickman, Ben. *Crisis and the United States Avant-Garde*. Edinburgh, UK: Edinburgh University Press, 2015.
Hills, Patricia, and Peter T. Nesbett. *Jacob Lawrence: Thirty Years of Prints (1963–1993)—a Catalogue Raisonné*. Seattle: Francine Seders Gallery/University of Washington Press, 1994.
Hines, Thomas S. "Then Not Yet 'Cage': The Los Angeles Years, 1922–1938." In *John Cage: Composed in America*, edited by Marjorie Perloff and Charles Junkerman, 65–99. Chicago: University of Chicago Press, 1994.
Hoeynck, Joshua S., ed. *Staying Open: Charles Olson's Sources and Influences*. Wilmington, DE: Vernon, 2019.
———. "Without a Mammalia Maxima, Charles Olson and Robert Duncan Apprehend a Cosmological American Poetics." In *The New American Poetry: Fifty Years Later*, edited by John R. Wozniki, 29–58. Bethlehem, PA: Lehigh University Press, 2014.
Hollenberg, Donna. *A Poet's Revolution: The Life of Denise Levertov*. Berkeley: University of California Press, 2013.
Homire, Cynthia. *Insights and Outbursts: Poems and Drawings*. Taos, NM: privately published, 2008.
Homire, Cynthia, and Connie Bostic. *Cynthia Homire: Vision Quest*. Asheville, NC: Black Mountain College Museum + Arts Center, 2014.
Hope-Gill, Laura, dir. *Hell's Hot Breath: Galway Kinnell at Black Mountain College*. Charlotte: North Carolina Humanities Council, 2016. 15 min.
Horowitz, Stephen. "An Investigation of Paul Goodman and Black Mountain." *American Poetry* 7, no. 1 (1989): 2–30.
James, William. *Pragmatism and Other Writings*. Edited by Giles Gunn. New York: Penguin, 2000. First published 1907 by Longmans, Green (New York).
Jarnot, Lisa. *Robert Duncan: The Ambassador from Venus*. Berkeley: University of California Press, 2012.
Johnson, Ray. *Not Nothing: Selected Writings by Ray Johnson, 1954–1994*. Edited by Elizabeth Zuba. Los Angeles: Siglio, 2014.
Jonas, Stephen. *A Stephen Jonas Reader*. Edited by Garrett Caples, Derek Fenner, David Rich, and Joseph Torra. San Francisco: City Lights, 2019.
Jones, LeRoi [Amiri Baraka], ed. *The Moderns: An Anthology of New Writing in America*. New York: Corinth, 1963.
Kane, Daniel. *All Poets Welcome: The Lower East Side Poetry Scene in the 1960s*. Berkeley: University of California Press, 2003.
Keenaghan, Eric. "Teaching Open Form Poetics through the Beat Generation and the Black Mountain School." In *The Beats: A Teaching Companion*, edited by Nancy McCampbell Grace, 105–20. Clemson, SC: Clemson University Press, 2021.
Kempf, Christopher. "Significant Craft: Robert Duncan and the Black Mountain Craft

Ideal." In *Craft Class: The Writing Workshop in American Culture*, 104–56. Baltimore, MD: Johns Hopkins University Press, 2022.
Kentgens-Craig, Margaret. *The Bauhaus and America: First Contacts 1919–1936*. Cambridge, MA: MIT Press, 1999.
Kienle, Miriam. *Queer Networks: Ray Johnson's Correspondence Art*. Minneapolis: University of Minnesota Press, 2023.
King, Basil. *Learning to Draw / A History*. Edited by Daniel Staniforth. Cheltenham, UK: Skylight, 2011.
———. *Mirage: A Poem in Twenty-Two Sections*. New York: Marsh Hawk, 2003.
———. *There Are No Ghosts, There Are Portraits*. New York: Center for the Humanities/Pinsapo, 2023.
———. *Warp Spasm*. New York: Spuyten Duyvil, 2001.
King, Martha. "Colored Men: The Distance between Flash and Boom." *North Carolina Literary Review* 2, no. 2 (1995): 86–88.
———. *Imperfect Fit: Selected Poems*. New York: Marsh Hawk, 2004.
Kinnell, Galway. *Collected Poems*. Boston: Houghton Mifflin Harcourt, 2017.
———. *A New Selected Poems*. Boston: Houghton Mifflin, 2000.
Kohn, Andrew David. "Black Mountain College as a Context for the Writings of Wolpe, 1952–1956." In Clarkson, *On the Music of Stefan Wolpe*, 111–32.
———. "Wolpe and the Poets at Black Mountain." *Perspectives of New Music* 40, no. 2 (Summer 2002): 134–54.
Koven, Katie Lee. *Black Mountain College: Shaping Craft and Design*. Asheville, NC: Black Mountain College Museum + Arts Center, 2013.
Lane, Mervin Louis. *Going to Town*. Santa Barbara, CA: Sadhe, 1985.
———. *The Houston Passage*. Santa Barbara, CA: privately published, 1978.
———. Poems. Mervin Lane Manuscripts. Western Regional Archives, State Archives of North Carolina, Asheville.
Lauria, Jo, and Steve Fenton. *Craft in America: Celebrating Two Centuries of Artists and Objects*. New York: Clarkson Potter, 2007.
Lawlor, William. *Beat Culture: Icons, Lifestyles, and Impact*. Santa Barbara, CA: ABC-CLIO, 2005.
Layton, Irving. *The Improved Binoculars*. Erin, ON: Porcupine's Quill, 1991. First published 1956 by Jargon Society (Highlands, NC).
———. *In the Midst of My Fever*. Mallorca, Spain: Divers, 1954.
———. *A Wild Peculiar Joy: The Selected Poems*. Toronto, ON: McClelland and Stewart, 2004.
Leibowitz, Herbert. Introduction to Williams, *Blues and Roots, Rue and Bluets*, n.p.
Lempert, Benjamin R. "Hughes/Olson: Whose Music? Whose Era?" *American Literature* 87, no. 2 (2015): 303–30.
Levertov, Denise. *The Collected Poems of Denise Levertov*. New York: New Directions, 2013.
———. *New and Selected Essays*. New York: New Directions, 1992.
———. *Tesserae: Memories and Suppositions*. New York: New Directions, 1995.
Litz, Katherine. "Reflections on Making a Dance." *Dance Observer*, no. 21 (February 1954): 21–22.

Longwell, Alicia Grant. *Dorothea Rockburne: In My Mind's Eye*. Southampton, NY: Parrish Art Museum, 2011.
Maass, Andrew. *The Black Mountain Connection: John Cage, Merce Cunningham, Irwin Kremen, M. C. Richards*. Tampa, FL: Tampa Museum of Art, 1992.
Mackey, Nathaniel. *Paracritical Hinge: Essays, Talks, Notes, Interviews*. Madison: University of Wisconsin Press, 2005.
Matterson, Stephen. "American Modernism from the 1930s to the '50s: Williams and Stevens to Black Mountain and the Beats." In *A History of Modernist Poetry*, edited by Alex Davis and Lee M. Jenkins, 341–58. New York: Cambridge University Press, 2015.
Matthews, Sebastian, ed. *From BMC to NYC: The Tutelary Years of Ray Johnson, 1943–1967*. Asheville, NC: Black Mountain College Museum + Arts Center, 2010.
Mattison, Robert S., and Loretta Howard. *Black Mountain College and Its Legacy*. New York: Loretta Howard Gallery, 2011.
Maud, Ralph. *What Does Not Change: The Significance of Charles Olson's "The Kingfishers."* Teaneck, NJ: Fairleigh Dickinson University Press, 1998.
Mayhall, Jane. *Cousin to Human*. New York: Harcourt, Brace, 1960.
———. *Discourse before Dawn*. New York: Qohéleth Press, 1960.
———. *Givers and Takers*. New York: Eakins, 1968.
———. *Ready for the Ha Ha and Other Satires*. New York: Eakins, 1966.
———. *Sleeping Late on Judgment Day*. New York: Knopf, 2004.
Maynard, James. *Robert Duncan and the Pragmatist Sublime*. Albuquerque: University of New Mexico Press, 2018.
Menand, Louis. *The Free World: Art and Thought in the Cold War*. New York: Picador, 2021.
Metcalf, Paul. "The Metcalfs in North Carolina." *North Carolina Literary Review* 2, no. 2 (1995): 135–41.
Metcalf, Paul, Fielding Dawson, and Michael Rumaker. *3 x 3*. Rocky Mount: North Carolina Wesleyan College Press, 1989.
Michahelles, Caroline. *No-Nonsense Poems*. Florence, Italy: Florence Art Edizioni, 2007.
———. *Nonsense-No Poems*. Florence, Italy: Florence Art Edizioni, 2013.
Miller, Leta E., and Frederic Lieberman. *Composing a World: Lou Harrison, Musical Wayfarer*. Urbana: University of Illinois Press, 2004.
Misiroglu, Gina Renée, ed. *American Countercultures: An Encyclopedia of Nonconformists, Alternative Lifestyles, and Radical Ideas in U.S. History*. New York: Routledge, 2015.
Moore, Robert Seaborn, ed. *Black Mountain College: The Visual Arts as Taught and Practiced at Black Mountain College*. Johnson City: East Tennessee State University Press, 1960.
Morley, Hilda. *Cloudless at First*. Mt. Kisco, NY: Moyer Bell, 1989.
———. "Organic Form." In *An Exaltation of Forms: Contemporary Poets Celebrate the Diversity of Their Art*, edited by Annie Finch and Kathrine Varnes, 325–33. Ann Arbor: University of Michigan Press, 2002.
———. *What Are Winds and What Are Waters*. Wakefield, RI: Asphodel, 1993.
Motherwell, Robert. *The Collected Writings of Robert Motherwell*. Edited by Stephanie Terenzio. New York: Oxford University Press, 1992.

Nelson, Howard. "Martha Treichler and the State of Poetry." *Hollins Critic* 57, no. 2 (2020): n.p.
———, ed. *On the Poetry of Galway Kinnell: The Wages of Dying*. Ann Arbor: University of Michigan Press, 1987.
New York Times. "Cooperative Education: A Social Experiment in the Carolina Mountain." 7 June 1936, 135.
———. "Cooperative Work at Black Mountain." 1 September 1935, 27.
Nichols, Miriam. *Radical Affections: Essays on the Poetics of Outside*. Tuscaloosa: University of Alabama Press, 2010.
Nielsen, Aldon Lynn. *Black Chant: Languages of African-American Postmodernism*. New York: Cambridge University Press, 1997.
———. *Reading Race: White American Poets and the Racial Discourse in the Twentieth Century*. Athens: University of Georgia Press, 1988.
North Carolina Museum of Art. *The Visual Arts at Black Mountain College, 1933–1956*. Raleigh: North Carolina Museum of Art, 1973.
Olson, Charles. *The Collected Poems of Charles Olson*. Edited by George F. Butterick. Berkeley: University of California Press, 1987.
———. "Katherine Litz Dance Concert: A Review." *Olson: The Journal of the Charles Olson Archives*, no. 8 (1977): 16.
———. *Letter for Melville, 1951*. Black Mountain, NC: Black Mountain College Print Shop, 1951.
———. *The Maximus Poems*. Edited by George F. Butterick. Berkeley: University of California Press, 1983.
———. *Mayan Letters*. Mallorca, Spain: Divers, 1953.
———. *Selected Writings*. New York: New Directions, 1967.
———. *The Special View of History*. Berkeley, CA: Oyez, 1970.
———. *This*. Illustrated by Nicola Cernovich. Black Mountain, NC: Black Mountain College Graphics Workshop, 1952.
Olson, Charles, and Frances Boldereff. *A Modern Correspondence*. Edited by Ralph Maud and Sharon Thesen. Hanover, NH: University Press of New England, 1999.
Olson, Charles, and Edward Dahlberg. *In Love, in Sorrow: The Complete Correspondence of Charles Olson and Edward Dahlberg*. Edited by Paul Christensen. New York: Paragon House, 1990.
Oppenheimer, Joel. *Collected Later Poems of Joel Oppenheimer*. Buffalo: Poetry and Rare Books Collection, State University of New York at Buffalo, 1997.
———. *The Dancer*. Illustrated by Robert Rauschenberg. Highlands, NC: Sad Devil, 1951.
———. *The Dutiful Son*. Illustrated by Joseph Fiore. Highlands, NC: Jargon Society, 1956.
———. *Lessons: Selected Poems*. Buffalo: White Pine, 2017.
———. *The Love Bit, and Other Poems*. New York: Totem/Corinth Books, 1962.
———. *Names and Local Habitations: Selected Earlier Poems*. Winston-Salem, NC: Jargon Society, 1988.
———. *On Occasion*. Indianapolis, IN: Bobbs-Merrill, 1973.

———. *The Woman Poems*. Indianapolis, IN: Bobbs-Merrill, 1975.
Ozenfant, Amédée. *Foundations of Modern Art*. Translated by John Rodker. New York: Dover, 1952.
Paul, Sherman. *The Lost America of Love: Rereading Robert Creeley, Edward Dorn, and Robert Duncan*. Baton Rouge: Louisiana State University Press, 1981.
———. *Olson's Push: Origin, Black Mountain, and Recent American Poetry*. Baton Rouge: Louisiana State University Press, 1978.
Payant, Felix, ed. "Black Mountain College." Special issue, *Design* 47, no. 8 (April 1946).
Perloff, Marjorie. "Charles Olson and the 'Inferior Predecessors': 'Projective Verse' Revisited." *ELH*, no. 40 (1973): 285–306.
———. *The Poetics of Indeterminacy: Rimbaud to Cage*. Princeton, NJ: Princeton University Press, 1981.
Pizza, Joseph. "'All That Is Lovely in Jazz': The Creeley-Rice Collaboration for *Jargon* 10." *Journal of Black Mountain College Studies*, no. 9 (2018). www.blackmountaincollege.org/lovely-jazz.
Porco, Alessandro. "The Life and Art of Mary Parks Washington." *New Americanist* 1, no. 1 (Fall 2018): 9–50.
———. "The Poetry of Jane Mayhall." In Bathanti, "Black Mountain College," 318–29.
Rasula, Jed. *The American Poetry Wax Museum: Reality Effects, 1940–1990*. Urbana, IL: National Council of Teachers of English, 1996.
———. *This Compost: Ecological Imperatives in American Poetry*. Athens: University of Georgia Press, 2002.
Redmond, Glenis. *Gwendolyn Knight: Discovering Powerful Images*. Asheville, NC: Black Mountain College Museum + Arts Center, 2001.
Redmond, Lois. "Women in Waiting: Women Writers at Black Mountain College." *North Carolina Literary Review* 2, no. 2 (1995): 95–97.
Rice, Barbara Stone. *Barbara Stone Rice: A Sampler of Poems*. Santa Rosa, CA: Clamshell, 1999.
Rice, John Andrew. "Black Mountain College." *Progressive Education*, no. 11 (1934): 271–74.
———. "Black Mountain College." *School and Home*, no. 16 (April 1935): 655–58.
Richards, Mary Caroline. *Backpacking in the Hereafter: Poems*. Edited by Julia Connor. Asheville, NC: Black Mountain College Museum + Arts Center, 2014.
———. *The Crossing Point: Selected Talks and Writings*. Middletown, CT: Wesleyan University Press, 1989.
———. *Imagine Inventing Yellow: New and Selected Poems of M. C. Richards*. Barrytown, NY: Station Hill Literary Editions, 1991.
———. *Poems*. Black Mountain, NC: Black Mountain Print Shop, 1947.
Roberts, Janet Heling. Notes: Creative Writing (1943–1947). Papers of Janet Chloe Heling. Black Mountain College Project. Western Regional Archives, State Archives of North Carolina, Asheville.
———. "Over All These Forty-five Years!" In Lane, *Black Mountain College*, 128–30.
Roberts, Richard [Dick]. "Egomania." *Voices: A Quarterly of Poetry*, ca. 1944–45, n.p.
———. "For Sale, or Trade." *Voices: A Quarterly of Poetry*, ca. 1944–45, n.p.

Rosenfeld, Isaac. "The Dedication of a House in Spring." *New Republic* 106, no. 23 (1942): 793.
———. *Passage from Home*. New York: Dial, 1946.
———. *Preserving the Hunger: An Isaac Rosenfeld Reader*. Edited by Mark Schechner. Detroit: Wayne State University Press, 1988.
Rosenthal, M. L. *The Modern Poets*. New York: Oxford University Press, 1960.
———. *The New Poets*. New York: Oxford University Press, 1967.
Rumaker, Michael. *The Butterfly*. New York: Scribner, 1962.
———. *A Day and a Night at the Baths*. Bolinas, CA: Grey Fox, 1979.
———. *Gringos and Other Stories*. New York: Grove, 1967.
———. *"Like a Great Armful of Wild and Wonderful Flowers": Selected Letters*. Edited by Megan Paslawski. Lost and Found: The CUNY Poetics Document Initiative, series 3, no. 6. New York: Center for the Humanities, 2012.
———. "Meeting Charles Olson at Black Mountain College." *North Carolina Literary Review* 2, no. 2 (1995): 56–67.
———. *Pagan Days*. New York: Spuyten Duyvil, 2013.
———. *Pizza: Selected Poems*. Nyack, NY: Circumstantial Productions, 2005.
———. "Robert Creeley at Black Mountain." *boundary 2* 6, no. 3 (1978): 137–72.
———. *Robert Duncan in San Francisco*. San Francisco: Grey Fox, 1996.
Sandford, Mariellen R., ed. *Happenings and Other Acts*. New York: Routledge, 1995.
Sarton, May. *Collected Poems, 1930–1993*. New York: W. W. Norton, 1993.
———. *The House by the Sea: A Journal*. New York: W. W. Norton, 1977.
Schawinsky, Xanti. "From the Bauhaus to Black Mountain." *Drama Review* 15, no. 3 (Summer 1971): 30–44.
———. "Spectodrama." *Form*, no. 8 (September 1968): 16–20.
Scroggins, Mark. "Coming Down from Black Mountain." *Parnassus* 33, no. 1–2 (2012): 340–67.
———. "From the Late Modernism of the 'Objectivists' to the Proto-postmodernism of 'Projective Verse.'" In *The Cambridge Companion to American Poetry since 1945*, edited by Jennifer Ashton, 16–30. New York: Cambridge University Press, 2013.
———. *Intricate Thicket: Reading Late Modernist Poetries*. Tuscaloosa: University of Alabama Press, 2015.
Shreffler, Anne Chatoney. "Wolpe and Black Mountain College." In *Driven into Paradise: The Musical Migration from Nazi Germany to the United States*, edited by Reinhold Brinkmann and Christoph Wolff, 279–97. Berkeley: University of California Press, 1999.
Sieden, Lloyd Steve. *Buckminster Fuller's Universe: An Appreciation*. New York: Plenum, 1989.
Smith, Anne Chesky, and Heather South. *Black Mountain College (Images of America)*. Charleston, SC: Arcadia, 2014.
Smith, D. Newton. "The Influence of Music on the Black Mountain Poets." *St. Andrews Review*, nos. 3–4 (1974–75): 99–115, 73–81.
Smith, Leverett T., Jr., ed. *Art and Education at Black Mountain College, 1933–1956*. Rocky Mount, NC: Rocky Mount Arts and Crafts Center, 1978.

———. *Michael Rumaker: Eroticizing the Nation*. Asheville, NC: Black Mountain College Museum + Arts Center, 1999.
———. "Twenty-Seven Batting-Practice Pitches for the John Kruk of American Letters: An Interview with Jonathan Williams." *North Carolina Literary Review* 2, no. 2 (1995): 98–111.
Sontag, Susan. *Against Interpretation and Other Essays*. New York: Farrar, Straus and Giroux, 1966.
Sorkin, Jenni. *Live Form: Women, Ceramics, and Community*. Chicago: University of Chicago Press, 2016.
Sorrentino, Gilbert. "Black Mountaineering." *Poetry*, no. 116 (1970): 110–20.
———. "A Note on Gregory Corso's *To Black Mountain*." *Yūgen*, no. 5 (1959): 38.
Stepanchev, Stephen. *American Poetry since 1945*. New York: Harper and Row, 1965.
Stern, Gerd. *Afterimage*. Woodstock, NY: Maverick Books, 1965.
———. *First Poems*. Sausalito, CA: Bern Porter Books, 1952.
———. Interview by Raymond Foye. *Brooklyn Rail*, July–August 2019. https://brooklynrail.org/2019/07/art/GERD-STERN-with-Raymond-Foye.
Sutton, Gloria. *The Experience Machine: Stan VanDerBeek's Movie-Drome and Expanded Cinema*. Cambridge, MA: MIT Press, 2015.
Taylor, Mabel Capability. "'It wouldn't have been like a history': M. C. Richards's Black Mountain." *Journal of Black Mountain College Studies*, no. 9 (2018). www.blackmountainstudiesjournal.org/wouldnt-like-history-m-c-richardss-black-mountain-mabel-taylor.
Tedock, Dennis. *The Olson Codex: Projective Verse and the Problem of Mayan Glyphs*. Albuquerque: University of New Mexico Press, 2017.
Theado, Matt, ed. *The Beats, Black Mountain, and New Modes in American Poetry*. Clemson, SC: Clemson University Press, 2021.
Thompson, James. *The Art of Fannie Hillsmith*. Asheville, NC: Black Mountain College Museum + Arts Center, 1996.
———. *Imagining the Landscape: Joseph Fiore's Rhythm and Sentiment*. Asheville, NC: Black Mountain College Museum + Arts Center, 1995.
Thomson, Julie J. *Begin to See: The Photographers of Black Mountain College*. Asheville, NC: Black Mountain College Museum + Arts Center, 2017.
———, ed. *That Was the Answer: Interviews with Ray Johnson*. Chicago: Soberscove, 2018.
Treichler, Martha Rittenhouse. *Black Mountain to Crooked Lake: Poems, 1948–2010, with a Memoir of Black Mountain College*. Kanona, NY: FootHills, 2010.
———. *Living on a Dirt Road*. Kanona, NY: FootHills, 2011.
———. *Variations on a Theme*. Kanona, NY: FootHills, 2014.
Troy, Virginia Gardner. *Anni Albers and Ancient American Textiles: From Bauhaus to Black Mountain*. Burlington, VT: Ashgate, 2002.
Turnbull, Gael. *More Words: Gael Turnbull on Poets and Poetry*. Edited by Jill Turnbull and Hamish Whyte. Exeter, UK: Shearsman Books, 2012.
———. *There Are Words: Collected Poems*. Exeter, UK: Shearsman Books, 2006.
Urbain, John. *No Ideas but in Things*. Asheville, NC: Black Mountain College Museum + Arts Center, 2013.

Vaughan, David, Connie Bostic, and Erika Zarow, eds. *Hazel Larsen Archer: Black Mountain College Photographer*. Asheville, NC: Black Mountain College Museum + Arts Center, 2006.

von Hallberg, Robert. *American Poetry and Culture, 1945–1980*. Cambridge, MA: Harvard University Press, 1988.

———. *Charles Olson: The Scholar's Art*. Cambridge, MA: Harvard University Press, 1978.

Voyce, Stephen. *Poetic Community: Avant-Garde Activism and Cold War Culture*. Toronto, ON: University of Toronto Press, 2013.

Wagstaff, Christopher, and Paul Alexander. *Paul Alexander: On Black Mountain College and the San Francisco Scene—an Interview*. Berkeley, CA: Rose Books, 2010.

Wagstaff, Christopher, and Tom Field. *Tom Field: On Painting at Black Mountain and in San Francisco—an Interview*. Berkeley, CA: Rose Books, 2006.

Washington, Mary Parks. *Atlanta: Remembrances, Impressions, and Reflections*. Atlanta: Auburn Avenue Research Library on African-American Culture and History, 1996.

———. "New Dungarees." *North Carolina Literary Review* 2, no. 2 (1995): 84–85.

Weber, Nicholas Fox. Foreword to Josef Albers, *Interaction of Color*, ix–xi.

———, ed. *Josef Albers: A Retrospective*. New York: Solomon R. Guggenheim Foundation, 1988.

Weil, Susan. *Moving Pictures*. Milan: Skira, 2010.

Weil, Susan, Vincent FitzGerald, and Olle Granath. *Illuminations: Bookworks of Susan Weil*. Stockholm: National Museum, 1997.

Wells, Zachariah. "The Mountain Came to Him: Situating Irving Layton in the Context of Black Mountain Poetics." *Canadian Poetry: Studies, Documents, Reviews*, no. 73 (2013): 123–36.

Wesling, Donald, ed. *Internal Resistances: The Poetry of Edward Dorn*. Berkeley: University of California Press, 1985.

Wicker, Roger A. *Black Mountain College: An Experiment in Education*. Nashville, TN: Southern Student Organizing Committee, 1968.

Wieners, John. *The Hotel Wentley Poems*. San Francisco: Auerhahn, 1958.

———. *The Journal of John Wieners Is to Be Called 707 Scott Street for Billie Holiday, 1959*. Los Angeles: Sun and Moon, 1996.

———. *Selected Poems*. London: Jonathan Cape, 1972.

———. *Selected Poems, 1958–1984*. Edited by Raymond Foye. Santa Barbara, CA: Black Sparrow, 1986.

———. *Stars Seen in Person: Selected Journals*. Edited by Michael Seth Stewart. San Francisco: City Lights, 2015.

———. *Yours Presently: The Selected Letters of John Wieners*. Edited by Michael Seth Stewart. Albuquerque: University of New Mexico Press, 2020.

Williams, Jonathan. *Blues and Roots, Rue and Bluets: A Garland for the Southern Appalachians*. Durham, NC: Duke University Press, 1985. First published 1971 by Grossman (New York).

———. *Elegies and Celebrations*. Highlands, NC: Jargon Society, 1962.

———. *Elite/Elate: Poems, 1971–1975*. Highlands, NC: Jargon Society, 1979.

———. *Get Hot or Get Out: A Selection of Poems, 1957–1981.* Metuchen, NJ: Scarecrow, 1982.
———. *Jubilant Thicket: New and Selected Poems.* Port Townsend, WA: Copper Canyon, 2005.
———. *The Loco Logodaedalist In Situ.* New York: Cape Goliard/Grossman, 1972.
Wilson, William. *Ray Johnson.* Asheville, NC: Black Mountain College Museum + Arts Center, 1997.
Woznicki, John R., ed. *The New American Poetry: Fifty Years Later.* Bethlehem, PA: Lehigh University Press, 2014.
Wrighton, John. *Ethics and Politics in Modern American Poetry.* London: Routledge, 2010.
Wunsch, W. R. "Plot Own Courses at Black Mountain." *New York Times,* 11 December 1938, 10D.
Yépez, Heriberto. *The Empire of Neomemory.* Translated by Jen Hofer, Christian Nagler, and Brian Whitener. Oakland, CA: Chain Links, 2013.
Young, R. V. "The Lesson of Black Mountain: Liberal Education's Short-Lived Utopia." *Weekly Standard,* August 1998, 31–34.
Yu, Timothy. *Diasporic Poetics: Asian Writing in the United States, Canada, and Australia.* New York: Oxford University Press, 2021.
Zipperstein, Steven J. *Rosenfeld's Lives: Fame, Oblivion, and the Furies of Writing.* New Haven, CT: Yale University Press, 2011.
Zommer, Cathryn Davis, and Neeley House, dir. *Fully Awake: Black Mountain College.* Elon, NC: ElonDoc, 2006.
Zung, Thomas T. K., ed. *Buckminster Fuller: Anthology for the New Millennium.* New York: St. Martin's, 2001.

www.ingramcontent.com/pod-product-compliance
Lightning Source LLC
Chambersburg PA
CBHW022101300426
44117CB00007B/543
* 9 7 8 1 4 6 9 6 8 3 4 4 7 *